DONALD DEAN VC

THE MEMOIRS OF A VOLUNTEER &
TERRITORIAL FROM TWO WORLD WARS

DONALD DEAN VC

THE MEMOIRS OF A VOLUNTEER & TERRITORIAL FROM TWO WORLD WARS

EDITED BY
TERRY CROWDY

Pen & Sword
MILITARY

First published in Great Britain in 2010 by
Pen & Sword Military
An imprint of
Pen & Sword Books Ltd
47 Church Street
Barnsley
South Yorkshire
S70 2AS

ISBN 978 1 84884 158 1

A CIP catalogue record for this book is
available from the British Library

Typeset by Acredula

Printed and bound in England
by the MPG Books Group

Pen & Sword Books Ltd incorporates the Imprints of Pen & Sword Aviation,
Pen & Sword Family History, Pen & Sword Maritime, Pen & Sword Military,
Wharncliffe Local History, Pen & Sword Select, Pen & Sword Military Classics,
Leo Cooper, Remember When, Seaforth Publishing and Frontline Publishing

For a complete list of Pen & Sword titles please contact
PEN & SWORD BOOKS LIMITED
47 Church Street, Barnsley, South Yorkshire, S70 2AS, England
E-mail: enquiries@pen-and-sword.co.uk
Website: www.pen-and-sword.co.uk

Dedication

My grateful thanks to Richard whose perseverance enabled this book to be realized; to my family and to all Daddy's friends who died in both World Wars.

Susan Bavin (née Dean)

Contents

Foreword by H. Richard Walduck OBE JP DL

Colonel D.D. was my father's first cousin. I was only privileged to know him when I succeeded my father as a fellow trustee of my grandfather's family trust in 1976 – a chance to tactfully probe a subject he avoided talking about – his experiences as a survivor of front-line active service through World War I (1914–18) and World War II (1939–45). These ten years, with nineteen spent as a volunteer Territorial officer between the wars, moulded a most effective 'amateur' colonel from a man whose destined career was the family brick business, Smeed, Dean & Co. Ltd. Had he chosen the army as his life's calling, we might have seen him commanding the 4th Bn of The Buffs at the front instead of the Pioneers in support situations – albeit never far from front-line fire – through World War II.

I only once saw him in uniform, when I helped him adjust his heavy medal bar to attend a Victoria Cross anniversary at Buckingham Palace. Although aged, he seemed fit and lean with very alert challenging eyes. Indeed he almost seemed to tilt with the weight of medals on his left breast!

I was to learn on my subsequent visits on Trust business to his Sittingbourne home, where, although bedridden with age, he always sat up to attention: alert was the word. He once asked me what had happened to the two previous cheques in the number sequence to the one I was asking him to sign – they had in fact been cancelled in error by the auditors. He certainly, as his army reminiscences show, knew some administrative tricks.

I became aware of the existence of these notes and once persuaded him to send me a sample page, saying to me he would give me an idea of what it was like. I received the page recounting his wounding at Passchendaele in 1917.

I pressed him often on bravery with a strategy, as I thought, like those 'Chateaux Generals' who had planned to take their objectives. He always, as in that crucial paragraph of his notes relating to his Victoria Cross, said I would find it in regimental records. He added: 'I wasn't brave that day, just fortunate to be seen doing my duty'. He said he certainly could tell me about bravery and brave men another time – and he especially mentioned Boulogne in 1940.

He showed emotion when he observed both colonels of the 2nd Welsh and 2nd Irish Guards receiving DSOs for holding the shrinking perimeter during the evacuation, which could not have been done without help from his Pioneers, using Welsh Guards rifles left behind. He was the last man to be evacuated on the destroyer *Vimiera*, and still chuckled when mischievously mentioning how he offered the Welsh Guards at Colchester their rifles back, when more than a third of the Pioneers returned to England, still an 'operational formation' under their own officers.

He spoke just as his account of events reads, without emotion or elaboration, but effectively making his point, with a twinkle in his eye reflecting some of the humour he recounts; like 'Gladys' in the 1916/17 winter lady's white cotton night dress camouflage, or General 'Hunter Bunter' Weston and the gas mask that was revealed to be old socks, not forgetting Wilfred the goat in 1944. He betrays much of what he appears to have felt – 'Dogsbody (never volunteer) Dean' was under appreciated – in the pleasure he took, as the only officer left in 'D' Company during the Asian Flu epidemic of spring 1918, recommending Lt Dean as 'an officer in whom he placed great confidence'.

He briefly describes dealing with gas, but once confessed to me the horror he really felt at the prospect of being blinded for life at the age of nineteen, as he shuffled back holding the man in front as the man behind held him, in a bizarre procession, only to recover sight, two or three days later.

He could be very direct with superiors, as with the women's uniform issue in 1939 or involving Lord Gort in obtaining a second uniform of fatigue denims in France for men working during the 'Phoney War' of 1939/40 (an attitude which, with his TA volunteer status, no doubt did not assist his promotion prospects). He ended World War I still a lieutenant, just twenty-one (age being a factor), although often mentioning he hoped to be confirmed in the rank of captain, having, due to heavy casualties, so often found himself acting as company commander.

Once when I was pressing him to reminisce, he said, 'With men it is all about leadership. You did not *order* that company of Pioneers from the Glasgow back streets to whom I gave Guard's rifles at Boulogne, and who had more reason to wish to kill me than the enemy.' After all he had kept most of them in and out of the 'glasshouse' he had personally opened for them in Doullen's jail, to deal with the indiscipline of boredom in the 'Phoney War' winter of 1939/40 in France. He just said, 'Follow me! Today we kill Germans – tomorrow you can have me!' When an enemy patrol entered the street ahead a clatter of rifles behind made him momentarily think he was on his own, only to see his men rush past and do what they did best in their native city – street fighting with knives and razors. He mentions how these same men remembered him, and the glasshouse, almost with affection when they came under his command again four years later in Italy.

Repeatedly, in both wars, he demonstrates how to win over reluctant and sometimes mutinous men. When attacks falter in 1917 and 1918, and he has to rally men from other units, he attributes this not to cowardice but to loss of officers to follow. The lessons learnt by a young subaltern who did not betray the stolen rum in his new command's water bottles, and who bought tea at his own expense for a train load of recovered wounded, being returned to a war of which they were more than weary, prepared him well to control the diverse and numerous labour force he inherited from the Vichy French regime in Madagascar, and to handle the difficulties that arose with African and Indian labour units in Italy. 'If that is how you wish to play it, so be it, Dean,' he quotes General Clark.

His observation and comments tell us much about him that he was reluctant to put into words, although he did once mention with an almost Cheshire Cat grin, the brothel he had found it expedient to open in 1939, and that he had learnt the value of carrying a German firing mechanism to enable him to turn their captured machine guns back on them. Apart from his comments about certain generals, particularly Major General Osborne, who passed him over for command of the 4th Bn of The Buffs, because he was not a regular (age was again probably a factor), and some specific failures like the impossibility of the ground at Passchendaele, and failure to exploit success, he was, like most soldiers of his time, respectfully confident of his leaders, and that they would win both wars.

Certain examples illustrate a civilian volunteer's view of military authority that cannot always have endeared him. There was the 'What shall I do with the hand grenade now I've pulled the pin out, sergeant?' teasing of one 'base wallah' instructor. Another telling incident was reported in his obituary. On a training exercise between the wars, when asked how he would defend a certain position Dean advised holding one line by day and another by night. This tactic was criticized by an instructor, but Dean replied, 'I once defended such a position for three days like that and the King gave me a medal for it'. He then unbuttoned his coat and exposed the VC ribbon on his chest. No more was seen of this instructor.

Did 'Dogsbody D' have a reputation for being difficult? He did once mention to me the absurdity of nearly being court-martialled for using the railings from private mansions as corduroy road to facilitate the beach landing under fire at Majunga necessitated by a wrongly packed landing ship – a certain Brigadier Lush did not enjoy his respect.

Because of his factual style we must re-read and use imagination to understand what it was really like, to know that of the twenty-two who were commissioned in his group into the end of the terrible Somme offensive, only he and one other were still alive after eight weeks. After several revisits his matter of fact accounts of excursions into no man's land in early 1917 begin to focus as an almost unbelievable picture that is certainly no boyhood game of hide and seek.

Four times he was wounded (not to include the explosion of what he told me were his own wire-breaking 'Bangalore torpedoes' hit by German shells during the VC episode, and the 'concussion gap' in his Boulogne experience) – three times so seriously as to be treated back in England, twice to return to the trenches, and the third time to survive being isolated and expected to die peacefully, to parade at Buckingham Palace and receive the Victoria Cross. He did once, with his teasing grin, mention to me he would be taking a few bits of German metal with him to his grave. The purse with the bullet-bent coins that saved his matrimonial prospects at Passchendaele still exists, but again, only when the reader brings imagination to his account can a little of the real horror of the blood and mud be pictured.

There are occasional glimpses of the Germans – the enemy. They tolerate each other, refraining from throwing grenades by mutual consent in Plug Street, and repairing wire within yards of each other only to turn a machine gun on them when the British finished their work first. In a world where wounded can be bayoneted whilst helpless there is still room for chivalry or humanity. If you shot the enemy first you kept his pistol, and his surviving colleagues were your stretcher bearers. The River Sangro in Italy was of necessity made as sacred as the Ganges, just as the same God marked all graves in Flanders' fields.

Between the wars, a brave and risky visit to Germany in July 1939, recorded elsewhere in letters to 'ransom' (an unrecorded but substantial sum was provided by his uncle Harold Walduck) his brother who had been caught by the Nazi regime trying to retrieve family valuables belonging to his newly wedded wife, gave him an interesting glimpse of the enemy he was so soon to be fighting yet again.

How incongruous it must have seemed to find himself back in 1939 near Ypres and Arras not far from where he had spent so much of 1915–18. He surprisingly does not refer to any memories revisiting must have prompted, although during the retreat to Boulogne he recalls the practice of dumping stores at strategic crossroads as during the Ludendorff Offensive of spring 1918.

I often reflect on his words to me: 'We knew what had to be done;' whether it be holding a trench against determined counter attacks, when he won his cross, or walking the plank as the last man out of Boulogne, or persuading the Franciscan Order to help with the wounded, and a Mother Superior to billet frozen men in her chapel.

Today, ten years into the twenty-first century, and when the very last survivors of the trenches, Henry Allingham aged 111, and Harry Patch aged 106, have so recently passed away, and when the Very Revd Richard Chartres,

Lord Bishop of London warns, 'a society that loses its traditions, loses it signposts and tends to become lost', I wonder how teenagers would respond to the call made to our Nation in both World Wars. Would they, without our traditional schooling to duty and family upbringing, venture into no man's land and know 'what had to be done'?

Editor's Introduction

I have been immensely privileged to edit the memoirs of Colonel Dean VC. As the experience of the trenches during the Great War has now sadly passed from living memory we have a duty to preserve the veterans' stories and to never forget their sacrifice. This is all the more so in the case of a man awarded Britain's highest decoration for valour and one who served in both World Wars of the twentieth century. On a more personal note, this memoir also has added poignancy for me as Dean's home town of Sittingbourne in Kent is only a few miles along the old Roman road on which my own house stands. In that capacity it serves as an important piece of local, as well as military history.

Donald John Dean was born in Herne Hill, London, on 19 April 1897. His life spanned a remarkable era in British and world history. It stretched from the late Victorian era, the two World Wars and into the age of space exploration, a time of remarkable change. Until his death at the age of eighty-eight on 9 December 1985, he was the longest surviving recipient of the Victoria Cross from the trenches.

His family managed one of the largest brick makers in England, Smeed, Dean & Co. Ltd. Formed in the 1850s by George Smeed and his son-in-law, George Hambrook Dean, by the time of Donald Dean's birth the company employed 1,200 hands and was producing 70 million hand-made bricks a year. The company owned ninety-six sailing barges upon which the bricks were shipped to London, where they were used on the great building projects of the age, including Tower Bridge, King's Cross Station and Westminster Cathedral.[1] On their return leg from London the sailing barges would be filled with the city's dustbin refuse. During the winter months this 'rough stuff' consisted of more than 50 per cent coal fire cinders. Enough of this fuel was recycled to burn all the bricks for the following season.

When war was declared in 1914 Dean was underage for military service. Having spent his youth re-enacting colonial actions such as Rorke's Drift with lead soldiers, Dean could have had little idea he too would one day receive the coveted medal awarded to so many of the heroic defenders of Zulu fame. In fact the defenders of Rorke's Drift proved a useful inspiration to him and were very much in his mind when he won his own VC defending a post against overwhelming odds.

Before the war he had been a member of the 1st Sittingbourne Troop of Boy Scouts and this no doubt imbued him with the sense of adventure and initiative Baden-Powell thought so necessary for the youth of the era. This, coupled with real concerns of being presented with a white feather, saw Dean sign-up for service at the first opportunity and we have documentary evidence he lied about his age to do so.

His first step into the armed forces may require some explanatory note here. As the account correctly states, Dean had to pay for the privilege of enrolling in the armed services. The 28th County of London Regiment (Artists' Rifles) was a London-based volunteer regiment first formed in 1860 in response to a perceived invasion threat from the French Emperor Napoleon III. As its name suggests, the corps originally comprised creative individuals such as painters, musicians and actors. During the First World War the regiment was a popular choice for those hoping to gain commissions. Based in France, the 1st Bn of the Artists' Rifles operated as an officer training corps. During the course of the Great War 10,256 officers were commissioned after training before being posted to other regiments. Of these 4,848 were posted killed, missing or wounded.[2]

From the Artists' Rifles, Dean was posted to the 11th Bn Queen's Own Royal West Kent Regiment. This was a local battalion formally established on 12 November 1915. By 'Local' this means the battalion was raised from volunteers by an individual or corporate body, which took care of all expenses and training until the unit passed a formal War Office inspection. In this case the task of raising the unit was given to the Mayor of Lewisham, Mr R. Jackson. Leaving its base in Catford for the front, the 11th Bn had its first real taste of action at the Somme, north of Derville Wood on 15 September 1916. It was a bloody baptism of fire. Out of eighteen officers and 592 other ranks going into action, only five officers and 262 men were left unscathed by the end of the day. The battalion was immediately reinforced and saw action again at Eaucourt l'Abbaye on 7 October. In this action German machine guns halted the battalion's advance after just 100 yards. By nightfall only four officers and 100 men were left in the line, from a starting strength of 481. Posted to the Royal West Kents on 3 October, Dean arrived shortly after this bloody affair, a fresh-faced 2nd Lieutenant aged nineteen.

After the Somme offensive the British turned their attention to the Channel coast with the intention of denying Belgian ports to the German Imperial Navy by driving northward from Ypres. Here the British front line created a bulge in the German front line, the result of which was that the Germans could shell Ypres from three directions simultaneously. In order not to expose their rear while driving up to the coast from Ypres, the British first had to clear German opposition on the Messines Ridge to the south of the city. To this end the 11th Bn was sent into the Ypres Salient along the southeastern sector near the Ypres/Comines Canal.

The winter of 1916/17 was particularly harsh and Dean's depiction of life in the trenches leaves us in no doubt about the hardships British and Commonwealth troops faced. As Dean describes, their position was made all the worse by a combination of a low water table and heavy shelling. From our modern perspective, to endure such conditions and such a high rate of casualties seems inconceivable. The British generals of the Great War have entered popular consciousness as aloof, ill-informed and uncaring. Of their leadership, Dean's paradoxical views are probably reflective of many when he noted, 'We felt that all the generals considered us as "expendable" and as "cannon fodder", but we also felt that our only chance of winning the war was to do as they ordered'.

While recovering from a wound in England, Dean missed the opening of the Battle of Messines and therefore did not witness the famous detonation of the mines under the German positions on 7 June. His account of the trenches continues from the end of this phase of the fighting to the Third Battle of Ypres, a battle more commonly known as Passchendaele. Dean's vivid description of the attack on 'Tower Hamlets' ridge on 20 September 1917 rates among the most memorable pieces in his account. In his papers I found a version of this account which had many of the more graphic details omitted from his final manuscript. In this early draft one can recognize a piece of writing, which although told matter-of-factly, has all the hallmarks of a cathartic unburdening of the horrors he witnessed and endured during that attack. Needless to say, it was the earlier account I included.

While his account of war in the trenches and in particular his gripping account of the attack on 'Tower Hamlets' at Passchendaele will no doubt capture the lion's share of attention among general readers, the second half of the memoir is equally, if not more important, for students of military history.

After the war, Dean returned to the family brick-making business. Not forsaking army life completely, Dean remained a Territorial officer in The Buffs. On Britain's declaration of war on 3 September 1939 Dean was the lieutenant-colonel of the 4th Bn. He had recruited this battalion from scratch and fully expected to lead it into battle himself. Instead he was rejected, he claimed, because he was not a Regular officer, although his age (then forty-two) was cited as the real reason. Bitterly disappointed he was instead sent to the Auxiliary Military Pioneer Corps. This set in motion a chain of events which led to one of the signal acts of Dean's career: the retreat to and defence of Boulogne in 1940.

The Pioneers deserve a special mention at this point as they are often overlooked in military accounts.[3] Until reading Dean's account of the work of the Pioneers in the Second World War I am ashamed to admit having only a passing knowledge of this vital component to waging war. The sheer scale and diversity of the enterprises Dean oversaw in his time with the Pioneers is staggering. While an army of Napoleon's day might be said to march on its stomach, in the Second World War, armies needed lakes of petrol, mountains of ammunition and supplies of every kind. As Dean's account shows, the logistical support of the Allied military endeavour was nothing short of epic. There was almost nothing the Pioneers could not achieve, from handling stores and ammunition, building camps, airfields and fortifications, clearing rubble, building roads, railways and bridges, loading and unloading ships, trains and aircraft, constructing airfields and aircraft pens, etc. Essentially they provided each field army with a pool of labour to support the Royal Engineers and the needs of the other armed services. Often, when the needs of the army outgrew the manpower available, Pioneer commanders like Dean became great hirers and organizers of civilian labour. This called for an enormous amount of tact, diplomacy and cutting through 'red tape' – something Dean revelled in. In fact, from reading the account, one is left with the impression that Dean's principal opponent was not the enemy forces on the other side of the hill, but 'the system'.

The Pioneers could also fight. Initially only 25 per cent of Pioneers were equipped with rifles, but it soon became clear to Dean in France that all should be trained in 'musketry', if only for improving morale. Although training had begun by May 1940, the other 75 per cent of rifles were not forthcoming in time for the German *Blitzkrieg* offensive. As the British in Flanders were outflanked by the German drive on the Channel though Amiens and Arras, a large proportion of Dean's command were without weapons. Hence we read of Pioneers tackling German tank crews with picks and shovels. It was only when Dean commandeered weapons from those soldiers embarking at Boulogne that anything like enough were available, but by then it was really too late.

On the barricades of Boulogne the Pioneers faced the tanks of German 2nd Panzer division with nothing but rifles and their inherent ingenuity. They made a stout defence: dive-bombed from above, mortared and shelled by tanks from in front and shot at by 'Fifth Columnists' and trigger-happy Guardsmen to the rear, they certainly gave as good as they got. Dean's account of the defence of the French Channel port in 1940 brings welcome light to an episode somewhat eclipsed by the events along the coast at Dunkirk. Dean's considerable anger and frustration over the debacle was clear – but the summer of 1940 was not a time to rock the boat. With the threat of Nazi invasion perceived to be imminent, the army hardly had time to mount an inquiry over the matter and Dean was ordered by an unnamed brigadier at Aldershot never to voice his views on the matter again. Seventy years on from Boulogne, this memoir at last sets out Dean's side of the story in full.

Dean's next foray abroad was to the French-held island of Madagascar. Operation Ironclad remains one of the less well known episodes of the Second World War, but it was vitally important to the British. The objective was to prevent the ports of Madagascar being used by Japanese submarines operating in the Indian Ocean against Britain's Eastern Fleet and, more importantly, against the supply routes to the Eighth Army in Egypt. With the entrance to the western Mediterranean then dominated by Axis U-boats and aircraft, British convoys travelling to Egypt would pass the long way round Africa. Japanese bases at Madagascar would cut this vital route and complete the strangulation of British links to Egypt, Suez and the oil fields of the Middle East. The torpedoing of the battleship HMS *Ramillies* by Japanese midget submarines on 29 March 1942 showed the Japanese threat off Madagascar was real and present.

While some French colonial possessions had declared for de Gaulle, Madagascar remained staunchly in support of the Vichy government. Given this regime's apparent collaboration with the Nazis and following Britain's attack on the French navy at Mers el Kébir on 3 July 1940, there appeared little chance the French would resist any Axis request to use Madagascar's three major ports as a base for military operations as described above.

On 5 May 1942 the first phase of the operation began with an assault landing near the port of Diego Suarez on the north of the island. This landing was opposed and the port was only taken after two days' heavy fighting. When it became clear the French authorities had no intention of surrendering the whole island, a second landing was organized, this time against the western port of Majunga. This landing took place on 9 September, with the port falling on the following day. Nine days later a third expedition was launched against Tamatave and only here did the French surrender after token resistance.

From Madagascar Dean took part in the invasion of Sicily. Following the Battle of El Alamein (23 October 1942) and the successful Torch landings, the capture of Sicily was the final step to secure the Mediterranean for Allied shipping. The invasion was a colossal endeavour, perhaps unfairly eclipsed by the later Normandy landings. Here 160,000 men, 14,000 vehicles, 600 tanks and 1,800 pieces of artillery were assembled in convoys and unleashed on the island on 10 July 1943. Needless to say the Pioneers again played a leading role in facilitating this enterprise.

After Sicily, Italy was invaded. While the Americans landed at Salerno, Montgomery's Eighth Army crossed the Straits of Messina on 3 September 1943. Dean had experienced Montgomery's leadership style before and was not an enthusiast. Despite bearing some physical resemblance to Montgomery, Dean, like many senior British officers, preferred General Alexander's quiet confidence to Monty's showmanship.

Each of these campaigns is described in great detail with a dry humour I have come to associate with the late colonel. I have also come to appreciate his observations of life outside the scope of the war. The complexities of logistical nightmares in Madagascar are lightened with such anecdotes as the mythology of giant crocodiles and the range of flying foxes. In Italy he confesses to having kept his sanity by taking long, solitary walks in the countryside, which he describes in vivid colours.

In their original form, the memoirs consist of two typed manuscripts, each containing an account of the First and Second World Wars respectively. In addition, there are dozens of papers, including handwritten notes, official reports, diary entries and press cuttings. Also made available to me were numerous private letters to his wife covering the periods when he was on active service. The letters mostly refer to domestic matters: to the family finances, the education and progress of Dean's two children and routine observations about life in the officers' mess. Some of these letters have been reproduced in the text as they shed light on several interesting areas Dean omitted from his manuscript, such as his meeting the King in France in 1939. In other places the text from certain important letters has been added into the general account.

I have edited these various documents into a single narrative as sympathetically as possible. Apart from the occasional alteration of syntax, the words produced here accurately reflect Dean's original accounts. In two places I have found it necessary to expand Colonel Dean's account. To ensure the reader distinguishes between them and the original account, Colonel Dean is referred to in the third person. One of these inserts is to add detail to the inter-war period. Typically modest, only the barest note was provided for the details surrounding his winning the Victoria Cross. Using these notes and, at his suggestion, the regimental history of the 8th Bn of the West Kent Regiment, I have expanded the original memoir to give the fullest possible account.[4]

I should like to acknowledge Colonel Dean's daughter, Susan Bavin, for giving me access to and entrusting me with the care of these precious family relics. Without the constant support and advice of Richard Walduck, this book would never have been realized. Great thanks must also go to Philip Sidnell at Pen & Sword for having faith in this project. I have been given much valuable advice from Lieutenant Colonel John Starling, the current Pioneer Regimental Historian, who was kind enough to comment on the Second World War account and offer his expert advice. For taking the time to read sections of the book I am also grateful to Colonel K.R. FitzGerald for his comments and Richard Dunn, Director RE Museum, Library and Archive. I also must acknowledge Christine Rayner, editor of the *East Kent Gazette* and Claire Laming for their help sourcing material from the EKG's archives. I should also like to thank Tony Butler and Lawrence Hannaford for their respective photographic expertise.

Lastly, but by no means least, for her patience and understanding, I would like to thank my wife Sarah.

Terry Crowdy

Maps

LIST OF MAPS

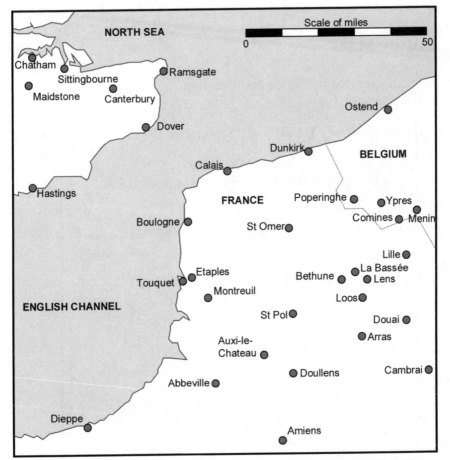

Dean's service in France and Belgium, 1915-18 and 1939-40

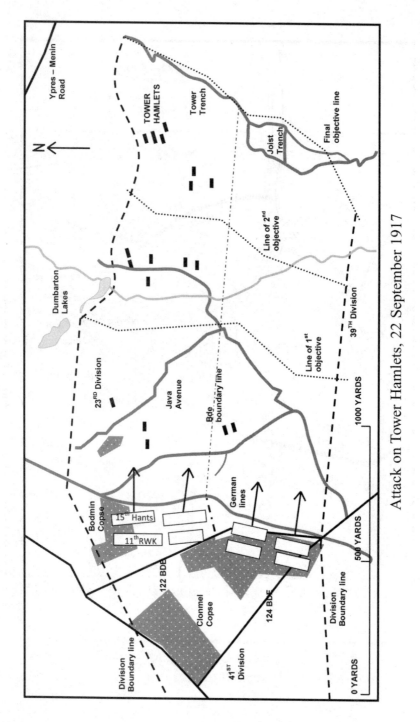

Attack on Tower Hamlets, 22 September 1917

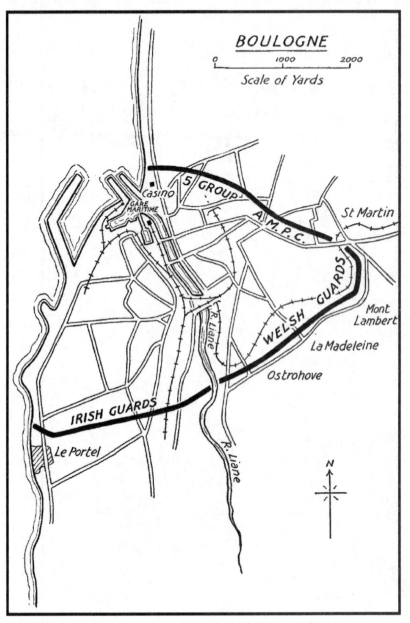

The Defence of Boulogne, May 1940
(courtesy of the Royal Pioneer Corps Association)

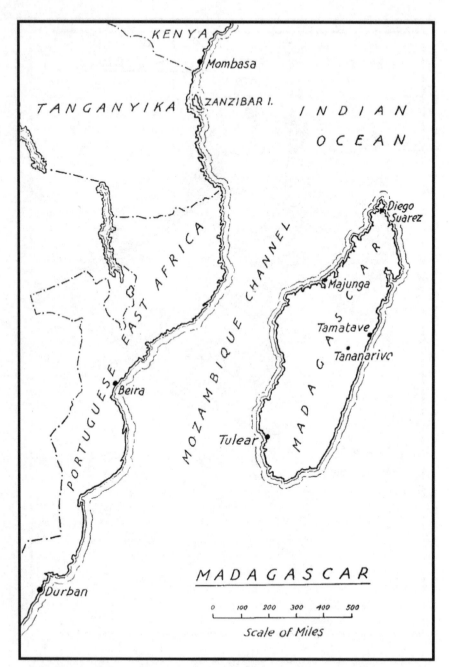

Madagascar (courtesy of the Royal Pioneer Corps Association)

Italy and Sicily (courtesy of the Royal Pioneer Corps Association)

DONALD DEAN VC

PART I

The Great War

While they are still fresh in my memory, I put on record the following details on my wife's suggestion that my war experiences may be of interest to our descendents after I have ceased to be able to answer in person the question set by the popular recruiting slogan: 'What did you do in the Great War, Daddy?'

Donald John Dean

CHAPTER 1

The Artists' Rifles

When war was declared in 1914 I was seventeen and, like most of my friends, I was anxious to play my part. We were faced everywhere with recruiting posters calling upon the young men to enlist to fight 'the war to end wars'. Girls were constantly giving white feathers to young men who appeared to them to be slow in joining up and practically the whole nation was united and solidly behind the government and armed forces; especially when it was seen that our valiant little Expeditionary Force was totally inadequate for such a massive war for which we of course were not prepared, in the traditional way.

There was no conscription at that time, nor was it at all necessary as men flocked to the recruiting stations to join either: 1) The Regular Army for long engagements; 2) The Territorial Force (known as The Terriers); or 3) The New Army, generally known as Kitchener's Army, for hostilities only. No. 2 was not encouraged to start with as the Territorial Force was for Home Defence at the time and the individual could only be sent overseas if they volunteered to do so. Shortly, however, they only took men who signed on for Foreign Service. We therefore had the three recruiting offices going in competition to some extent.

My elder brother, Graham, was very keen to join up and tried the Terriers but was turned down on eyesight, as he had to wear spectacles. He therefore memorized the three smallest lines of type on the sight card and tried again. They were very suspicious of him when he could read the small print easily but not the larger print higher up the card. Nothing daunted he learned the lot and was accepted on the third try at a different recruiting station. He joined our local company of The Buffs and later saw service in Gallipoli and what we later called 'The Middle East'. But this is not his story.

My younger brother, Harold, first of all made munitions after leaving school and then trained as a ship's wireless operator. At the age of eighteen his first ship was a cargo vessel and he was the only wireless officer on board. He later served on transports etc until the end of the war and received the Merchant Navy medal.

I tried twice to enlist locally, but was sent home as they knew I was way under age. I was reluctantly persuaded to wait until I was older before enlisting so I joined the Special Constabulary and also a newly formed Volunteer Corps which was really intended for home defence for those too old or too infirm for active service abroad, or in some essential job. I am the only case I ever heard of who joined it because he was *under* military age.

I'd decided it would suit my purpose best to join the ranks, learn my job and then take a commission in a smart London Territorial battalion. I wrote to Uncle Harold Walduck asking him if he would kindly make enquiries about the best London battalions. So on my eighteenth birthday, 19 April 1915, I went up to London and Uncle Harold sent me round in his car with three suggested battalions to call on if found necessary. The nearest address was the headquarters of the Artists' Rifles, the 28th County of London Regiment in Dukes Road, off Euston Road, so I made first application here. The minimum age for enlistment was still nineteen, so giving my age as nineteen – of course – I enlisted, becoming Number 3692, Private Dean. I wired home jubilantly, being thankful that I had managed to join up before the war was over because at that time we still expected it to be settled in our favour within a few months.

The entrance fee charged to all recruits permitted to enlist in the Artists' was 25/-. We started off by doing squad drill, tent pitching etc in Russell Square Gardens for the first few weeks and living out. My living and ration allowance for the first week came to 19/3 as far as I can remember, anyway just under £1, but as Uncle Harold Walduck very kindly allowed me to live free in the Premier Hotel, Russell Square, this did not unduly worry me and he would accept none of the allowance.

Early in May we marched down to Richmond Park which gave us ample training area for everything then required of the army. We were brigaded with the London Scottish; the Queen's Westminsters and the Honourable Artillery Company. At first we formed 3rd Bn and later 2nd Bn. By this time 1 Bn was in France and the 2nd Bn consisted of those few men who had not felt able to volunteer for Imperial Service.

To start with we had part only of our uniforms but were gradually issued with the balance as and when available. We must have looked a queer lot with some in army caps as their only sign of uniform, some with tunics only and so on. The uniform at that time consisted of a stiff cap, tunic with brass buttons and numerals, both of which had to be kept in a high state of shine, and long trousers worn with puttees. The last were yards of khaki bandage which had to be neatly wound from ankle to knee. This was no mean feat and they had to both end at the same particular point of the legs. As there was only a little stretch in most of them there had to be also several turnovers, all to pattern, to get them to fit snugly. The British Infantryman was reputed to be the only male with ankles looking bigger than his calf. We had to provide our own underclothing, washing and shaving tackle, also cleaning materials and two pairs of marching boots, for which we received a total payment of £1. If the total was not complete we got nothing.

Again owing to acute shortages of equipment we were armed for about two months with short, cavalry Martini-Henry carbines and bandoliers from the Boer War. Later we also received some bayonets, which did not fit these carbines.

Our commanding officer was a Lieutenant Colonel Shirley who had recently changed his name from Sharleib and being of foreign parentage was apparently not allowed to go into a theatre of war, or at least that is what we firmly believed.

Our pay was then one shilling a day, but those receiving marriage allowance, or separation allowance as it was then called, had 6d per day docked off their rate of pay.

In camp we all slept in bell tents, generally eight men to a tent, which meant very little room round the centre pole for eight rifles and eight pairs of feet! We had no mess tents so fed outside our bell tents when fine or inside them when wet. The food was brought round and dished out onto our mess tins or plates, if we provided them ourselves, and quite naturally the last tents to be served had cold food, but we all made very light of any discomfort.

After we had been in camp for a few days the orderly officer came round as usual one morning, together with the orderly sergeant who called in the approved stentorian voice 'tent 'shun, any complaints', whereupon I, being at that moment the senior soldier in our tent by nearly two days said to the officer, 'Yes sir, the fish issued for breakfast is bad'. He replied, 'I know it is but I can't do anything about it, have you got enough?' This taught me a lesson never to make a complaint again in the army but I took care later on when I was orderly officer that a legitimate complaint received attention.

About this time I started a very great friendship with two other recruits, Kingsley Thompson Smith (always known as 'Katie') [Out of respect, Dean refers to him by his initials K.T. for the rest of the account – Ed.] and Vernon Baynes, an Englishman who had recently emigrated to Australia but had returned to enlist. We soon had a working arrangement which was most successful. When any one (or two) of us was detailed at the last moment for fatigue duty after normal parades the one of the trio next on our private rota would answer and act for him. Our NCOs were a little puzzled sometimes to find a man they knew as Dean answering to the name of Baynes, but as long as they got the number of bods they wanted they did not really bother and this gave us three some chance of keeping any date made for that evening.

Owing to a case of measles occurring in our tent the whole tent was shifted and pitched well away from camp near the public boundary. We entertained several of the public to tea (girls of course) while in isolation here. This led indirectly to my being written to later as 'a Lovely Soldier' by a girlfriend of one of these casual visitors.

There was considerable rain at one time and the lower part of our camp was flooded at least a foot but we just moved a line of tents higher up the slope and dried our blankets etc when the sun shone.

Shower baths were later installed but we never of course got any hot water for them. But nobody complained seriously about this or anything else as there was a wonderful feeling of all-out endeavour to fit ourselves as quickly as possible for the overseas service for which we had all joined and the only fear was that the fighting might all be over before we could get out to do our bit. This, remember, was early in 1915! The idea of losing the war never entered our heads for one moment. We prayed in all our churches for victory in our righteous war just the same as the Germans were doing, to the same God.

About this time there was rioting in the East End of London where shops with German or Austrian names over them, or thought to be belonging to enemy aliens, were broken into and smashed up. Half our battalion was ordered to stand by as an 'inlying piquet' to be rushed out to reinforce the civilian police if necessary at a moment's notice. This piquet was chosen by detailing any man who had fired a rifle, then to make up numbers, any man who had fired a shotgun and finally any man who had fired an air rifle. They were issued with live ammunition in readiness. After several days of this business they complained about being confined to camp night after night so then the live ammunition was handed over to the other half battalion who had never fired even an air rifle and they were the emergency squad. Providentially for the population of the East End and themselves, they were not required to perform.

Later we moved to High Beech near Loughton in Epping Forest to continue our training and were armed with long Lee Enfield rifles and short bayonets. These rifles had been discarded by the Regular Army but naturally were quite good enough for the Territorial Force and actually were a good and accurate rifle even if a trifle clumsy for trench warfare. These rifles were all sighted for mark 6 ammunition, which was no longer made and so we were issued with mark 7 ammo. We fired our rifle course on the Purfleet and Rainham ranges and merely had to adjust our sights by trial and error with sighting shots at each distance before firing the course. One of the most important tests then being to fire fifteen aimed rounds in one minute starting with only five rounds in the magazine. It could be done but needed much practice. We also in those days fired regularly at 600 yards and a few shots at 1,000 yards. But this it must be remembered was before the day of the light automatic rifle or light machine gun.

One wet day we had a lecture by our company officer, Captain (Pigeon) Rust, who decided that he should read out to us from King's Regulations and

The Manual of Military Law all the offences that one could commit in the army for which a man could be shot. We volunteers thought this really funny.

After we had been in the army for fourteen weeks we were pronounced trained men. We were called at this time 3rd Bn Artists' Rifles. The 2nd Bn consisted then of all those who could not agree to going overseas for business or family reasons or just 'cold feet'. About this time there was considerable excitement as a draft of 250 men was prepared to go to the 1st Bn in France. All those known to be under nineteen years old were carefully weeded out of this draft.

Suddenly we received leave from 1pm until midnight. I wired Mother and I met her for a few hours at Auntie Jessie's house at Bromley, Kent. This was our only leave before going abroad. The next morning, early, we marched off and entrained for Southampton where we waited for ten days expecting every day to embark. Owing to this unexpected delay we all spent all our money thinking each day would be our last in England, perhaps for all time.

When we were lined up at Loughton camp ready to move off, Lieutenant Colonel Shirley gave us a farewell speech which ran as follows: 'Trust in the Lord and keep your bowels well open may God go with you I'm sorry I can't move to the right in fours form fours right Quick March'; all this without a punctuation pause.

We finally sailed in a small boat about 10 August 1915. We followed the usual custom of crossing by night to Le Havre, where we lay outside the minefields until daylight before entering harbour. We had a pleasant surprise, however, when we found that our boat was going right up the Seine as far as Rouen – the day was a perfect one for this trip which we all very much enjoyed.

We disembarked, marched up a steep hill and spent the night lying in mud, crammed into leaking bell tents. We were visited by a succession of small boys soliciting in broken English for their sisters with Rabelaisian remarks about their feminine charms and skill.

We entrained next morning in the trucks (with which we were to become so very familiar in the next few years) each labelled '*Hommes 40 chevaux 8*' and on the third day since we embarked arrived very late at night in St Omer and joined our 1st Bn which was living in ancient French barracks and acting as GHQ Troops. Directly opposite to these barracks was of course the usual 'licensed premises'.

On parade at 7 am the next morning I was roundly told off because I had not, before getting on parade, polished the tiny buckle on my chin strap! This was of course to give us an indication of the extremely high standard of spit and polish expected of us.

Our barrack rooms literally had nothing in them except grime when we arrived and we had to live and eat in them. The food was brought round in dixies and dumped on the landing where it was dished out into our individual mess tins or plates. It was not long before we remedied this in our room, as in most of the others, by acquiring a trestle table, homemade forms (benches) and later, a food cupboard for storing our opened tins of butter, jam, milk, bread etc which both kept the place tidy and also the many flies at bay.

The General Officer Commanding GHQ Troops, a General Stopford, came round one Sunday and made a surprise inspection of the barracks. Later he issued orders to our CO (Lieutenant Colonel 'Auntie' May), a good officer and a gentleman, that as he was horrified to find that The Artists' had made themselves far too comfortable and had acquired furniture not issued by the army and would therefore not be able to move off at two hours' notice as all good soldiers should when on active service. Everything that could not be carried on the person was to be disposed of at once and that he would inspect the barracks again on the Thursday to see that his orders had been complied with. Colonel May finally won permission that those of us who had them could keep our food cupboards, on health grounds, but that was all he could do. He therefore issued his orders and the general duly inspected in four days' time as stated, found bare barrack rooms and went off satisfied.

There was an interesting sequel to this as follows. About ten years later this same General Stopford, then retired, was the guest at a Rotary Club luncheon at Ramsgate of which I was a member. After lunch he was due to make a discourse in the usual manner and he mentioned that he was down at Ramsgate that day to inspect the local Red Cross detachment. He went on to say that though on this occasion his inspection was expected it was not a bad thing sometimes to make a surprise inspection and that he had in mind one that he had made in France in 1915 when he found things most unsatisfactory etc. After the talk our president asked if there were any questions or observations any member would like to make before the vote of thanks was passed. I got up and said that I was particularly interested in the remarks of our distinguished guest as I happened to be a private soldier in the French barracks in 1915 at the time of this surprise inspection and it might be of interest for the gallant general to hear another side of the affair. I then told the assembly that on the morning of the second inspection the whole battalion rose early and packed away everything not Government Issue. The smaller items were packed in cases and sacks and placed out of sight in the barrack roof and my platoon at any rate clubbed together and subsidized the driver of a lorry belonging to the Army Service Corps. We filled his lorry with furniture and off he went into the country for the day. The general inspected, found bare barrack rooms, went off satisfied, the lorry returned and was unloaded and we carried on as before and everyone was satisfied. There was only one man at the luncheon table who was not doubled up with mirth!

K.T., Vernon and I still kept together and shared food parcels and everything in common. I was the total abstainer of the trio and had certain responsibilities in consequence.[1] I remember one evening we three had been out together for a birthday celebration and the other two had rather overdone it. I escorted them back to barracks; K.T.'s legs gave him some difficulty but his head was clear, on the other hand Vernon's head was his weak point but his legs good; I managed to get them safely past the quarter guard and into barracks, Vernon doing what I told him and the two of us casually supporting K.T. while I answered the guard for the three of us.

After a while in France I joined our battalion machine gun section. We were then, like all the Territorial infantry battalions, in possession of two Maxim guns passed on to us by the Regular Army who had the lighter but equally effective Vickers guns. Ours dated from the Boer War. Later I qualified as an instructor in the new Lewis guns which were just beginning to be issued to the British Army. Although they were essentially a light automatic they were originally used on fixed mountings together with the Vickers guns.

Our main work as GHQ Troops was in providing a number of guards which were mainly ceremonial, for instance to the C-in-C General Sir John French, Staff HQ, Chaplain General, etc. also an examining guard on every road into St Omer where we checked the identity of every officer or other ranks entering or leaving the town. This was once again rather a farce as when any of us wanted to go for a walk out of town and had not first obtained a pass we merely used one of the several well known footpaths which were all unguarded. One day when I was on duty on a road guard I stopped a young captain riding a cycle out of town and, as usual, glanced quickly at his pass and noted the official stamp and signature, which being in order I saluted and allowed him to pass. On looking round I spotted a cavalry orderly some fifty yards behind so I looked at the captain's face for the first time and saw it was the Prince of Wales, I immediately called out the guard and we presented arms to his departing back. This was typical of the Prince in those days.[2]

Later on, when King George V came out to visit the troops in France the Prince naturally stayed with him. Our battalion supplied the guard during that period and it was noted that the Prince of Wales used to get up early and take a cross country run, vainly followed by his personal detective who could not keep up with him at all. After the first morning they tried two detectives, posting one at the chateau gate and the other part way along the route taken the first day, but the prince took another route that day! The third and subsequent days the detective or guard was mounted, to the apparent disappointment of the Prince.

Sir John French used to take his exercise walking alone in the public gardens after they had been closed for the day to the public but Sir Douglas Haig, when he took over as Commander-in-Chief, took his exercise on horseback. We were pleased that one of his aides-de-camp, Sir Phillip Sassoon, generally rode a striking piebald horse so if a group of horsemen were seen approaching, one riding this piebald horse, we had ample time to turn out the guard or warn everyone that the C-in-C approached.

When on the march, Vernon, K.T. and I used to carry several unauthorized articles. I generally had the primus stove, K.T. had the kettle and Vernon the teapot etc. At a suitable time we brewed up and always saw that the CSM and platoon sergeant had a cup at the same time, which no doubt helped.

GHQ was later moved to the ancient (largely) walled town of Montreuil and the C-in-C, now Sir Douglas Haig, lived in a nearby chateau.[3] The Artists', less one company, were moved to barracks in Hesdin while one company at a time did guard duty at GHQ. This included ceremonial and security guards at Haig's chateau. For the first time we as guards were allowed a bit of common sense duty as at night two men rambled round the estate, silently watching and sleuthing about, in addition to the double sentries marching up and down who would have been easy enough to dodge.

These guards, while on ceremonial duty, would have been hard to beat by anyone. We were trained under a Guards sergeant major and really knew our stuff. One day one of our sentries was nearly court-martialled because while on duty it was noticed that the end of one of his boot laces had protruded under the bottom of his puttee. For the C-in-C we had double sentries who worked as one man without a glance at each other. When it was necessary to come to the salute, present or to move in any way the selected leader gave a faint tap with the butt of his rifle on a sounding board and everything was done in perfect unison. I was proud to work my way up to being one of these chosen guards.

I later got seven days' leave and proudly showed myself off at home as a veteran, though from the photo taken at that time I must have looked very youthful all the same.

In 1915 there were a certain number of deserters who collected in Clairmarais Forest, near St Omer, and who sallied forth for food at intervals. It was decided to clear them out so some troops, including a detachment of the Artists' Rifles, formed a line of beaters as in a pheasant shoot and swept through the forest to flush them out while other troops waited on the outside.

While I was a private soldier in the barracks in St Omer there was one man we knew who had been appointed from army Details as batman to an army padre in that town. The padre moved on leaving the batman behind, who never reported back to the town major as unemployed, but continued to be fed in the barracks and draw his pay weekly but slept in the town with some French woman. This went on for months but as we moved from St Omer we do not know if it was ever reported.

Then there was the case of a man who was detailed from his unit to look after a certain divisional bath installation. His division moved away and the incoming division appointed a new man to the bath job; but the first man remained without a job and forgotten but continued to mess with division details as before. He feared to draw his pay, getting a remittance from home, but after a year or more he managed to get leave to the UK (how I never heard) and when in England he is reported to have drawn all his back pay. On his return from leave he got swallowed up in the depot at Étaples and I never heard any more of him.

Early in 1916 Vernon was commissioned so our trio of 'the three musketeers' was broken up. Later both K.T. and I were chosen to go to the cadet school. We did not have to produce birth certificates in France to prove age as it was naturally assumed that we must be over the minimum age of nineteen years to have got out to France at all. While waiting to go to the cadet school at Blendecques (near St Omer) we were made acting corporals and put in charge of prisoners from the local army detention camp to do certain sanitary work in Hesdin and district. One day there were insufficient prisoners to do this work so we, as acting NCOs and potential officers, had to empty the buckets ourselves!

Although the war was fierce for all combatant men, some of the staff officers during 1914 and 1915 had their wives or lady friends out in France and it was not unknown for them to be as near to the front as Amiens, though as far as reports went, most of the ladies stayed in Paris and the officers got weekend leave fairly freely. It was always understood that Sir Douglas Haig was the one to put a stop to this.

We had a turn in the trenches at 'Plug Street' where one section of the line was only twenty feet from the German trench but things had been so impossible for both sides with bombing (hand grenades) that by mutual, but unspoken agreement, both sides now refrained from throwing grenades at each other while we were there.[4]

At the cadet school we had a very intensive course of six weeks during which a certain number fell out and were returned to their units, but at the end we were commissioned. Quite a lot of stress was placed on ceremonial company and battalion drill which was considered both essential to an officer, however junior, and good value for discipline etc. I was roundly told off myself because when we were asked for any suggestions on the training we had, I suggested that we might with advantage learn something about strategic retreat, which had always been the role of the British Army in every major war up until then and even in 1914 was not done too well from all accounts. I was told that 'the British Army never retreats' which was so obviously untrue that it sounded farcical, bearing in mind the retreat from Mons.

We had to get our officers' clothing and equipment from the army officers' shop in St Pol but as usual there was not enough of anything in stock to go round for the fifty-odd of us, newly commissioned. There never was. Those of us who got valises could not have sleeping bags and those who had revolvers (at that time each officer bought his and it remained his personal property), could not have binoculars and vice versa. We had an allowance of £35 to buy revolver, binoculars, prismatic compass, Sam Browne, valise, sleeping bag, two tunics, one pair officers breeches, one pair officers trousers, puttees, brown boots, khaki shirts, socks, ties etc. A further £15 was given if or when we returned to the UK and could buy and use camp furniture (bed, bath etc) but not on active service as we in the infantry could not carry them round with us. We had no mechanical transport of any kind and for the horsed transport officers were allowed to put on the wagon a valise or bundle not to exceed 35 lbs in weight, which of course included blankets, training manuals and all that could not be carried on the person, so only the very barest minimum could be taken. Naturally infantry officers were expected normally to sleep on the ground. The pay of a 2nd Lieutenant was then 5/- per day.

There were twenty of us cadets in our division or class at the cadet school and we kept tabs on each other; all had gone to infantry regiments. Within eight weeks eighteen of us were dead and my great pal K.T. Smith was killed a few months later, leaving me as the sole survivor of our class, all within about six months. K.T. and I asked to go to the same unit and I gave The Buffs as my first choice and The Queen's Own Royal West Kent Regiment as second choice. We were commissioned in the latter regiment and ordered to report to the 11th Bn which we duly did together with other officers and a draft of fine men from the Kent Yeomanry who, to their disgust, were turned into infantry. We were all received with pleasure as our battalion had just had a shocking number of casualties. They were in the 41st Division which was then taking part in the bloodbath of the Somme, which we saw the end of.

My platoon, No. 16, contained some hard bitten toughs. One section came from Wapping and I, being young and inexperienced, had great difficulty in controlling them to start with until one day when we were out of the lines a parade of the battalion was ordered in marching order, which of course included full equipment. When we were on parade we were told that two jars of rum had been stolen from the QM store and that every platoon officer, or sergeant if there was no officer, was to sniff his men's water bottles to see if they smelt of rum. We accordingly did this and the first of my platoon's water bottles not only smelt of rum but contained rum. The man and I looked hard at each other but no word was spoken. Half of the men in my platoon still had rum in their water bottles but I kept silent. The CO called to us in rotation 'No. 1 Platoon any sign of rum?' 'No sir' 'No. 2?' and so on while the tension behind me mounted until finally the question came 'No. 16 Platoon?' and in a firm voice I replied 'No sir' and from that moment there was a bond of understanding between us.

CHAPTER 2

The Ypres Salient

Early in August the battalion machine-gun officer was made assistant adjutant and I was picked to replace him. The 49th Division to which I was posted was the most northerly of the British line. We marched up from the holocaust of the Somme to the Ypres salient and went into the line with our left flank on the Ypres/Comines Canal.

Our rest billets were huts in Reninghelst and one of our early jobs there was to make horse lines with brick hardstandings. We took over from the Canadians who, like all colonial troops, lived only for the day and did no work that could possibly be left undone, either to the line or billets. We obtained lorry loads of bricks from the smashed up town of Ypres. We went in by day in ones and twos, collected and stacked bricks behind some form of cover, and after dark the lorries came in and we loaded them up.

The Second Battle of Ypres (22 April – 25 May 1915) had left the British trenches much knocked about. Astride the Yser Canal the depth at which dugouts could be made was severely limited. Some trenches were on the east bank and some including the communications to the rear, on the west. The whole of this area was waterlogged and as soon as we tried to dig a trench it filled with water so we had to build breastworks most of the time there.

When the autumn rains came, liquid mud ruled our days. Puttees, rolled upward from the knee, were worn by infantry and the mud came up nearly to the knee. When you wanted to wash your hands you dipped them in the mud and dusted it off when dry. In these conditions living in the trenches presented many problems for everyone. The officers' mess consisted of three or four sheets of corrugated iron laid across the trench, very likely with a thin rubber ground sheet at one end to keep the rain out. Candles, or rations, were stuck in bottles or other receptacles. Six feet along the trench the batmen, also under corrugated sheets, cooked a meal for four or five officers. Each officer contributed an enamel plate, knife, fork and spoon. How they got washed during and after a meal one did not ask, but after meat and pudding I have known sardines on toast to be served.

A daily ration of rum for all ranks came up, which was welcome. Communications to the rear were impossible by the day and the REs had installed on the muddy surface a track of wooden rails and a four-wheeled trolley to carry the rations up and any casualties down. On 8 December my machine-gun section remained behind in the trenches to cover the company's relief. On the following morning – I had to wait until after dark – I stopped a small splinter from a whiz-bang in my right knee. After dark when the rations had arrived I was put on a stretcher on the wooden trolley. This took me to Essex Farm – the nearest road traffic could come. As well as serving for rations, there was a forward dressing station there. There were two or three other cases and our stretchers were laid in the mud outside to be loaded into the motor ambulance. I was unlucky. I found myself in the lowest slot and got a face-full of mud.

The winter of 1916/17 was a very hard one. As we had very few dugouts we slept as and where we could when in the line; quite a usual spot would be a very shallow dugout or shelf in the back of the trench or breastwork, above ground level to avoid flooding but of necessity low enough to have a sandbagged roof which did not protrude above the parapet level; when necessary we just stretched out on the fire-step wrapped in a blanket and groundsheet. We took one blanket per man into the trench with us but even so I well remember waking up one night after a short sleep and finding that the muddy gumboots I was wearing were frozen to the ground. Naturally one of our worries was 'trench feet', a complaint brought about by wet, cold and constant wearing of boots. We did our best to fight this with changes of dry socks, when available, and a daily rubbing of the feet with whale oil. The atmosphere in a crowded dugout with men rubbing this on dirty feet can be imagined.

The usual routine when things were comparatively quiet was one week in the front line, one in the support line and one in rest billets, but this was later changed to one week in and one week out wherever possible. We normally had two companies in the front line and two companies in the support line at this time. As it was quite normal for an attack to be made either just after dark or just before daylight, the orders were to 'stand to' (man the posts in readiness) at both dusk and dawn. After the stand down in the mornings we cleaned all weapons in rotation, a few at a time; shaved as and when possible, generally washing in the shaving water owing to the shortage of clean water; posted single sentries to peer through periscopes, repair trenches, etc. After dark we would fix bayonets, post double sentries looking over the parapet, send out wiring parties and patrols as ordered and snatch a little sleep if at all possible. It was necessary to have two men on sentry at night both to keep each other awake and alert and to take turns at looking over. If a man on his own peered too long straining to see the approach of any enemy it was not long before the objects in no man's land seemed to be moving and the wiring stakes forming fours.

One never knew of course when to expect shelling, rifle grenades or trench mortar shells. The heavy shells and howitzer shells one could hear coming and duck a fraction of a second before they arrived but the high velocity field gun shells (whiz-bangs) burst before one heard them coming; ditto the rifle grenades but the latter were proceeded by a sound as of a rifle being fired (as of course it was); and we could generally detect the sound of a trench mortar being fired and looking up could often see them en route and could often dodge the fall of the mortar shell whether it was the plum pudding type or the Minnie (Minnie-Werfer).

The British Army formed trench mortar sections quite independent of the infantry units, under brigade command. These would try and sneak into our front line while we were not looking, fire a few rounds and then run like hell out of it before the enemy retaliation came down on the trench. Not unnaturally they were not looked upon as friends and brothers, but as a real danger to us. We made friends with our own trench mortar section, however, and as we were worried at that time by German rifle grenades, we arranged with our mortar-wallah to have one of his mortars permanently in our trench for a while and every time a rifle grenade came over this Stokes mortar fired two shells in response. The first time or two this brought down on us the Minnies but in a few days the enemy took the hint and stopped firing grenades.

At one time a notice board was put up one night in front of the German breastwork which read something as follows: 'Bavarians here, you no shoot, we no shoot'; but a few days later it was altered to read 'General inspecting, shooting today'.

It was the custom to send out wiring parties at night to fix barbed wire entanglements sufficiently far in front of our trench to prevent enemy patrols creeping up to within bombing distance or rushing a trench undetected. At night a rattle in the wire was soon noted and we even hung up empty tins on the wire to increase the rattle but on windy nights we had many a false alarm. All sides started off by using stakes to hold up the wire but hammering these in on a still night was not funny, however much we muffled the sound with empty sand bags. We later copied the Germans who started using corkscrew pickets which were comparatively quiet in use.

On the unique occasion when our divisional commander, General Sir Sydney Lawford ('Swanky Syd'), came round the front line, he saw through a periscope that the wiring at one point was very poor and he ordered this to be rectified that night and that our CO was to report to him when this was done. As the Germans had a saphead only forty yards from our trench, just there, this was not easy; but orders are orders. Our colonel said to one of my brother officers, 'You've got to go out' and that night, to that particular spot, so that he could report back to the divisional general the following day. Unfortunately they had not been out there very long when our wiring party was fired on by the German machine guns and came in without the work being done. A similar thing happened the second night to another company and on the third I was the one detailed to take out a party and do the job. I didn't like the idea at all. Poor Colonel Corfe hated giving the order to me, but was acting under extreme pressure by this time from the divisional commander.[1]

With considerable misgivings I did the usual thing; sent two men out in no man's land crawling up well in advance, much nearer the German lines than ours, so as to give a warning if any German patrols came out. We started wiring; they began to fire at us. I got a bullet that grazed my neck. We all flattened ourselves of course and I put up a hand and felt the blood. Telling my party to stay in the shell holes, which was hardly necessary, I crawled back to get bandaged up but by the time I got back into a shelter and had a look the bleeding had stopped so there was nothing for it but to return and try again.

As I was crawling out again one of my lookouts crawled over to me and said that he thought the Germans were gathering in their trench for a raid so we waited out there to receive them, but before we fired we found that it was a German wiring party to cover the same ground as us. We immediately got on with our wiring a few feet away; no words passed between us, we just ignored each other. I got a second wiring party out and we wired like hell, until I was satisfied, when on a given signal we all scuttled back into our trench. Then, perhaps not quite playing the game, we gave the Germans what they had given us: a couple of Lewis guns on their wiring party. A dirty trick perhaps, but who can blame us if after living like animals we behaved badly. We did, however, refrain from firing on their stretcher bearers removing their casualties.

For my sins, I suppose, I got appointed battalion patrol officer, which meant taking a patrol out into no man's land at a different time every night, taking a different route and varying the time spent out so as to fox the enemy and to deny the ground to him. For a time the enemy had had mostly his own way out there, but we soon changed this. I got quite familiar with the gaps through ours and the enemy's wire, best shell holes, ditches, etc. It was not quite as simple as it might sound as there were sections of old trenches and scattered lines of wiring running in various directions and both front-line trenches weaved about quite substantially with odd saps running out of them.

It was really my own fault that I got this thankless job, mainly because I did not know when to keep my big mouth shut. I was originally told to take out a patrol and try to find a hole in the enemy wire. I took out a sergeant and two privates and got to the enemy wire when I left them in a shell hole while I crawled along it testing likely-looking gaps. I found a passage through

15

presently but then I discovered that there was a German patrol between me and our front line. When he spotted the enemy my sergeant took himself and his two men back unseen but I was spotted and I shot a German who was in my way and made it to safety myself. I was immediately as sick as a dog but reported to the company commander what had happened and was told to get out there again quickly and try to bring in the German, dead or alive, for identification. (We were always trying to check up what German units faced us so that the pattern could be put together by our Higher Command.)

I tried to do as ordered but was met by the enemy party waiting for just such a move. In my report I suggested going out the next night and finishing my reconnaissance. Colonel Corfe said 'as he seems to enjoy himself in no man's land he had better be permanent patrol officer'. I must say that we did shortly after this have control out there and the enemy cut out reconnaissance patrols and only occasionally sent out fighting patrols.

That winter we had a newly commissioned 2nd Lieutenant join us one evening in the trenches and our company commander sent him out on patrol that same night with an experienced sergeant as tutor. I voiced a protest as the poor fellow had no idea of his job and had not even seen no man's land in daylight, but I was very curtly told to mind my own bloody business. They went out and only the sergeant returned. The officer, 2nd Lieutenant Knight, was most foolishly wearing a trench coat when he went out and, when a Verey light was fired, he did not keep stock still but tried to dive for cover; his coat got caught in the barbed wire when the enemy opened up with machine gun fire. I went out with the sergeant as guide to try and bring him in but the Germans had removed him before we got to the spot. It was not until several weeks later that we heard details of his fate. One of our men who happened to come from the same town as 2nd Lieutenant Knight had his local paper sent out to him and it reached him while we were in the same trenches once again. The paper informed us that he had been wounded while on patrol, had been captured by the Germans and that he had died of wounds while in captivity. Although he had been wounded only 100 yards from where we then stood the information travelled from Germany to the Red Cross in Switzerland, from them to our War Office who had informed the parents who informed the local paper and had sent a copy out to us in Belgium.

But to return to the question of patrols in general – during the bitter winter months of 1916/17 it was imperative to take off one's greatcoat before going on patrol as one cannot crawl in a coat at any time and especially with strands of barbed wire lying around. We got back at times merely muddy and wet but other times shuddering with cold, hardly able to move and it was on such occasions that a tot of rum probably saved us from pneumonia. This is when I stopped being a teetotaller.

When the snow lay thick on the ground we showed up badly against the white so I indented for six white patrol suits which we heard were available. When they arrived they turned out to be nothing but women's white cotton nighties. As one had red featherstitching round the neck and short sleeves I decided it must be an officer's pattern and so took it myself. At that particular period we were using as a password, changing daily, a series of girls' names. That night I led my patrol party up the trench wearing our new white nighties (which while only covering us down to the knees and elbows did at least break up the outline). There was a challenge from the sentry, 'Halt, who goes there?' Answer: 'Gladys'.

My company commander for some months was Captain F. who was capable enough when sober but often took too much while in the line. We all covered up for him and this was not discovered. One night he would keep getting out of the trench and wandering about no man's land making so much noise that he was bound to have been shot sooner or later even if he did not wander into the German line, so I had to deal firmly with him. After bringing him back twice, with help as he was more powerful than I, I put him in his funk-hole and put a sheet of corrugated iron over the entrance and staked it down but even then he fired his revolver through the metal so I had to put a sentry over his funk-hole also. He was killed in action at Messines a few months later. RIP.

Our opposite number at that time was 11th Bn The Queen's and while we were both very rude to each other, the two units really got on very well together. There was an occasion when the line was raided while they were in and they lost the only Lewis gun belonging to that particular company. The first I knew about it was when they came to relieve us and one of their officers, whom I naturally knew, begged me to leave my Lewis gun with him when we were relieved, explaining (what I already knew) that he would be court-martialled if this loss was officially reported. He said that they were trying hard, but so far unsuccessfully, to get a replacement and say nothing about it. Between us we got a few spare parts and a fragment of a destroyed Lewis Gun and he successfully got a new one in exchange for 'one almost totally destroyed by enemy shellfire'.

During that same winter there were times when we got very short of water, all of which had to be brought up in two-gallon petrol cans. Things were difficult when the filling points froze up and the cans had to be filled far back. By the time they in turn came up they were frozen solid. We often used water for washing from the nearest section of the Ypres/Comines canal but had to chop a hole down for that. We could only use this for drinking water in an emergency and then only after heavy chlorination, as we knew there were bodies in it.

Baths were difficult to get at this time also and the division laundry was inadequate, so naturally we all got thoroughly lousy. When out of the line the custom was for men to go to the combined bath/laundry, undress and hand in their dirty underclothing, pass through the bath house which sometimes had showers but otherwise tubs, and receive clean towels and underclothes as they emerged. This system was better than nothing, but it presupposed that all men took the same size and also, while the laundry mostly killed the vermin but not the eggs, this really made little difference as the untreated uniforms were donned again. Very occasionally both blankets and uniforms were deloused by being placed in autoclaves and superheated steam under pressure was injected; this did the trick but if left in too long, a man's clothing came out boy's size. We had no powder other than Keating's in those days and this merely seemed to nourish rather than destroy vermin.

Our rest billets at Reninghelst were about 8 to 10 miles away from our section of the line and the final 2 miles had to be done after dark of course as we were within clear view of the Germans who had nearly all the higher ground round there. After a bad time in the line it took us nearly four hours to walk out to Reninghelst. We did not mind the wet trenches so much coming out, but wading through water and deep mud going in meant, as a rule, just letting one's clothing dry on one.

So passed the worst of the bitter winter of 1916/17, when the temperature dropped at times to zero. March came in and the Germans started pulling back slightly in some places to shorten their line where there was perhaps a bulge. Opposite us all was quiet for several days so it was thought possible that this had happened on our front. The company on the right of 'D' Coy, in which I served, was ordered to send out a reconnaissance patrol to find out. The officer concerned was most mortified to lose his way in no man's land, an easy enough thing to do, and on his return with his tiny patrol I was told to take his place as I knew no man's land so well. I decided to take only one man with me, but the first officer was so upset that he asked for and, very wrongly, received permission from his company commander to be this second man. Officers were far too scarce to be allowed to go in pairs like this.

Off we went and when I had led us to just outside the German wire, opposite a point where I knew there was a gap, I told my friend to lie still in a shell hole, both to guard us, and so that if anything happened to me he could return with a report. I crawled on without hearing a sound from the enemy and decided of course that the only thing to do was to look in the trench to see whether or not it was occupied. It was. In a moment all hell seemed to be let loose, rifle and machine gun fire swept no man's land and grenades were thrown out along the enemy front.

I nipped back promptly and dropped smartly into a shell hole, breaking the ice and getting my legs down in the water, face against the ground and with my arms covering my head as far as possible, fingers laced at the back of my neck. This was just as well because one of the stick bombs burst under water and I got a small leg wound but another burst on the edge of the shell hole close to me and a large splinter penetrated my left forearm and cracked a bone, without the arm protection it would have been my head. A small splinter did, however, get through my interlaced fingers which partially broke the force before it entered the back of my neck.

Things were a bit too warm for me there so I jumped up and dashed back to another shell hole just out of bombing range being joined in this mad scramble by my friend who, stout hearted fellow, had started crawling up to my first hole to see if I needed help. We lay there for quite a time as the enemy artillery had started firing on their SOS line which was between us and our trench, because the German front-line troops had fired their SOS rocket thinking that they were being raided. Fortunately our artillery did not also join in, partly no doubt because we were still down to four shells per gun per day.

Finally things quietened down a bit and we were both very cold and I was in some pain so we started back for our trench, or where we thought it to be, but would you believe it, I had lost my way. It was too overcast for us to see the stars so I used my compass, though as we had to keep changing direction, even then I was not too sure. However, we got near a trench which I judged to be ours but we were neither of us certain. After a few minutes discussion in a shell hole I finally called out and was answered by an English voice. We thankfully climbed in and found ourselves on the next battalion front. The sentry said 'I'm glad you called when you did as we had you covered for several minutes and although I had been warned that a patrol was out next door we did not expect you back here.'

I finished the night in our support line, after sending in a report that there was no truth in the rumour the enemy had vacated his front-line trenches, and next morning walked back behind the line alone as a walking wounded case until I finally made the ambulance waiting at the nearest point possible in daylight. I then went to the Advanced Dressing Station, the Casualty Clearing Station and finally by train to a hospital in Boulogne where they operated and got the piece out of my arm but did not remove the neck splinter, although they had a go at it, as they said it was too near the spine. They unsuccessfully tried again later in a London hospital and I finally had it removed by a civilian surgeon six years later in Chatham.

I was sent to England, to King Edward VII's Hospital in London where we had every possible care and thoughtful attention by Sister Agnes ('Kaiser') and her staff. I later had a few weeks' convalescence in the home of Sir Henry and Lady Samuelson at Hatchford Park, Cobham, Surrey, where they were giving hospitality in their own home to a number of us.

One day in March my parents received a telegram from the War Office saying that they regretted etc that Graham Dean had been severely wounded and then the next day, before my letter reached them, they had another similar

WO telegram saying that Donald Dean had been severely wounded. They naturally imagined that 'severely' meant 'dangerously' and one can imagine their feelings for a while.

After coming out of the convalescent home I asked for a medical board and told them I was fit. They never examined me in any way at all and I was passed for General Service again. This was the usual happy way in which the boards worked then. I was sent to join the 3rd Bn The Queen's Own RWK [Royal West Kent] Regiment, then stationed at Fort Horsted, Chatham; a place where ex-BEF men were *not* welcomed by the permanent staff, few, if any, of whom had seen active service.

K.T. was sent home sick and we met again at Chatham where we were together for a while. He went back to France again shortly before me and got sent to another battalion where he was killed. His grave is unknown and his name is among those of the missing on the British memorial in Arras.[2] Vernon survived the war and returned to Australia where he died of old age. For the last forty-odd years, whenever Armistice Day comes round, these two, but particularly K.T., are especially in my mind – our friendship, tempered by dangers and discomforts shared, is difficult to be understood by those who have not been together through such times.

CHAPTER 3

Passchendaele

My battalion was again very badly cut up in the Messines Battle and I rejoined in time for the tail end of this.[1] One incident that I shall always remember is that at Hollebeke, a village on the right bank of the Ypres/Comines Canal, we attacked one morning and got a lodgement in the shattered village. During a pause in the fighting we collected some of our wounded and laid them under the shelter of a section of wall still standing. The Germans counterattacked and drove us out. We pulled ourselves together and retook and held the ruins. We found that during our temporary absence our row of wounded had been bayoneted as they lay there helpless! It was some months before we took a German prisoner again, and I for one never forgot.

After the war we learned that some of our men, who were attacking with our right hand company against a different enemy unit, were wounded and taken prisoner and the Germans shared their rations with them; both events taking place at the same moment in the same action.

Then there came what might be called the Third Battle of Ypres, though when the Second Battle ended we never knew, but this Third Battle just merged into what we called Passchendaele. But what's in a name anyway? Our 11th Bn was taken out of the line exhausted and decimated, together with most of the 41st Division, where we had some rest, training and reinforcements to prepare us for the next attack.

Our next attack as far as our division was concerned was to take Tower Hamlets ridge south-east of Ypres and I propose giving in some detail the personal side of it rather than to try and give it historically. It was by no means unique, but was as bad as any attack I was in myself.[2]

This may sound simple, but as a rule, very great care was taken over the planning and briefing of the troops before going into action. The point over which they so often fell down was the state of the ground. Arrangements were made weeks if not months beforehand and during that period we steadily pounded the area with heavy shelling which both churned up the ground and probably upset any watercourses. In any case, in the Ypres Salient the water table was just below ground level in much of the area so shell holes quickly filled with water. When therefore we came to do the actual advance we generally found that it was a waterlogged tract through which the troops floundered and over which the guns could not travel to come up in support if we were successful. Fighting under such conditions was a nightmare.

It was arranged that our communications would be made via two tanks fitted up with full signal equipment. In actual fact of course, the state of the ground was so bad that the tanks were quite unable to approach anywhere near the area. An infantryman going into action normally carried on his person rifle and bayonet, entrenching tool, haversack containing iron ration, a day's ration, filled water-bottle, about 200 rounds of ammunition, respirator of course, ground sheet, spare pair of socks and razor and washing gear, either a pick or a shovel on his back and often several hand grenades.

At one time we used to attack also carrying our greatcoat, but not latterly as it was too bulky and as we already had on us about 60 lbs weight which was as much as a normal man could stagger, slide or walk with over trenches, barbed-wire and shell holes and then engage in hand-to-hand fighting. If gas were used by the enemy around our support lines or approach lines (by gas shell of course) the troops had to advance wearing gas respirators which very considerably increased the difficulties.

Up in the Ypres Salient where it was always muddy and watery, summer or winter, many a man was hit or just slipped and went into a mud-filled shell crater never to get out again with all this equipment and weight hampering his movements. We were sure that if such senior people as corps commanders and upwards really knew personally the ground over which we had sometimes to attack they could hardly have ordered some of the impossible operations.

Our attack was to be made on 20 September 1917 and I was once again chosen to command 'D' Company in it, though still only a lieutenant, but I certainly expected my captaincy if I could get through unwounded. We moved up to the sector and went into some already overcrowded dugouts and tunnels (Larch Wood tunnels) on 18 September. On the 19th we started at dusk to move to our assault position.

All the officers of 'B' Coy became casualties on the way up, but my 'D' Coy got off fairly lightly in the shelling.[3] As we marched northwest up a specially prepared track we called Towsey's Track, after our brigade commander, we got mixed up with another battalion moving at nearly right angle across our front going northeast. I kept calling out 'D Company Queen's Own this way' and the other battalion officers were doing the same. I presently found out that the other unit was our 10th Bn of the Queen's Own. We finished up by losing some of our men who went on with the wrong unit but collected about the same number of theirs.

We got up to some dead ground behind our assault position and waited there for some hours and had our breakfast about 2 am. Mine consisted of only half a tin of pork and beans which was not the ideal meal before an attack. I asked my batman for my rations for the day, which he had drawn for me earlier but he said that they were all together with his and he could not divide them very well in the dark but he said 'I'll see that you get yours during the day whatever happens'. This man was an elderly private who suffered from bad feet and it was for this reason mainly that I had chosen him as my batman to help with less arduous duties than drilling and route marching etc. I heard afterwards that he was wounded later that morning but in spite of this he crawled from shell hole to shell hole for some time looking for me to keep his promise, before he heard that I had also been wounded. This was typical of our men.

One of my men had fallen into a shell hole full of water but although he was soaked I could not let him go back out of the line as it might have encouraged someone else to do the same. I got one of my runners, all of whom were first class men with common sense as well as guts, and sent him back to try and find dry clothing or at least a dry shirt. He came back later on with some clothing which he had obtained, he said, from the Advanced Dressing Station but which I have no doubt came off one of our dead. We then got quietly onto the jumping off line which was marked off by tapes laid on the ground during the night by one of our officers. Two of our companies were in the front and two directly behind them with Battalion HQ centrally just behind them.

A battalion of the Hampshires was in front of us and the idea was that the first half should take the first objective, then the second half of the battalion should pass through them and take the second objective while we passed through both lots to take and hold the third and final objective. There was a carefully timed programme for the barrage in front of us and it was highly advisable to keep as close behind our creeping barrage as was possible so that we were on the enemy before he realized the barrage had passed him.

Zero hour arrived half an hour before dawn when our guns all started together with a deafening crash and continued thundering out, aided by heavy overhead machine gun fire, in a tornado of sound which made it almost impossible to hear any speech unless it was shouted in one's ear. Quite soon the air was filled with very fine particles of mud which fell gently over everything and everybody and added to the murk. Needless to say the German guns were also firing as fast as possible on their SOS line (the so called no man's land which we had to cross).

We had to wait a few minutes for the Hampshires in front to do their part but there was a check as their first two companies did not take their first objective and their two rear companies just caught up with them and also stopped. What probably happened was that their officers got wounded early on

23

of course and with the only partially trained troops that we had received as reinforcements, bewilderment set in if they were not able to see their leaders. Anyway, whatever the reason, the first objective was not taken as planned and we were waiting to go forward and we just waited for the moment. I was in command of 'D' Coy, one of our leading companies, and had just decided that we must push on anyway as the barrage was getting away from us, when the matter was solved for me.

In the half light I saw our very popular CO, Colonel Corfe, coming up with his Battalion HQ Group from my rear and although I could not hear a word he said he was waving us forward with his walking stick so his intention was clear enough. I immediately took my company forward with him and passed the word to our other leading company to go forward, which of course immediately conformed.

We passed through all four companies of the Hampshires, picking up a few of them en route. I found one lance corporal cowering in a shell hole apparently unwounded so I kicked his backside really hard and he came on like a lamb. He probably only needed a little encouragement to do his duty. We got into the German lines and Colonel Corfe was badly hit with a smashed shoulder. Even so he continued to stagger forward and shot one German before falling down.

We got him on a stretcher and ordered four of our German prisoners to carry him back. One of these whom we took to be either an officer or warrant officer evidently felt it beneath his dignity to take a corner of the stretcher as he haughtily drew himself up and refused. We could neither hear what he said nor understand probably if we heard but his actions were clear enough so we quickly found a substitute (we were definitely not in a mood for arguing) and sent the colonel back under the charge of one of our walking wounded to see fair play. This was the usual custom of course as we could not trust unescorted enemy stretcher bearers not to kill, or at best, abandon our wounded at a convenient moment.

Long before this I had picked up a rifle and bayonet as was my custom in an attack. For one reason I liked and felt at home with these weapons and for another thing it made it more difficult for enemy snipers to spot that I was an officer. For the same reason we discarded officers' clothing, up to a point, in an attack and merely wore other ranks tunics with shoulder rank badges and webbing equipment instead of the Sam Browne.

About this time I was hit in the left arm by hand grenade splinters, one of which went 9/10ths through my forearm and stopped close under the skin the other side (where it remains for life). Dropping the rifle and getting out my trusty revolver I of course carried on. One German had two shots at me with a miniature automatic pistol but missed. My .45 revolver did not miss. I collected his pistol and also took a trench dagger from another who had no further use for it.

We got on to the second objective, which again was not supposed to be our job, and I got in the way of a burst of machine gun fire and was hit by three bullets; one of them went through my unlucky left forearm, one cleanly through my left thigh, while the third entered my breeches pocket, passed through my purse buckling several coins in transit and stopped against my flask which was stuffed into the same pocket. It spoiled the flask but that probably helped to save my matrimonial prospects!

I dropped and rolled into a shell hole and had not been there for many seconds before one of my brother officers, 2nd Lieutenant Came, fell landing on top of me frothing blood over me before dying. I could not move him off me but two of my men came up and did so.[4] They then collected two prisoners and put them in the shell hole with me while they scouted round for a stretcher; presently they returned with a German one. Meantime I had rather a job to keep my stretcher bearers as on-coming troops seeing them wanted to kill them naturally and there was I, with two cowering Germans behind me, shouting 'Don't touch my stretcher bearers, leave my stretcher bearers alone'. When my men found this stretcher one of them, who was one of my runners, asked if I would let him have Lieutenant Came's revolver, which I did of course. (Runners preferred to carry a revolver instead of a rifle but there was no issue of same for them and we had no objection to their doing so when one was available; we could always get hold of a rifle).

We started back, naturally with a walking wounded in charge, and all went well until a shell (either ours or Bosch – it made no difference) burst close to us and the Germans dropped the stretcher and lay flat. I groaned as I hit the ground so my irate walking wounded stirred the Germans up with his bayonet. En route down a trench our progress was impeded by a group of our dead and wounded, one of whom was in two halves while another was holding his entrails in with a pair of muddy hands, I recall.

We finally got back to an advanced dressing station cut into the steep slope away from the enemy, half dugout and half shelter. My two stretcher bearers were then sufficiently far back for them to be harmless, so we just pointed the way for them to go and they departed to the prisoner collecting point under their own steam, thankful to be alive.

I was bandaged up a little better there, but as I lay on the ground just inside the shelter the whole dugout was blown up and caved in. When I recovered consciousness I found myself completely buried and unable to move hand or foot. My steel helmet was partially over my face and I could just breathe. Someone dug out my face and I asked them to hurry up and get to a man I could feel underneath me moving so I knew he was alive. They got him out but a man next to me was not so lucky. They continued to dig me free but found that my left leg was pinned by a piece of timber and while they were levering this up to free me the earth once more cascaded down again and covered me again. I lost consciousness, but when I came to I found a padre there with a flask to my lips so I took a good swig. I found my jaw was dislocated while my nose was crooked and has never been straight again.

Later on a civilian YMCA helper brought cups of tea round to us wounded which he had brewed up himself. One can imagine how grateful we were to him and his association! The horsed ambulances tried unsuccessfully to get us over the shell-pocked ground but finally a Ford ambulance bounced its way through and was loaded up. They put as many of us as possible into it and we started off, the driver did not know where to go, but I knew where the nearest casualty clearing station was and directed him, though not too fit myself, as can be understood.

A lieutenant colonel lying alongside me begged me to shoot him as he had decided he was done for anyway and was in such great pain. I refused but gave him instead a dose of morphia in capsule form which I, like many other officers, unofficially carried with me when going into action. I marked a cross on his forehead in indelible pencil, which was a well recognized sign that he had had a dose, to make sure he didn't get another without doctor's orders.

We duly arrived at the casualty clearing station and while I was waiting there, either asleep or unconscious, someone pinched my wrist watch off my wrist but did not take my souvenir automatic pistol or trench dagger, nor of course my revolver which was, in those days, personal property and not an issued item.

I was sent to a hospital at Étaples for a while and one of the first things they did after getting me into bed was to burn all my blood-stained clothes except my field boots. It was here that I found someone had removed my souvenir pistol, but I got hold of the corporal orderly and he said that he had seen one like I described on the QM's desk. I bribed him and he produced it but whether or not from the QM I never knew of course as I asked no questions.

LETTER FROM HOSPITAL IN FRANCE: 30 SEPTEMBER 1917

Dearest Mother,

Two lovely long letters have just arrived from you and have been enjoyed very much. It must indeed be difficult for you to write every day but I have much enjoyed your letters. I wonder if Auntie Jessie has mentioned to you anything about a Bosch card I sent to her to be sent on to you. It is rather a good souvenir I think. I found it in a Bosch dugout at [censored]. I'm progressing by leaps and bounds towards perfect health and I can walk about now a bit without a stick. I have begun to use my left arm again; also my jaw, that was dislocated when I was buried is absolutely alright again. By the way Harold's birthday is of course on the 4th, so I am writing to the YMCA Tottenham Court Rd.[5]

I don't know if that is still his address. The book arrived yesterday also and I am much enjoying it. I have not read either of the books you mention by the same author but have read one which is all short stories. I think it is called 'Proff. Keene' or something like that. I am not reading so many books now that I get up all day. I haven't any clothes or anything yet as my valise has not come so [I] go about all the time in a dressing gown. The other day some travelling party gave us quite a good concert. The fellows here are all very decent. I have plenty of money with me and can always get plenty as an officer so don't trouble about that at all. I was so glad that Gr[aham] got his registered letter. I was very interested to hear about Uncle's hotel. Hope it was well insured but it is sure to have been.[6] Glad the potatoes have done well, what about the lantern light for storage. We are perched among sand dunes here with a little bit of pine wood just at our back door enclosed with barbed wire where we can sit or lounge which is jolly fine [in] this warm weather.

Very much love to all,

From Don

One day while I was still a bed case, the ward sister came to me and said they were clearing the hospital as much as possible and that a hospital ship sailed next day but there was no room on her for any more lying cases; but I could go to England on her if I could get up and go as a sitting case. Naturally I at once said that I would go. Having said that, the next problem was something to wear going over. I got hold of the hospital quartermaster but found that he had no clothing available for officers or other ranks, other of course than pyjamas or similar. I then asked for the corporal in charge of the incinerator who managed to pick out of the condemned clothing, due for burning, a very tattered and torn pair of breeches and a blood-stained private's tunic. These, together with my field boots, hospital pyjamas and two large red cotton handkerchiefs, which I still have, supplied by the hospital (one to hold up my breeches and one round the neck) had to suffice. As it was now October, and getting rather chilly for a sea crossing, I insisted on taking an army blanket also, to cover my deficiencies.

I found myself in the war-time hospital in London, converted out of the old Great Western Railway Station Hotel in Euston Road, now called the Prince of Wales Hospital. Next morning I managed to get into a taxi with a little help, dressed in the same garb, and went straight to an outfitters where I stayed until I could emerge looking once more like 'an officer and a gentleman'. A girl friend sent me anonymously a poem, one verse of which went something as follows:

About this time round London strolled
A weird young man in blankets rolled.

'Twas not his fault so I have learnt,
The reason was his clothes were burnt.

While in that hospital we had air raid warnings several nights in succession and a few bombs dropped but most of us did not bother to go down to the basement until chivvied by the ward sister, who had to be obeyed, but there was soon a two-way drift; patients being shepherded down in the lifts and then slinking up the back stairs back to bed.

The medical attention was so bad that I finally got so fed up when my bandages had not been changed for a week (they were put on in the hospital in France and no examination of my wounds had been made on arrival in England) that I applied for a medical board so as to get out. The president of the board asked me how I was and I replied, 'I am applying for a fortnight's sick leave and then to go back to my home unit'. Without any medical examination at all he replied, 'All right you can go home for a fortnight tomorrow and we will mark you as A1 now'. I asked for and received one month's light duties and my papers were marked accordingly. Then I walked carefully out the room, picked up my two sticks that I had left outside the door (having left my walking sticks outside and managing to walk into the room without them) and on arriving home the next day got my own civilian doctor to do my dressings. This was a typical medical board. Unless a man said he was unfit when the doctors examined him, they would pronounce him fit as long as he had no temperature and his wounds were not actually still open!

I joined the 3rd Bn RWK who were then in winter quarters, mostly in empty houses in Rochester. I got phlebitis in one leg but was merely told to go to bed in my billet; but after five days there with cold food brought up by my batman from the mess I got up and sat in the mess for a week, when the trouble cleared up by itself fortunately.

There were a number of us temporary New Army officers there who had come out of hospital and were waiting to go overseas again and, not unnaturally, we were very unpopular with the permanent staff who had had no overseas service but had been retained at home year after year either because they were good instructors, good athletes, good for a concert party or good at something which made the home battalion wish to keep them.

I expect we were a bit of a problem to the staff as they really did not know what to do with us, so once again they put us under instruction in such things as Lewis guns and bombing. As we had all used these weapons in action we reckoned we knew more about them than the instructors. One sergeant who 'taught' us bomb throwing was particularly disliked. So, when we got to the stage of instruction when we went with him into a trench, one by one, and solemnly threw a Mills hand grenade over the parapet, we decided to play a game on him. These grenades had a five-second fuse which started operating as soon as the safety pin was removed and a lever was allowed to fly off as it left our grip. My turn came to throw but I pulled out the pin, let the lever fly off, retained the bomb in my hand and looked foolishly at it for two seconds saying 'what do I do now sergeant?' By this time the sergeant was dashing round the traverse so I quickly got rid of the bomb having judged the safety time to a split second. My brother officers from a distance were doubled up with laughter meantime. This sergeant did not take any more of us under instruction for some time at any rate. Two of us applied for and got sent on a Vickers Gun course at Grantham where we were quickly qualified as instructors. This was the Machine Gun School for the MG Corps, as long before this all heavy MGs had been taken away from infantry battalions to be used by specialists in these guns, the infantry being by this time supplied with a fair number of light machine guns, mainly of the Lewis gun type, for their own use.

I got back to the 3rd Bn and found that a draft of BEF men, like the officers, newly out of hospital, had been prepared for overseas once again, to their great disgust as they felt that they should have a longer spell in England and let those troops who had no foreign service go first. Anyway they decided that they would not go. They were, however, put into a train in Chatham station and locked into their compartments; the draft conducting officer was an inexperienced youngster with no foreign service, the last man suitable to take charge of this particular draft. As soon as the train cleared the tunnels at Chatham and Gillingham, the men climbed out of the carriage windows while the train was moving and some climbed on the roofs, while some just sat on the buffers. They got down to Folkestone but refused to embark. This of course was plain mutiny but the War Office did not know what to do about it with over 200 men. Anyway they were all brought back to Chatham and only the officer, company sergeant, major and CSM were court-martialled; not because they had mutinied themselves, but because they had not been able to stop the others doing so.

A week later the draft were ordered abroad again and I was detailed this time as draft conductor. This time the draft was to go to Italy via Southampton and Le Havre. I did not even see my draft until they were locked into the special train and handed over to me at Chatham railway station. My first action on taking charge of this draft, after signing for them of course, was to order the railway guard to unlock the carriage doors. This was immediately criticized by the senior officer who had handed them over to me but, as it was now entirely my responsibility, all he did was to have Military Police posted to see that the men did not leave the station. I put my head into each door in turn and introduced myself to the men and had a chat with them; I found that some of them were men I knew personally from my own 11th Battalion so I neither expected nor had any trouble at all on the journey. I organized hot tea for them all (at my expense of course) when changing trains at Basingstoke and finally arrived on board without losing a single man.

We left Southampton soon after darkness and had a very rough crossing. There were a number of mules on part of one of the decks and during the tossing about, one or two broke adrift and went mad down there and we finally had to shoot them.

There were several other drafts on board and I got friendly with one of the draft conducting officers. We lay outside until daylight before entering the Le Havre defences. Our men needed their rations for the day, as did all the other drafts, so my new-found friend and I had to look round for the OC Troops to enquire about them. He was seasick and had locked himself in his cabin and would not answer the door. We finally asked one of the ship's officers if he knew anything about rations and he told us that the army rations were on the top deck under a tarpaulin. We went up there and found some of the troops helping themselves. Naturally we stopped that and while I stood guard my friend passed the word round for each detachment to send a ration party up with numbers. We then issued the food and found plenty for all. Later that day when we had landed there was an enquiry as to how two days' rations came to be issued for one day but no one knew anything about it and OC Troops was left to explain why he did nothing about rations himself nor detailed anyone else if he was unfit himself! I left the draft there and the following day returned back to Chatham.

When I felt sufficiently recovered from my wounds I asked for a medical board, telling them I was fit. They never examined me of course; they passed me A1 and I spent my twenty-first birthday en route for France once again. The night before I had to travel up to London to be there in time to catch the early morning train, so I decided to go to a theatre that evening. Not unnaturally I was feeling rather 'browned off' and as I sat alone in a seat in the front row of the stalls I got more and more fed up generally. At the end of the show we all stood up for 'God Save the King' but a man near me put his hat on and started walking out. I grabbed him with one hand and snatched off his hat with the other and told him that if he did not stand still for the National Anthem I would knock him into the orchestra. He stood like a lamb, to my regret.

CHAPTER 4

Reflections on Trench Warfare

Arriving in France in April 1918 I went to the staging camp at Étaples to which most of the men were sent when waiting to go to a unit in France or Belgium, or for small drafts of men out of hospital etc. While I was there on this occasion, waiting to be posted on my return from hospital, some trouble started.

As far as I could gather it all began when two Irish soldiers were having a quiet drink on the veranda of the canteen in the camp area and were reviling England and the English in a typical Irish way when a Portuguese private soldier who could speak English joined in unasked and said, 'Yes English no damn good', whereupon one of the Irishmen knocked him down for daring to speak so disrespectfully about the English. The Portuguese went off and came back with his rifle and bayonet accompanied by a party of his countrymen and went for the two Irishmen. Naturally all British in the neighbourhood joined in against the Portuguese and when the Military Police (Red Caps) tried to stop the trouble and arrest a few men every one turned on them and so the trouble spread.

We heard about it in the officers' mess of the RWK depot and a young inexperienced subaltern there, who was orderly officer for our depot, buckled on his revolver and, although white-faced and nervous, was prepared to do his duty at all costs. I, who had quite a considerable service by that time, told him not to be silly but to leave his revolver behind and that I would go along with him. We went to where the main mob of shouting men was and one after another winkled out the men of our regiment, telling them to get back to their own camp as we could see serious trouble brewing. They all did so as far as we could see and later on a few men got killed, but our chaps were not involved. No one in any case was rough with their own officers as far as I know and, in my opinion, much of the trouble arose from the fact that to keep the waiting men at the various depots busy, and no doubt also to try and smarten them up, they were sent daily to the 'Bull Ring' (the Étaples parade ground) where loud-mouthed instructors drilled them hard to their great disgust and a considerable annoyance: they hated it!

I could not rejoin my own old 11th Bn as owing to acute shortage of man power we just could not replace casualties in the army, so instead of having four battalions in an infantry brigade it was decided to have three and to break up the 4th for reinforcements. The 11th Bn was one of the unlucky ones to have to go.[1] Needless to say each brigade was expected to do as much fighting with three battalions as before so it meant longer in the line and less time out. I was therefore posted to 8th Bn The Queen's Own West Kent Regt. I was not too happy in the 8th Bn, but needs must.

Once again after a while I got command of a company with the acting rank of captain, but this time I lost it, not through wounds, but because a subaltern, Jack Orchardson, with seniority over mine, but only a fraction of my fighting experience, came out from England and took over from me, so I of course reverted to lieutenant yet again. I may say that 'Orchie' was a very good chap and we soon became staunch friends.

We had of course been much diluted by this time and our battalion, like all the others out there, consisted of a small proportion of good men, some who had been good but were now really tired and war weary, some over forty who had family cares and were not so fit perhaps as the younger men and a large proportion of 'A4 Boys'. These A4 Boys were enlisted under conscription at the age of eighteen and it was arranged that they should do a year's training and go overseas at the age of nineteen. We were getting desperate for reinforcements in 1918 and there was not much help as yet from the American Army, which had started coming out but was not yet ready in any numbers, so these A4 Boys were suddenly sent out as reinforcements to us in France at the age of 18. This meant that instead of having done an inclusive six months training they had only done half a twelve-month training course, which was quite a different matter.

When I got a bunch of these A4s I put them under an experienced and fatherly sergeant and warned him to treat them very carefully while they were learning their job with us. He said 'I know just how to handle them; I'm an old soldier and have sons of their age'. Next morning he said to me 'I'm not such an old soldier as I thought I was because last night one of those young b–s changed his old pair of boots for my new ones'!

It was the much disliked duty of officers to read and censor all letters written while on active service by the other ranks. The only exception to this was a green envelope issued once a week, per man, on which he had to sign that the contents contained only private and personal matters – such letters might be opened at the base but not regimentally. Shortly after I had been posted to 8th Bn one of my platoon wrote, 'Dear Mother, we have a new platoon officer, I will tell you what I really think about him next week in a green envelope'.

It was not unusual to get a letter from a worried mother saying that her little 'Willie' was always delicate and would his officer please see that he changed his socks when wet, or something in similar strain. I always replied something to the effect that I would keep special note of her 'Willie' and, as far as active service conditions permitted, would look after him. I once had a letter from an anxious mother enquiring whether in my opinion, Private 'Snooks' would make a good husband for her daughter. I replied that Private 'Snooks' was a good soldier but that I could not recommend him as suitable to marry her daughter as he was already drawing separation for one wife. I had 'Snooks' in and showed him the correspondence before sending off my reply.

To start with there was no leave but when things settled down in 1915 home leave for seven days was started and later increased to ten days; this could be given every six months but naturally front-line troops could not get this as every time there was a 'push' all leave for us was cancelled, so it worked out for us about once a year in consequence.

As so many men arrived at their homes lousy, great efforts were made to send them back in a more sanitary condition, with varying success. When one's leave was due in a short time one took extra care of oneself and it was a standing joke with us that even the sound of a rifle shot might make a seasoned soldier dive for cover if he was due for leave in say forty-eight hours.

My second leave was fourteen months after the first one. We got on a train at the railhead near Ypres and I was detailed to be in charge of the leave party of all units, numbering about 120. I reasoned that if a man missed his leave after having once got on the right train it was entirely his own fault so I tore up the nominal roll and took no further action at all. After arriving back after this same leave I spent the night at Wimereux above Boulogne, and was put in charge of a large party of Australians, with orders to see them back to their divisional railhead, but I could not find out from anyone where this was. Every time an Aussie got thirsty he would drop off the train as soon as it stopped and make for the nearest estaminet [small café selling cheap wine or beer – Ed.] and I could do nothing about it if the train moved off before he or they returned. At intervals during the day or night a Railway Transport Officer would walk along the stopped train and call out 'men for such and such a division out here.' After several of these stops an Australian officer RTO called out for Aussies to detrain; I turned out the balance of my draft saying that I was probably twenty men short. He said 'don't worry about that they will all find their way back sooner or later and it's a long way from Australia', which relieved my troubled mind considerably.[2]

Very occasionally a man could get compassionate leave from France. One of my men applied for such leave in order to marry a girl in the family way. Not to be hoodwinked I wrote to the vicar of the girl's parish and asked him to confirm the facts before I put the leave forward with my recommendation, which he did. After 'Snooks' had got his leave I also wrote to the local police officer asking him to confirm that Private 'Snooks' had in fact got married on his compassionate leave. The police confirmed that he had got married, but to a different girl!

We had mainly Church of England chaplains of course but also some Roman Catholic and a fair number of mixed Free Church. At the beginning of the war it was arranged with the Chaplain General that the Free Church padres should receive equal treatment to the C of E. The C of E padres were allowed to go into the fighting line but apparently the Free Church were not allowed to do so, at least at the start, by their administrator or whatever he called himself.

After a while there was a complaint that twenty Military Crosses had been granted to the C of E padres and this was not in accordance with the arrangement for equal treatment etc. Accordingly twenty MCs were presented to the Free Church authorities and they were told to pick their own deserving cases. One was given to a padre down at Southampton who had not left England, but the troops made such a fuss about it that he hastily left, no doubt for overseas.

Certain C of E padres used to wander around the trenches quite freely and I expect RCs did as well, but I didn't run into any myself. The men admired the padres. Most naturally, going into an attack from which we knew positively a number would not return, some of us attended Communion, if available, and neither we nor the padre would enquire whether he or we were one denomination or another. It was the same with battlefield burials. We did not unduly trouble if a Christian burial service was read over the graves by an Anglican or a RC though we did our best in every case and the identity disc gave the man's religion.

Rations were supplied by the Army Service Corps and units drew theirs daily from some depot, or ration point when too far forward from the depots for their horse transport to reach. Such ration points would often be at a cross roads a few miles behind the line where unit NCOs met a ration lorry bringing up their rations for which the units had indented two days before. When we were in the line our horse transport would bring up food, water and sometimes mail as close behind the trenches as they could approach at night. They would then be met by men to carry it up to their sub-units, mainly by hand but in a few places a narrow gauge trench tramway was used as this was also so useful for bringing up Royal Engineer stores such as V frames, sandbags and barbed wire etc. Our dead and sometimes our wounded went back in the reverse way.

Food was normally cooked in the support line by night so that smoke did not give us away, and was then carried to the front line where possible in hay boxes or insulated containers. Water was normally brought up in two-gallon petrol cans which we hoped had not been used for petrol first as the taste never left them. The ration supplies were really good as I never remember a case where rations were not available, although that did not mean that they always reached us. We often had to make do with biscuits in lieu of bread. Such biscuits were made the size of large dog biscuits and were often very hard indeed. There was also a regular supply of excellent bully beef of which we got heartily tired, pork and beans, McConnachies meat and veg tinned stew and Tickler's plum and apple jam. Our transport and QM sergeants did a first class job bringing up our nightly rations, often under shell fire or even machine gun fire.

I remember one occasion when I, with my platoon, was holding a forward post which could only be reached after dark, and the meat ration consisted of Australian frozen rabbits. By the time they reached us they had become unfrozen and smelled far from fresh. However, I asked for volunteers to skin them, but found that there was not a single man who knew how to skin a rabbit. One man thought that one plucked them. I therefore had to give a demonstration of skinning, but they finished by tearing off bits of fur. I told a man to bury the fur as soon as possible, which he did. Next night word came that all skins were to be returned for salvage. I therefore had the skins disinterred, put in sandbags and passed back to the ration party on the following night. By this time they were really ripe and some very pithy remarks were made by the CQMS when we next saw him after we came out of the line.

We did not have any Army Catering Corps in that war and our cooks were generally men who were so scruffy on parade that they were told to be cooks so as to get them out of sight. It was no wonder cooking was often unreliable. One man so detailed strongly objected but had to go. The first day he was in the cook-house the men complained that their stew tasted of paraffin, the second day stew and tea got mixed up apparently, while on the third day a pair of army socks were found in the stew. Nothing was proved but it was felt that this reluctant cook had made his point and he was returned to normal duties.

After the Somme battles in 1916 all our cooks had become casualties as we had had to use *everyone* in the line and after coming out of the battle I was detailed to be in charge of the cooking for the battalion. Rations were plentiful as for three days we got rations for the strength we went into action with and we now had less than half the mouths to feed. Anyway I asked for volunteers, but found none so I detailed men, all of whom had been Boy Scouts, and we did our best. If the meat was not cooked enough we put it on half an hour earlier next time and if the potatoes were over boiled we gave them ten minutes less and so on. Providentially we got hold of a sergeant cook after about a week, as our need was so great, and I thankfully handed the job over to him.

A good cook was rare and a man to be looked after. One day we were marching from one part of the front to another and I was acting company commander so was riding the company charger. A man I knew, a cook from another of our companies, had fallen out with bad feet. As we could not afford to let a cook drop out like that I said to him 'can you ride a horse?' and he said 'no'. 'Well you are going to learn now' I said and put him up in the saddle while I walked. After about an hour he was so stiff and sore that he decided he was well enough to march then. Years afterwards he used to talk of the only time he rode.

In an infantry battalion we only had horsed transport which consisted of a few General Service (GS) wagons drawn by two draught horses or, later on, four mules; also GS limbers. These were two-wheeled box-type bodies normally linked together in pairs and drawn by two light draught horses, one ridden by a postillion; these could go over any rough ground that horses could go over. Then there was one gig for a medical officer and one gig as officers' mess cart. The CO, 2i/C, transport officer, quartermaster and each of the company commanders had a charger. On many occasions the light draught horses were also used as chargers if limbers were not needed. If a chaplain were attached he generally also had a gig for himself and church furniture, which also came in useful taking casualties to hospital on occasions. Other people had to ride bicycles, such as signallers, post corporal etc. Owing to a shortage of horses we used a number of mules during the closing year of the war. These mules were extremely useful. Some came fourteen hands high, many of them from South America, and they were so hardy that they needed, and got, very few oats. We gave them to the horses that could not get on without them.

Some of these mules made good riding animals. One of my friends in the Machine Gun Corps used to ride one as his charger as he was not entitled to a charger anyway. A particular mule he had was very fast and one day when the division was out of the line resting and training, divisional sports were held which included a race for officers' chargers. This friend entered his mule in the race and won his heat and might have done well in the finals but for the fact that after winning his heat he could not stop his 'charger' until about four miles away. By the time he got back to the sports ground the final had been run.[3]

Expeditionary Force canteens were established at most of the base towns used by the British and sometimes as near as maybe six miles from the trenches. These supplied necessities such as soap and bootlaces and luxuries such as drinks (whisky was 5 shillings per bottle), coffee and sweets and a variety of tinned foodstuffs which one could buy to supplement army rations. The YMCA did very fine work in bringing small canteens and rest/writing rooms nearer the front line. The 1 penny cups of tea were much in demand. The Church Army also did good work but on a much smaller scale.

In March 1918 when the Bosch pushed us back many miles in a hurry, one of my friends, a Lt Bacon, in the MG Corps, saw an Expeditionary Force canteen thrown open for the troops to help themselves as the Bosch were expected there not later than the next day and the staff had gone. He galloped back to the CO and told him about this and was told to hurry back with a double limber and fill up with all the drinks he could lay hands on, champagne for preference. Dick Bacon did his best but there was not of course time to open all the cases, so he loaded up with likely looking ones and that night, when they bivouacked some miles further back, they opened the cases. Instead of champagne found that they had a gross of boxes of Beecham's Pills.

I was detailed to run our company officers' mess at one time. In 1917 we got into rest billets at Noeux-les-Mines, a small mining town close behind the line, and our mess consisted of a room and part use of a kitchen in a miner's house still occupied by him and his family. There were two daughters. Alsace was aged about nineteen and was married; Lorraine was about seventeen and was a dainty little thing. As the locals grossly overcharged me for everything we bought, I got a list from Lorraine of the current prices for vegetables etc. Armed with this I sallied forth and refused to pay more but the locals just refused to sell to me except at their inflated prices.[4] I finally got over this by getting Lorraine to shop for me.[5]

Naturally when the war started we were extremely short of everything, but while great efforts were made to rectify this in some directions, there was much misunderstanding of the basic requirements by Lord Kitchener and other senior generals.

As far as rifles were concerned we bought a large number from the Japanese of their own type. These were .300 and had short stocks to suit their rather small men. My brother Graham, when guarding German prisoners at Fort Pitt, Chatham was armed with one of these but was issued with British .303 ammunition, which of course would not fit his rifle!

Artillery was a very sore point with us in the British Expeditionary Force in France as it was years before we had enough artillery support, but because shrapnel (a bullet-filled shell which burst overhead and scattered the shot over an area) was in demand during the Boer War a very large proportion of this was supplied in France when it was high explosive shells that were required for trench warfare. This affair was finally brought to a head when the press was brought into the matter and exposed the scandal but we always understood that this was the reason why Lord French lost command of the BEF to Sir Douglas Haig.

Kitchener, French and Haig were all obsessed by the idea of a breakthrough by the Allies when cavalry could be used with great advantage. For this reason large numbers of cavalrymen and horses were kept in France for years doing no good at all until finally the cavalrymen were used as infantry, to their great disgust; a job for which they were neither trained nor suitable.

Hand grenades were much needed in trench warfare, though once again, as they had not been used much in the Boer War, we were not supplied with them for a very long time. We used to save the German stick bombs as far as possible for use against them in emergency, but we started making home-made jam-tin-bombs. We saved some of the 1lb jam tins, filled them with a mixture of nails, small scrap or even stones, together with black gunpowder and tied in a detonator into which we inserted a length of fuse. We aimed to use enough fuse to burn for five or six seconds but if we cut off too little the bomb might burst before we got it thrown far enough; if too much fuse then the enemy could throw it back. When we had no tool, the job of crimping the end of the detonator over the end of the fuse, to hold it in place, had to be done with our teeth, not the best of jobs. We then lit the fuse with a match and hoped for the best. A number of small grenade shells were cast by local foundries in France, but the really good hand grenade on which the British Army finally settled was the Mills Bomb. This was heavier than the German egg bomb so they could normally out-throw us, but neither their egg bombs nor their stick bombs had anything like the lethal effect of our Mills. Their stick bombs in particular went off with a much louder bang and could put the wind up inexperienced troops, but I still have several pieces in me, many years afterwards, with no ill effect.

It is interesting to note that during the First World War the Americans did not think much of our type of artillery. They spent so much time and effort in trying to produce better types of their own, that by the time they required artillery they had to use the British guns after all. The same applied to tanks!

Owing to the great shortage of automatic weapons, for years we used Hotchkiss and Brownings to supplement the Lewis Guns which came along so slowly. Lewis Guns were designed, if I remember correctly, by Colonel Lewis who offered the design both to the USA and Great Britain, both of whom turned him down. The Belgian Army took him up and it was because of this that the rifling in the barrels was the opposite way from our weapons. The French had their machine guns of a pattern something like the Maxim guns but with an addition that permitted it to shoot single shots automatically at a given speed as slow as twenty seconds between shots. This was most useful if the machine gun was trained on a cross roads or other suitable target and set going and left until the belt of ammunition was exhausted. The French would not permit us, their allies, to know the mechanism to copy it.

The German machine guns were a type of the Maxim gun with which I was very familiar as I had trained on them in 1915. If the Germans had to hurriedly abandon a machine gun in an attack against them they used to immobilize the gun by removing the 'lock' (a small but vital part of the mechanism). In several attacks I carried a German lock into action with me and on one glorious occasion I was thereby enabled to get a captured machine gun into action against a German counterattack, to the cheers of my men. We always understood that Hiram Maxim's patent belonged to the British but that the Germans only made their guns under a licence from us, on which they only paid royalty up to the start of the War, and that even during the War they, with Teutonic precision, continued to credit us with the dues. We never heard that they were ever paid however.[6]

Much of the .303 ammo was made for us by the USA but there were many rounds of irregular size; a 'giant' would cause a stoppage in the Vickers or Lewis Gun while a 'dwarf' did the same because the case split. British officers were armed with swords to start with, but these were soon ditched as useless for trench warfare. We were also armed with revolvers, .45 cal with lead bullets, which flattened out when hitting a hard object. They might go into a man the size of a pencil but come out the size of a fist. The Germans took great exception to this and said that we were using a type of dumdum bullet, which if hollowed and recessed in the nose, as the originals were, was probably correct and against the Geneva Convention. However, when we made them pointed nosed they had just as good a stopping effect and we used them until the end of the war. Nickel nosed pistol bullets did not come in until after the war except for automatics of course. Many of us carried a captured German automatic but I always preferred our own pattern as they never jammed however muddy they got. I ought to know as I used my Webley for years.

When 'Stokes' trench mortars were first introduced into the British Expeditionary Force in 1915 they were propelled by explosive packed into a 12-bore cardboard cartridge case which was inserted into the narrow tube at the base of the projectile. When lying about, primed with cartridge, such cartridge absorbed the damp and caused misfires. It was decided that a 'French Letter' (*Capote Anglaise*) was the ideal cover for the cartridge so two subalterns were detailed to go into Amiens and buy a quantity. They asked the young lady serving if she had any French Letters and she replied, 'but of course, how many please?' They said, '1,000 please', whereupon she looked at them in admiration and said, 'The young British officers, what stamina!'

Unfortunately, we in the New Army had rather a poor opinion of the average senior Regular Army officer for what we considered excellent reasons. They were very often so out of touch with realities. For instance we were constantly asked for 'returns' by staff officers in the rear, while we were in the line, on unimportant and often absurd matters. One I remember was 'give map references of all latrines in the front line trenches and state whether they are all properly provided with latrine screens, if they are not why not?'

At that particular moment we did not dare use latrine screens as they could so easily be spotted from the air and in any case we did not have proper latrines, just a bucket placed as and where possible. Another query was 'give a return of all anti-gas stores in the front line', the answer was of course nil as none were available anyway. Another one was 'give map reference of all reserve ammunition and hand grenades in the front line'. We had a few boxes of spare rifle ammo, which we kept covered up as best we could, also a sand bag full of Mills hand grenades which I used as a bolster under my air cushion (an article I always tried to carry throughout the war), but I gave a careful list of map references which of course bore no resemblance to the facts, but 'they' were satisfied and they never came to check up anyway.

A young lieutenant was posted to us and it was only after he had been with us for some weeks that he admitted he was a regular, but as he did not act in a superior way because of it we did not hold it against him.

Until 1918 our orders were never to exploit success in an attack but always to reinforce failure. In other words, if the left formation got hung up and the right formation met with success, the reserves were thrown in to attack again on the left so that a tidy line with no salient could be formed. It would have been quite wrong to push our reserves through on the right and take the enemy in their flank, as I found once to my cost. Of course the same machine gun and gun fire and/or uncut barbed wire that held up the first attack generally did ditto with subsequent attacks and casualties mounted accordingly even if we gained our left objective. In one attack the two companies on my particular front were mown down in succession as they advanced over a slight ridge and it was then my turn to take my company forward. In the interval I had had time to reconnoitre the ground and I found a little dead ground on my right flank. Instead of going straight forward, I took my men round in the slightly dead ground and we gained our objective with comparatively small casualties. When we came out of the line I was sent for by the brigadier general (as they were in those days) commanding our brigade and I fully expected to be congratulated for having used my initiative successfully and even possibly that I had been recommended for the Military Cross, but not a bit of it. I was roundly told off for having moved my men into the next unit's sector in order to use the dead ground!

General Sir Hunter Weston ('Hunter Bunter') was the well known and highly respected exception because when he commanded an Army Corps he frequently went unannounced into the lines to see for himself and he would chat to any private soldier. Hunter Bunter was a very big man and he used to go up the communication trenches as fast as any man I have seen, followed generally by an aide-de-camp who had to break into a smart trot at times to keep up with him. There were many stories told about him but probably the best known one was as follows: In the front line a private soldier had broken into the rum and was nearly paralytic as a result. Just then word came through that Hunter Bunter was on his way round the front line. There was no time to remove the man and nowhere to put him out of sight anyway, so they covered him up with a ground sheet after laying him out on the fire step. When H.B. came up he said to the subaltern, 'Who's that under the sheet?' The sub said, 'a shell burst and killed one of my men sir', and as H.B. drew himself up to attention, saluted and said, 'I salute the glorious dead', a voice from under the ground sheet said, 'What's that the silly old basket is saying?'

Another time H.B. was entering the trenches when it was pointed out to him that he was not carrying his gas mask so he stopped a private soldier on his way out of the line and said, 'Give me your gas mask'. The soldier demurred but H.B. said, 'That's all right my man, just tell your officer that your Corps commander borrowed it and you will get a replacement without any trouble to you'. The soldier handed over his gas mask and hurried off. After the tour of the trenches, while on the way out, H.B. saw an officer coming in without his gas mask so he stopped him, reprimanded him and said, 'Here, take mine', and then he said, 'I suppose you know how to wear it?'. 'Yes of course Sir.' 'Well put it on and make sure that it is the right size.' The officer then put his hand into the satchel and pulled out a pair of dirty socks and a candle end!

Talking of gas masks, when the Germans first used gas in the Ypres Salient in 1915 it came as a very nasty surprise and we had no protection of any kind against it.[7] To lessen the effects we used, in turn, first a sock, soaked in urine tied over the face. Then we were supplied with a length of gauze folded with a cotton wool pad centre which we were supposed to moisten from a bottle of liquid which smelt strongly of chlorate of lime, and probably was, and also on issue were goggles to use against tear gas. Later followed the PH helmet which was a flannel bag with eye pieces and after that was the PHG helmet similar to the former but it had as an addition a one-way mouth-piece through which to expel air. Both the PH and the PHG were strongly impregnated with chlorate of lime and caustic soda.[8] They were worn over the head of course with the open end tucked tightly under the collar of shirt or tunic. As soon as we began perspiring the caustic nature of the impregnation made our necks extremely sore but it did keep out moderate concentrations of chlorine gas, sneezing and lachrymatory gasses and was reputed to be some good against phosgene gas, but I never proved this. Later of course we had the highly efficient box respirator which kept out everything used against us, if donned quickly and correctly. I got gassed once but not badly. I was blinded for two or three days by mustard gas. Gas shells had come over and we weren't quite quick enough in putting on our respirators. You can imagine my feelings, at the age of twenty, thinking that I might be blind for life, but fortunately it wore off.

Reverting to the subject of reinforcing failure – it was not until after the March 1918 'push' by the Germans, where they so successfully exploited their gains by pushing their reserves hard through any gaps breached in our line, that we finally learnt the fundamental lesson the hard way.

When the Portuguese Division (a token force sent to fight alongside us), was hit hard in March 1918 and ran away, led by their officers, quite a bunch of their other ranks were collected by our battalion. And, because they could do nothing else with them at the time, they were mixed with our men and taken forward again. Within quite a short time these same Portuguese fought quite well under our command, proving yet once again 'there is no such thing as bad soldiers, only bad officers'.

It was the custom both for the Huns and us to fire coloured flares or rockets as a signal that the front line was being attacked and that artillery fire was wanted quickly on the SOS line. This was an imaginary line between the enemy's and our trenches. (For the first two years of the war we did not always get a satisfactory reply from our guns owing to acute shortage of shells, but they always did their best even if it was just a token round or two.) This signal method was generally much quicker and more reliable than trying to phone through by land lines, which might or might not be working and we had not any wireless equipment in that war. Such flares or rockets were changed from time to time naturally so as to fox the enemy. On one happy occasion the Bosch put up a rocket as a signal to their troops to launch an attack on us which happened to be similar to our SOS signal, that had been brought in less than a week before, so they brought our artillery fire down on themselves somewhat quicker than we could have done; result: attack easily repulsed.

One day in 1918 we were in the line near Loos when it was decided to try out a signal in the form of a mortar shell fired from a papier-mâché case. All along our divisional front, these were to be fired up into the air at 2 am on a certain day. Captain Orchardson, my company commander, forgot all about it until too late to fire it off, but he thought that we had got away with it as the artillery observation officer said he had not seen ours 'probably because of the mist' (he was a personal friend of ours). However, an order came through about 8 am to return the empty mortar cases! We decided that the best thing to do was to point it down an unused dugout in the front line; this we did and returned the empty case. However, the dugout continued to belch out smoke for an hour or so and we expected enemy shelling on that spot at any moment as it might well have been a cook-house. We countered this threat by withdrawing our men to either side of the smoke area until all was clear. The next fear was that the CO might choose that day to walk round the line, but fortunately he did not do so and all passed off safely.

CHAPTER 5

The Lens Front

In May 1918 our 8th Bn The Queen's Own R.W. Kent Regt was moved down to the Lens sector where the subsoil was mainly chalk and what a joy it was to be able to dig trenches which needed little, if any, revetting and which had natural drainage and into which we could dig dugouts without roof props etc. This was a coal mining area and there were numerous slag heaps about. One of them was smouldering and had been alight for several years (the 'Burning Byng') and as one trench ran up one side across the top and down the other side, there were times, especially in high wind when it still glowed at night.

We were for a time near Lens where our front line ran through several of these mining villages, Cité St Pierre, Cité St Laurent, etc and here we were most amply supplied with cellars instead of the inadequate supply of dugouts to which we had become inured. Our rest billets at that time were in Bully Grenay which had sufficient houses still undamaged for us to live in and there were even a few hardy civilians hanging on in the town. One night a shell burst in the road just outside our company officers' billet and we were just congratulating ourselves on a near miss when there was a crash through our roof and we expected to go up at any moment but the seconds ticked by and nothing happened so we said to ourselves, 'Another dud.' One of us finally got up to make sure and found that it was only a paving slab that had evidently gone high in the air with the near miss!

Part of our front line had originally been part of the German trenches and at one point the trench ran under a low railway embankment. Each time I had to pass through this short tunnel I had a feeling of acute mental discomfort and I had to force myself to walk that way when alone, especially past a roughly timbered-up bit that looked as if it might have been a doorway. Some weeks after first going into that sector I heard a story that I think worth repeating. When our 8th Bn captured that exact same sector of the line some months previously, before I joined them, there was a German dugout opening off this tunnel under the embankment, which was naturally used by us as a company

HQ. Hanging from a nail on the end wall they found a German helmet which, on examination, seemed to have a wire leading from it and was in consequence suspected of being a booby trap, so everybody was warned not to touch it until the REs had had time to examine it. The next day there was some shelling and an explosion occurred leaving a small crater above where the dugout had been; whether in truth the suspected booby trap had fired or whether a heavy shell had fallen exactly there is not known but the result anyway was that the dugout was destroyed and apparently everyone in it. The batman of an officer thought to have been in the dugout, who was at the time further up the trench, hurried to the spot and started frantically digging. Everyone round him told him not to be a fool as he could not dig down some twelve or fifteen feet and even if he did there was no object in trying to recover the bodies. The batman, however, persisted and close under the surface he came upon his officer unconscious but alive; with aid he was dug out and subsequently recovered! The explosion had apparently blown this officer nearly to the surface without killing him.

In that sector I recall we dug up the body of a soldier of another regiment which had been there for some months. In his pay book he had two photographs of girls, and a letter asking that if he was killed he would like the photos sent back to the girls whose names were written on the back. We could just make out the writing of the letter but not the names on the photos. As we always tried to comply with the expressed wishes of our dead comrades I wrote to both girls stating that we had found the body and had given him a Christian burial etc, but that I was not able to comply with his wish, that her photo should be sent back, as damp had made it fall to pieces. Thus we avoided any possibility of both girls getting the wrong photo!

We kept pushing the enemy back gradually, but still had some fighting in the streets and mine buildings. We were short of men and officers during all this time and when in the front line for a week at a time, we were on duty all night and took turns of duty during the day. During the remainder of the day we had meals, shared censored letters and slept for a few (very few) hours.

My greatest fear about this time was that my nerve would crack as had happened to so many officers and men. One day we were told that we were to be heavily attacked that night. I was in command of some scattered advanced posts in front of our main line of defence and in front of where our machine gun fire would fall. Our job was to try and break up the enemy's attack so that the main positions would not receive the full force! I wrote a farewell letter for home and sent it back with the ration carriers to the transport lines to be posted in certain eventualities, but for some unknown reason the attack never materialized.[1]

While still in that part of the line we were attacked by a strange malady. One morning one of our 2nd lieutenants and all his platoon, who had spent a night together in a dugout and tunnel excavated in the chalk under the front line, were all found to have high temperatures and some were unable to walk. The entire platoon was evacuated to hospital. We concluded that some form of gas poisoning had taken place, but later the same day others kept going down with similar symptoms and we finally heard that it was Asian Flu which was quite a new thing to us then. While we were still holding the line during that particular tour about three-quarters of our strength went to hospital where a number died. I was the only officer left in 'D' Coy with about thirteen men out of the 150 we started with. Our OC of the battalion (a stranger major drafted in as there were none left of our own senior officers) sent a message up addressed to OC 'D' Coy saying that a German deserter had given warning of a raid to be made on my company front that night and that I was to detail a reliable officer, and give his name to Battalion HQ, who was to take a strong party that night and lie out in no man's land well on the left flank while the company on our right was to take similar action and that we were to close in behind the enemy raiders and capture the lot. I replied that I had detailed Lieutenant D.J. Dean for this job, 'an officer in whom I placed great confidence', and signed it D.J. Dean OC 'D' Coy. I took out half my depleted company that night as ordered and left my senior remaining NCO in command in the trench.

After lying out there for an hour or more under sporadic shell fire one of my young soldiers, who was then some months under nineteen years of age, and looked a bit of a sissy, crawled up to me and reported that he had a shell splinter in his leg; I told him to crawl back into our trench and get it attended to at once. Some half an hour later I found that it was the same youngster who was crawling back to me and he reported that it was only a slight flesh wound and he did not feel justified in staying in the trench or being evacuated when we were so short of men. I noted him down as a stout hearted youngster on whom I would keep a special eye and I was very heartened to find that some of the spirit that animated our original volunteers still could be found. Incidentally the German raid never took place and just before dawn we crept back wet and very cold to our trench and I issued a stiffish rum ration in hot tea. We heard later that the Germans had flu just about as badly as we had, so no doubt that accounted for the fact that they did not trouble us when we were so under strength.

I got flu myself but just managed to hang on until we were relieved when I went to bed for a week and only got up an hour or two before I had to take my company back into the line for the next tour of a fortnight.

By this date in 1918 we had begun to get the Huns on the move but they were by no means finished. I was told one day to take my platoon forward then and there, in broad daylight and to establish a post at the junction of the Lens/Arras, Lens/Béthune roads in the shattered outskirts of the town of Lens. This I did without any *real* trouble from the enemy and when I had been there for an hour or more a platoon from the battalion on our left came up to hold the identical strategic position. I told their officer to go away as we were already there but he said that he had prior claim to that spot as he had come up there the night before. I told him that I did not believe him or he would have been there when we arrived. He replied that the Germans counter-attacked him and he had to leave and that in doing so he lost two of his men and all the rations for his platoon for twenty-four hours. At the sound of the friendly but loud argument his two missing men popped up from a nearby cellar, with the rations on their backs, where they had been hiding from the Germans, but hearing English voices they decided to show themselves. I had to give my opposite number best after that but did not budge from the position naturally, so he went off to report or take up another post a bit further on my left.

Later that same day my sentry reported some Germans behind us. I promptly took a few men to cut them off, but could not find them although my look-out said quite positively they had not re-crossed the road to get back to their position from which they had presumably started.

After some abortive searching for them we noticed a hole in the road which, on investigation, led straight down into a main sewer of the town. It was circular, about twelve feet in diameter and led straight up under the main road towards the part of the town held by the Germans, who still held most of Lens. Leaving men posted at the top of the hole I crept alone very quietly down the sewer with the aid of my torch muffled in a handkerchief (I was carrying my torch as I was constantly searching out the cellars in our new post). I finally came upon an obstacle of, apparently, sheet iron, blocking my way; passing my hand carefully over it I found a closed door and could hear German voices the other side. I crept back and investigated an opening I had noticed further back. This led into the cellar of one of the houses bordering the road and on going further I found that a number of cellars were joined up by holes knocked in their side walls, so connecting them up for quite a distance underground. We later used these to stage several surprise bombing attacks on the Germans.[2]

I reported my sewer and cellar finds back to Battalion HQ and they then sent me a complete map of the main sewers of Lens that had been in their possession for some time. I was a bit peeved about that as I might have been saved quite a bit of bother had I had it first of all.

We had been ordered to nibble away at the enemy line so as to prevent them from withdrawing troops for use elsewhere by thinning out their line, but we were not to become engaged in anything that required reinforcements on our part as we would not get them. Although the Americans had started coming over by the end of 1917 it was not until 1918 that they appeared in sufficient numbers to make any real difference to us; but owing to our crippling losses our own reinforcements had so largely dried up that it was still impossible to keep our fighting strength up to scale. However we did keep up our fire power by gradual increase in the numbers of Lewis Guns.

I was never very happy with the 8th Bn RW Kents and most of my friends had already been killed off or so badly wounded that they had to go home. Also, most of us had got really 'war weary' and in my own case I had got to the stage when I had to keep a very tight hold over myself so as not to show the slightest signs of nervousness to the men whose lives often depended on me. They would still follow an officer they could trust, but certainly not one whom they felt was a coward. In consequence I had sometimes to do damn silly things just to show my men, and perhaps myself, that I was not afraid. In addition I had by now become rather annoyed that I had been acting captain so many times and had then to revert as I was either wounded or superseded before holding the rank long enough for it to become 'Temporary'. Several times a more senior officer would come out from England with little or no fighting experience and take over command of the company from me.

I put in for a transfer to the Machine Gun Corps for which I was qualified as I had been in the battalion MG section as a private and had qualified at Grantham MG school while on light duty waiting to get back to France after an earlier wound, so it was difficult for my CO, Lieutenant Colonel Wenyon, to refuse my request. Then came the little action for which I was recommended for the VC so I felt that it was only playing the game to withdraw my request for a transfer when again asked to do so by Lieutenant Colonel Wenyon.

CHAPTER 6

Dean's Post

No account of Dean's career would be complete without a full description of the circumstances behind his winning the Victoria Cross in September 1918. Alas the original manuscript contains only the following note:

> For details of how I won the VC please see either the War History of the 8th Bn The RW Kent Regiment or the Regimental War History for the First World War, RW Kents. If I get down to it one of these days I may even add a few notes of explanation or further details.

Unfortunately Dean did not expand his memoirs much further on this subject. All that was added is a modest, single page of handwritten notes on what he described as a 'general action' which he was lucky enough to get the VC for. The account reads:

> Our line during Sept 1918 was on the outskirts of Lens – we decided that the German front line opposite us was only being held at night but to prove it I had to crawl in daylight across no man's land through the long grass, weeds and shell holes. I found their trench empty and only about 2 to 3 ft deep. We decided to take this so I and my platoon walked over at stand to that evening (during the twilight period) and arrived there without being fired at and apparently unobserved. Very shortly after we arrived the Germans came gaily up their communication trench and met with a surprise. My instructions were to hold this sector as it was thought to be a good jumping off spot for further operations. My only touch with my battalion was at night above ground.
>
> Five times in three days the Germans tried to dislodge us – on the fifth occasion they trench mortared us out of one end of our position at the head of their communication trench and occupied it themselves under cover of this shelling. When the shelling ceased we found the enemy in strength on our side of the blocks we had put in the trenches. We finally bombed them out again but lost heavily in so doing. That

night our troops finished digging a communication trench to us across from our old front line and I and my platoon were relieved. I had the extreme good fortune of receiving the VC for this general operation.

Fortunately, where Dean was typically overly modest in accepting he was any more deserving of praise than his comrades, in particular those that did not survive the war, his contemporaries were lavish in their praise. As Dean suggests, the official history of the 8th Bn, co-authored by Dean's commanding officer Lieutenant Colonel Herbert John Wenyon, does contain a full account of the action.[1] More information is contained in the after action intelligence summaries of the 8th Bn and in several other fragments of information. By collating them all, it becomes clear that during this action Dean pushed himself to the limits of his endurance and fully deserved such high honour.

To set the scene, Dean was with his battalion in 'the shattered outskirts of Lens'. As recorded in the previous chapter he was beginning to feel extremely war weary. He had lost so many friends and the experience of fighting in the tunnels and cellars around Lens had been particularly difficult, causing him nightmares later in life. On one occasion in the sewers his path forward was blocked by the corpse of a German soldier. Dean's belts and equipment prevented him from being able to turn round in the tunnel, so he was forced to keep moving forwards, pushing the corpse ahead of him until the passage widened sufficiently. No wonder then Dean noted, 'My greatest fear about this time was that my nerve would crack as had happened to so many officers and men'.

After a period of six days in reserve at 'Bully' the 8th Bn moved up to the front line on 18 September, relieving the 9th Bn East Surrey Regiment. After several days of active patrolling it became clear that the map references they had been given by the East Surreys showing the forward posts did not tally with the actual posts held. On the night of 23/24 September it was decided to rectify this and a party of 'C' Company was sent out to seize the proper positions.

The post in question was at a junction of Canary and Claude Trenches. These battered trenches meandered along a northeast axis and intersected one another on the remains of a track known as Twisted Alley.[2] The Germans had been disputing this position bitterly for several weeks and neither side had managed to hold onto the position for anything more than a couple of hours. The British held the southwestern end of Canary Trench and the Germans the northeastern end.

'C' Company took the post and spent the remainder of the night vigorously trying to improve the trench. At about 06.40 hours the Germans began to shell the British communication trenches with 5.9' [150-mm] shells. Under the cover of this bombardment a party of about forty Germans advanced on the post. Some of them came straight down Canary Trench while the rest entered Claude from the Twisted Alley, quickly capturing an NCO and five men.

The British response was swift. A counterattack was organized by 2nd Lieutenants Trenchard-Davis and Beynes and was preceded by a bombardment with rifle grenades fired up from Canary. While the grenades whistled up the length of the trench, Trenchard-Davis and Beynes took a party of men on each side of the trench and rushed the Germans.

Realising they were at a disadvantage, the Germans climbed out of Canary and bolted for safety over the open ground. One was cut down by Lewis gun fire and others may have been wounded in their disorderly flight. Inside the post two of the British prisoners had been left behind along with a wounded German soldier and a guard. In the face of the British counter raid, the German guard turned the tables on himself and handed his rifle over to Lance Corporal Binks. By 07.30 hours order was fully restored in the British favour.

That evening, at 21.00 hours, Lieutenant Dean was sent with 16 Platoon of 'D' Company to relieve the 'C' Company garrison in Canary Trench. The men of 16 Platoon were mostly young and inexperienced troops, as yet untried in the 'rowdy-dow' of a fight as Lieutenant Colonel Wenyon would later put it. Despite the best attempts of 'C' Company, the post was still in very poor condition. In places the trench was only two feet deep and very little cover was offered to the occupants.

Unfortunately for Dean there was little time to make improvements. Within ten minutes of his arrival the Germans began yet another attack on the post. Under cover from machine-gun fire the Germans attempted crossing the open ground to the northeast. Despite the risks from the machine guns, Dean moved among his men, directing them to fire on the Germans with their rifles and a Lewis Gun. The attack was driven off and the Germans again opened up with heavy machine-gun fire on the post.

Despite the constant fire, Dean wasted no time in making improvements to the position, deepening it and putting blocks into Claude and Canary trenches. Just after midnight another attempt was made to capture the post. Dean saw how close the Germans had got to his position and only drove them off by leading his men out of the trench in a surprise counterattack. With the attack repulsed, Dean and his men returned to their digging. As the sun began to rise, they were exhausted from their labour, but there was no chance to rest.

A third attack began at 06.00 hours. This time the Germans put down a barrage of heavy shells behind Dean's post, cutting him off from his own lines. They then directed trench mortars at the position. Dean held his men together and drove off an attempt down Canary Trench with rifle grenades. One of the Germans was killed at the entrance to the post from Canary and others were shot down by a withering rifle fire as they moved across the open ground. As the Germans began to turn tail, Dean and his men charged after them, but were themselves subjected to heavy rifle and machine-gun fire, forcing them back.

The rest of the 25th was relatively quiet. In the hours that followed this attack Dean could see enemy working parties moving through the opposite trenches. Although the Germans were suspected of planning another attack, it became clear they were in fact removing their casualties from the previous attacks. Dean pressed on with improving the position and by the following morning could be satisfied it was greatly strengthened. At the same time a reinforcement of two fresh sections was sent up to relieve the platoon. Dean remained behind, retaining command of the post.

At 10.15 hours the Germans began shelling the post and the communication trenches with 5.9s. Dean got his men into their firing positions and held off a fourth attack. In response the German bombardment resumed and came down very heavy. One of the German shells had a lucky hit against two Bangalore torpedoes which the British had brought up to the position for a raid planned for the afternoon. Dean was very close by when these charges detonated and was severely shaken by the resulting explosion.

Although he still would not relinquish command of the post, he realized help was required. During the previous night Dean had got a telephone line brought up close to his position. He went back down the trench to call his lieutenant colonel saying, 'They are shelling us rather badly. Can we get some retaliation? The shells seem to be coming from all directions.'

While Dean was on the field telephone the post received several direct hits and casualties were sustained. The sergeant left in charge decided to withdraw the men fifty yards back to avoid suffering any more casualties from the shells. No sooner had he done so when about fifty Germans sprung up and finally seized the post.

While on the telephone Dean saw what was going on and broke off the conversation he was having with his commander with the words, 'The Germans are here! Goodbye.' Despite having recently been blown up, seeing his post lost, Dean collected his remaining sixteen men and prepared to launch a bayonet charge to recapture it.

From a vantage point in the nearby Cinnabar Trench 2nd Lieutenant Cambrook could see what Dean was planning. He launched another two sections of the Royal West Kents out of Cinnabar Trench, which ran parallel to the right of Canary, hoping to take the Germans in the flank and cut off their retreat. As he charged forward Cambrook was severely wounded in the chest and the attack began to fizzle out. Seeing this, the remnants of Dean's command rushed forward and counter attacked. Their attack was fierce and the fighting bitter.

Although Wenyon's official account of the action says the Germans did not wait to receive the attack there is evidence to suggest otherwise. Dean later recalled to his daughter that during the action, after they ran out of ammunition, they fought with stones, clods of earth and their bare hands. In an unguarded moment Dean later spoke to a local journalist about the fighting. The journalist recorded that Dean spoke 'in the most matter of fact air' and said, 'I shot four of the Germans and we cleared them out.'[3] This was the fifth attack Dean had withstood in forty-eight hours. When relieved on the night of 26 September the battle-hardened survivors did not want to leave. The piles of discarded German weapons and equipment strewn around the post bore testimony to the scale of the attacks made against them.

On the following day, 27 September, Wenyon posted a Special Battalion Order. It began:

> In the past few days the battalion has passed though experiences which have tested the soldier-like qualities of all ranks to the utmost degree. You have stood the test in the finest possible way, and the fact that our line still remains intact and stronger than ever, and that very heavy casualties have been inflicted on a brave and resolute enemy, redounds very greatly to the credit of all concerned.

Specifically mentioning Dean's action, Wenyon wrote:

> I wish to mention the magnificent defence put up by 'D' Company during two days of very great stress and difficulty. Five times a determined enemy, supported by all means at his disposals, has attempted to drive in our post, and five times he has been thrown back with heavy loss. ... The fine work of the past few days is worthy of the best traditions of our magnificent regiment, and the Queen's Own will always be proud of the officers, NCOs, and men, many of whom have laid down their lives, who have done such sterling work during this week of stress.

According to the battalion history the defence of Dean's Post was talked about across the length and breadth of England. In his official recommendation for the VC, Wenyon described how Dean had:

> ...worked unceasingly and with utter contempt for danger in an exceedingly difficult situation. His garrison was suffering casualties continually, but he himself bore a charmed life ... Throughout he inspired his men with his own contempt for danger, and in consequence they all fought with the greatest bravery, though most of them were very young soldiers with little experience. He set an example of personal gallantry, initiative, splendid leadership, and devotion of the very highest order.

Colonel Dean's original narrative continues:

About the end of Sept 1918 we moved south to the Cambrai sector. The Germans had by this time been pushed back and we had a taste of open fighting instead of from trench to trench. In a little village called Awoignt we had rather a sticky time in our company, although the rest of the battalion got off fairly lightly in the attack.

I captured a machine gun post at Awoignt and collected a German automatic from a man who had no further use for it and kept it for nearly forty years as a souvenir, but finally turned it in to the police and only kept the holster as a reminder.

In this attack on Awoignt I was a platoon commander and while we had many good men left we also had a few who could not be relied on in a pinch, so I followed my custom and detailed a good NCO to follow behind as whipper-in. I quickly noted that one gun in the battery that was helping to produce the creeping barrage on our immediate sector was firing about 100 yards short every time and, as I could not drop an extra 100 yards back for it I moved my men so that there was a gap immediately behind the line this gun was firing on. Our platoon on my immediate right, commanded by Lieutenant Green, suffered in the same way with one gun firing short but poor Green got both his legs blown off by one of our own shells and of course died before he could be given proper medical attention. (Our medical officers were not allowed on the battlefield or in the front line trenches so all casualties had to be carried back to some advanced medical post.)

We got into a village whose name I have forgotten [probably Cagnoncles, 4.5km northeast of Awoignt – Ed.] close enough after the Germans to find German food on the tables in some houses. The village was very knocked about, but we did not dare of course to drink water from the wells as it does not take long to drop a dead body or so into them when leaving.

There was one action in 1918, of a comparatively minor nature, after we had finally burst through the trench system over which we had fought backwards and forwards for nearly four years and were getting more into the open country. We attacked and finally gained our objective and in so doing we captured some German field guns, including the horses of the gun teams which they had brought up trying to save the guns. Some of our men had started life in the Kent Yeomanry before coming, much against their inclination, as reinforcements to the infantry, and they jumped on the horses with much glee and started riding them round and round.

Our final objective had been a railway embankment and from the top of this we saw a German counterattack being mounted about a mile away. We tried unsuccessfully to signal back about this, both by flag and lamp. There only remained a 'runner' which would take too long to be much good anyway. The runner probably himself suggested using a horse; anyway we stuck him up on a German artillery horse and sent him back with our message. After what seemed to be a very long time waiting, during which our guns did not start up but the counterattack was approaching us, there was suddenly a clatter and a rattling and up came six guns of the 18-pounder battery that was supporting us, at a smart trot; they broke into a gallop and went up over the low railway embankment, loudly cheered by our men of course, wheeled round in front, unlimbered and the teams were led back over the embankment while the guns opened up and the counterattack vanished. Quite a parade ground action in fact and the only time I ever saw guns firing over open sights in real action. Naturally it was only possible now because we had at long last got through the trench systems and into open country fighting.

Then came 10 October 1918, a day when our battalion was, for a change, in divisional reserve. Our 24th Division was advancing on the right hand flank of Cambrai, a town which had long been in the hands of the enemy and which they had mined and filled with booby traps and set alight before evacuating it. The British plan was to refrain from going through the town but to advance on either side of it and then join up on the east. Of course, we did not know for certain whether or not there were any Germans left in or around the town, so our battalion took over our exposed left flank facing towards Cambrai just in case of a counterattack from that direction.

We were treated to an occasional heavy long distance shell, so ordered our men to dig in a bit. This only meant chipping out a shallow bit of individual trench and pushing the earth up in front of them as they lay there. This they mostly did with their entrenching tools. While I was supervising this work round my company area another shell burst at a moment when I was the only man in the company standing up and I was hit really hard by shell splinters both in my right hip and left thigh. This was particularly unfortunate as after going through so much fighting with the 8th Bn I was the only casualty in the battalion that day.[4]

Anyway I was carried back on a stretcher to a collecting point where we were later picked up by Ford ambulances and taken to an advanced dressing station set up in a marquee pitched behind a sugar factory. These were the most painful wounds I had sustained, as the shell splinters were so hot that they burnt me as they penetrated the hip and went a long way in. As I was carried from the ambulance into the marquee we passed an improvized operating table fixed up in the open to get more light. There was a patient on the table being treated, while on the ground at the end was a pile of amputated limbs which was not a very cheering sight for a badly wounded man.

While I was lying face downwards on the stretcher, waiting either for a doctor to see me or for a further move back, an army padre who was in attendance bringing a drink of water, or whatever he could to help, brought me, at my request, an envelope. I wrote a note to my parents on a sheet from my field message pad, saying that I was slightly wounded, they were not to worry and I was sure to be home soon. This actually arrived home a few minutes before the War Office telegram, 'I regret to have to inform you that Lt D.J.

Dean has been severely wounded' etc. This allayed their worry but I was most annoyed later on to see in our local paper, while I was lying critically ill, that I had received a slight wound but would soon be well again. No doubt my father had shown the reporter my letter.

A side light on all this – several years later, about 1927 I should think, I was in camp with the 4th Bn The Buffs together with other battalions in our Territorial Brigade, and was riding my charger back to camp after a day's training when I passed a field cooker belonging to 4th Bn The Queen's Own Royal West Kent Regt. I thought that the face of the sergeant cook looked familiar but could not at first place him. However, a bit further on I recalled something, so I went back and said, 'Hullo Sergeant Smith, you won't remember me I expect.' He said 'I most certainly do as I was one of the cooks in 'D' Coy 8th Bn when you were wounded near Cambrai.' He went on, 'Do you remember that morning I asked you not to forget the cooks when the rum ration was issued and you said you would see that we got it? Well later that day you were badly wounded and as you were being carried past the cooker you said, sorry I can't get you your rum ration today.' When he told me this I dimly remembered something about it, so that evening I got a bottle of rum and sent it round to the neighbouring battalion with a note to Sergeant Smith: 'Here's the rum ration. I'm sorry it's nine years late'.

I finally got to England and was sent to the Cambridge Military Hospital at Aldershot for a few months and it was while there that we heard the Armistice had been signed. In the large ward where I was, several of the wounded officers just cried when, at 11 o'clock on the 11th day of the 11th month of 1918, a gun was fired, the church bells rang out and cheering in the streets was heard.

This hospital was all staffed by Regulars and most of the nursing sisters were really tough. There was one wearing the Mons Star and she was always known, ironically, as 'The Angel of Mons'. Another, who used to walk heavily around at nights, flashing a torch in our eyes, waking us up and saying, 'Can't you sleep?' was known as 'Flat-footed Fanny'.

I had rather a bad time in that hospital as my wounds turned septic, as was usually the case in those days. They operated several times to get the shell splinters out and even after that they opened one hole up and made another fresh one just to drain out what they were unable to drain from the original wounds. I dare say that I was also in a state of war weariness which did not help.

My parents visited me there more than once, but after one such visit Mother turned up only two days later and I found that a Sister had suggested that she should as I was not any too well. However, when a few days later they moved me from the large ward into the single bed adjoining room I really took notice, as I had had far too much hospital experience to be taken in by their explanation that it was to give me a better chance for rest and sleep. For the sake of anyone who would not understand, I might say that it was done to allow a man to die without unduly depressing his fellows.

This, taken in conjunction with my Mother's quick return, stimulated me because I reasoned that if that was the staff's opinion of my condition, I had better do something about it. Accordingly I bestirred myself and tried more effectively to eat and gradually improved so that about six weeks later I was able to get home on sick leave for Christmas.[5]

Early in the New Year I was still on sick leave when one morning Uncle John Doubleday came running round from next door to tell us that my name was in the papers as having won the VC. This was the first official intimation I had had of it. In fact I never did receive any direct notification of this award, which surprised me. When the 8th Bn heard it out in Germany the Pioneer sergeant made a wooden box and the CO had a letter of congratulation written with the signatures of every officer and other rank still left with the battalion which was being rapidly disbanded then. The box was to pack the letter in, for transmission to England.[6]

Some time towards the end of January 1919 I went to the 3rd Bn in Chatham, on light duty. While there we had several alerts owing to men from hospitals in England on draft back to France arriving at Folkestone and then refusing to embark; they in fact mutinied but without violence. We were all warned that we might be called out to quell these mutinies, but as it was very uncertain whether or not our men in the 3rd Bn would obey orders, or would just side with the mutineers, the government gave way and discharged those who had jobs waiting for them, irrespective of their release class. After this the army only gave home leave from France after the men out there individually gave an undertaking that they would return at the end of their leave.

I applied for release from the army and a disability pension but was informed that I could either stay on in the army up to a year, during which time my disability might either disappear or get less than the minimum warranting any pension, or I could get a quick release if I signed that I would make no claim.

Not unnaturally I got out just as quickly as I possibly could. Peacetime soldiering held no attraction for me, and I wanted to restart my civilian job after the loss of so many years when I should have been getting on. So I went up to the Crystal Palace and was demobbed, being marked as 20 per cent unfit only, which meant no pension or wound gratuity.

When I wished to restart work with Smeed, Dean & Co. Ltd, I had considerable difficulty in getting my grandfather, old G.H. Dean, to agree to my being paid as much as £3 per week which, with the very long hours I was expected to work was equal to something like 1s 3d per hour. I was then 21 years old, had been abroad for some years, off and on, and had had quite a lot of responsibility, so I finally said that if they were not prepared to pay me £3 per week as a start, I did not wish to come back to the firm, but would take a Government Training Course, for preference as a Forestry Officer, and would probably go abroad. At that time there were forestry jobs in a number of our colonies besides India. I got my £3.

A few months later I went to Buckingham Palace to receive my VC accompanied by my parents and Aunt Jessie Walduck. Dear Mother, in her excitement, put on her garden coat for the occasion to her extreme disgust. It was not as bad as it sounds as her garden coat was her previous best black coat demoted when she got a new one.

The investiture was most impressive. I was the only one receiving the Victoria Cross on the day, so I went first.[7] King George V was keen eyed and quick witted as (no doubt having observed several wound stripes on my left sleeve) he asked me if I was fully recovered from my last wound and how long had I spent in hospital etc.

There was a very large number who fully qualified for decorations and never got them. I don't know of any case where any major decoration did not go where it was deserved. There was the story of the Australian officer who got the MC because he was the only man at Brigade HQ who had a corkscrew. That I can't vouch for. There were so many cases where people did marvellous jobs, but there was nobody there to recommend them.

For instance, I recommended a Sergeant Smith for jolly good work he had done when we were fighting on the Hollebeke Ridge, near Ypres. I recommended him for the DCM and then I was wounded. The colonel looking through the recommendations saw Sergeant Smith recommended for the MM. He said that won't do. He wrote to me in hospital saying he had seen him bayonet three Germans. He said he would put him in for the DCM. It was the wrong Sergeant Smith. Anyway, that was righted afterwards. When I found that my Sergeant Smith had got nothing, on my return from hospital, I spoke to the colonel about it. He got in touch with the brigadier, who righted it.

Of course, a certain number of officers got the MC, not for any particular job, but after several years of doing repeatedly good jobs without anything spectacular. They were given in the New Year's Honours. Well deserved, but nothing outstanding.

That was the end of the First World War as far as I was concerned. My elder brother, Graham, had been most seriously wounded out in Mesopotamia and never quite recovered from his privations and wounds. I was wounded four times as previously recorded. My cousin Leslie Doubleday lost a lung through wounds; 'Laddie' Doubleday won the DSC and was drowned. Cousin Spencer Edwards died and Cousin Norman Hudson lost a leg. An average for that war – six of the family went, four came back, all seriously wounded. We were very lucky compared with others.

PART II

The Second World War

These notes are written by me in case they may be of interest or help to anyone who, in the future, may write a history of the Royal Pioneer Corps, as by that time those who served in the earlier part of the late war may well have died off or forgotten many of the details of our early struggles, sorrows and triumphs.

Donald John Dean

Introduction

Donald Dean was invested with his Victoria Cross by King George V at Buckingham Palace on 15 February 1919. On his return to Sittingbourne he was greeted with a civic reception, recorded in the local newspaper, the *East Kent Gazette*. A mass of townspeople turned out for the reception at the train station where an enormous temporary platform had been erected and dressed in 'gala appearance' with a large banner reading 'DONALD' across the top.

Dean and his parents arrived back from London to be met by this throng and a guard of honour from his old Scout Troop. A band struck up 'See the Conquering Hero Comes.' The newspaper recorded that young Lieutenant Dean looked 'astonished' at the reception, and noticed he had his coat done up so no one could see the medal. The full citation for his award was read out to loud cheers.

After speeches by various local dignitaries, Dean addressed the crowd with the following words:

'Ladies and gentlemen – I must say I am overwhelmed with the reception I have received. I little expected to have a reception like this. I would like to say I am proud to belong to one of our Kentish regiments, in which so many Sittingbourne men have served with distinction. As one of the speakers truly said, there are many deeds done that deserve the Victoria Cross; but I am fortunate to be one of those individuals to be picked out for the honour. I am proud to belong to Sittingbourne – and I have nothing more to say.

At this the crowd laughed and applauded. After 'three cheers for Lieutenant Dean VC' and the National Anthem, the official ceremony came to an end. Dean was urged to unbutton his coat and show the bronze medal. He did this and saluted at which the crowd surged forward on mass to shake his hand. Only when this multitude dispersed could Dean walk home.

On 26 June 1920 he attended the famous garden party given by George V at Buckingham Palace to the recipients of the VC. In 1923 he married Marjorie Emily Wood at St Michael's church, Sittingbourne. The couple's first child, Laurence, did not survive infancy and died aged two months. He was followed by two more children, Michael and Susan.

Although he did not wish to make soldiering a fulltime career, Dean gave continued service to the Territorial Army. In July 1921 he was promoted to captain in the 4th Bn (East Kent Regiment) and major in April 1930. He took over command of the battalion in 1936, gaining the rank of lieutenant colonel. This period of his military career is described in the next chapter.

There is one important incident from the interwar era, which Dean does not refer to in his military memoirs, but which are of general interest to the story. In 1938 Dean's younger brother Alan married Gertrude 'Gerti' Bürger, an Austrian who spoke very little English. The wedding was in Vienna, but they were told to get married in Britain for the union to be considered legal. The reasons behind this have been lost to the family now, but Gerti was half-Jewish and Austria then formed part of the Nazi *Reich*. Given the Nazi's laws on racial intermarriage, this may have been a factor. The couple therefore came to Britain in early 1939 and married in a second ceremony attended by Alan's family. Many of Gerti's personal possessions had been left in Austria, so, with the political situation deteriorating, Alan somewhat imprudently decided to go and collect her valuables himself. The plan backfired on 31 May when he was caught at Aachen trying to leave Germany with his socks stuffed with Gerti's jewellery. Placed under arrest at the behest of the foreign currency control authorities, Alan Dean was returned to Vienna where he admitted trying to export currency from Germany.

Learning of the arrest, Dean contacted the British Consulate-General in Vienna to enquire after his younger sibling. Thinking the German authorities would respect him for his military rank and decorations, Dean flew to Vienna in order to secure Alan's release. He was told this could be accomplished on receipt of what can only be described as a substantial ransom. Much of Dean's time in Vienna appears to have been spent ironing out bureaucratic obstacles to organizing the money transfer. Writing to his wife on 3 July 1939 he explained the predicament:

> This is a wonderful country but unless a personal attention is given or you can get an introduction to some individual, letters to any department may lie there for weeks without receiving any notice at all.

Knowing his letter would be subject to censorship, Dean described the prison where Alan was being held in very guarded terms, writing:

> The hotel where A. is staying has had some plumbing troubles and he has not been able to get a bath for some weeks. He has plenty of English money still. He has some difficulty in getting fruit but had plenty to eat of course.

He then continued with a general description of the city which is interesting for its closing remarks, given they were made just over eight weeks before the start of the Second World War:

Yesterday afternoon for the first time I felt that I could devote some time to sightseeing so I booked a seat (4 marks) in a charabanc complete with guide and did a Cook's tour. Most of the passengers were of Teutonic (*very* Teutonic) extraction but there was also one American lady, an Irish couple and me as the sole English representative. The guide did his work extremely well and won my sincere admiration for his broadcasting work, first in German and then in English in double-quick time. It is true that I sometimes mistook the latter for the former, but I got the gist of it all. I was interested to see it all, but I think the best of the lot was the Castle of Schoenbrunn where we saw 45 of the state rooms most of them with their original furniture and decorations etc. I did so wish we were seeing it together. I went out to dinner and found a little restaurant that suited both my taste and pocket. ... All the Germans and Austrian Germans seem quite friendly just the same as our people at home are to alien visitors. What a funny thing it is that both countries are afraid of war and we seem constantly on the verge of it. 'The world is out of joint' (Hamlet).

As the Second World War approaches Dean's narrative continues.

CHAPTER 7

Disappointment with
The Buffs

When the Territorial Army was starting to be re-constituted after a lapse of time during which it had been disembodied following the end of World War I, I applied to the depot of The Queen's Own Royal West Kent Regiment at Maidstone to join the TA and serve, as a subaltern in the 4th Bn, travelling either to Maidstone or Chatham as these were their nearest drill stations.

The Queen's Own told me that they did not want me as they wished to sign officers living in the towns where their drill halls were.

I accordingly talked the matter over with my friend Gordon Stevens and we both went down to Canterbury and signed on with 4th Bn The Buffs. Their nearest drill hall was in Sittingbourne.

The adjutant then was Major Howard Smith and he told me that as I was senior to Gordon Stevens I would, for the time being, be commanding 'B' Coy. I asked him how many there were in the company and he replied, 'One – you are it'.

The CO at that time was Lieutenant Colonel Mainwaring Dunstan who had been the last CO of that battalion before demobilization. He was, unfortunately, not popular with the officers who had been with him in India and in consequence the only two to sign on again were Lieutenant C.S.F. Witts and Lieutenant John Sherwood.

In due time I became brevet major and, in January 1936, I attained the rank of lieutenant colonel.

After the Munich Affair in 1938, or rather during that period, we were on the very brink of war and a selected number of my 4th Bn The Buffs, including of course myself, were embodied and prepared for full mobilization.

We sandbagged part of Battalion HQ in the St Peters Lane Drill Hall at Canterbury and all our other drill halls did the same where this was possible.

Those who had the ground dug slit trenches to retire into if bombing started from the air.

We had orders to open a secret document that had been reposing in our safe at Battalion HQ for some time, this read something as follows:

> You will have opened this on War Office orders and you will now, without waiting for any further orders, raise three companies of Women's Auxiliary Territorial Service, one at Canterbury, one at Folkestone and one at Tenterden.

No details were given of their ages, physical fitness, what they were expected to do, rates of pay, conditions of service, etc, but orders were orders so we proceeded to advertise the cause immediately by town crier, posters, local papers, etc. When the ladies presented themselves all we could do was take their names and addresses and tell them that we would give them fuller details as soon as we had any. These very patriotic and enthusiastic ladies called round almost daily to know what they should do and how they could help. After about a week of this, during which we got no further direct details but gathered from the national press that these companies were to replace male soldiers as clerks, store women, possibly as cooks etc, I decided that in any event they would need a little drill instruction whatever their jobs might be, so I ordered a parade the following night in the drill hall and detailed RSM Tom Burt to take the parade.

The morning after I asked Tom Burt how he had got on and he replied, 'Fine, I got them on parade and told them to stop talking and they stopped talking. I'm advising my wife to join up today'.

The Munich crisis died down and we gradually got further information about our 'girls' who almost became part of the battalion. We finally chose company commanders for all three companies, submitted their names to the Kent Territorial Army HQ and they were duly commissioned. Shortly after this Lady Harris was appointed County Commandant. She became very upset because of the long delay in getting uniforms for her women and naturally consulted us as to what she should do. My adjutant, Roscoe Reid, advised her to go to County Territorial HQ, see the county secretary, Captain Stopford, hammer on his desk with her umbrella and demand action.

She said, 'Oh, I couldn't possibly do that,' so I said to her, 'If I write a letter as from you, in strong terms, will you sign it?' She said that she would, but when she read the letter she was horrified and said that she would never send a letter like that couched in such terms, almost abusive as far as I can remember. We finally persuaded her to sign and posted the letter before she could change her mind. A few days later she said to me, 'That letter actually worked!'

Shortly after the Munich Affair it was decided that the Territorial Army should double itself, so 4th Bn took all possible steps to do so. Such was the spirit of the times that we had recruited something like 60 per cent over strength by the time we went to camp in June 1939, as far as the other ranks were concerned. We were to get a number of our officers from the Territorial Army Officers Reserve. In the next two months we were up to full strength of ORs for two battalions; 4th and 5th Buffs, TA.

As some of these reserve officers were rusty it was obviously desirable that they should come to camp with us if possible, both to get up to date and also to shake down with the officers and men they would serve with if or when mobilized. I accordingly asked for permission to take them to camp with us, but this was refused and we were only allowed sufficient pay for about half of them. We arranged with our brother officers that they would in fact come for at least a week and that the pay allowed by the War Office should be divided between them as far as it went. They all agreed to this and much valuable training was done. We had about fifty officers in camp at one time.

A week before war was declared in 1939 our advance party was mobilized and final arrangements were made for splitting up into 4th and 5th Bns. We were then at full strength in both, but naturally as we had doubled the number of WOs and NCOs in a twelve-month period, they'd had very little time to exercise themselves in their new ranks. It must also be remembered that a full 50 per cent of the privates in both battalions had, at most, twelve months' Territorial Army training, some even only a few weeks and no camp.

The War Office had recently instituted a new rank, that of Warrant Officer Class III, to command platoons or similar sub-units normally commanded by a subaltern. We had a few of these posted to us. This unfortunate experiment by the War Office to find junior leaders was a grave mistake which was shortly proved. They had certain duties normally reserved for officers, such as paying out, were unpopular with WOs Class I and II, and were not liked by the men. As soon as war was declared the mistake was noted and the suitable ones were commissioned and the remainder were made WO Class I or II as and when vacancies arose. No new ones were appointed, so this bastard rank died out with sighs of relief all round. We attributed this scheme to the Minister of War, Hore Belisha.

When full mobilization was ordered we assembled at Canterbury, the 4th Bn with Battalion HQ in the St Peter's Lane Drill Hall and companies scattered round the city in private billets and all available halls, etc. The mobilization worked according to plan and nearly everything worked smoothly. We had arranged a year previously that two days' dry rations should be delivered within twenty-four hours of mobilization by Messrs Vye & Son Ltd and this was punctually done.

We were ordered to send fifteen NCOs to the depot of The Buffs to go through a short refresher course and then act as instructors to help train the National Servicemen who were soon pouring in. This still further handicapped us as we had so recently doubled our strength and could not possibly spare our best men like this, but it had to be done.

To start with there was no issue of rations as our Divisional Royal Army Service Corps had themselves to be mobilized so we had a cash allowance in lieu and had to arrange civilian catering at local restaurants and cafes, but this again worked very well.

We were able to draw imprest money to pay our men but officers were not paid at all for several months as the paymasters staff had to be mobilized first and anyway officers' pay was always a month in arrears. This meant that a certain number of young officers, particularly those with family commitments, were desperate and I had to lend them a total of £150 from my own pocket which was all repaid in due course.

Our three companies of Women's Auxiliary Territorial Services were of course mobilized and one company went to The Buffs' depot to the great disgust and distrust of Colonel George Howe, who was then the CO. However, they soon proved their worth and he later handsomely admitted he had been mistaken.

The 4th Bn gave the newly thrown off 5th Bn cash for their officers' and sergeants' messes. (The 5th was then commanded by Lieutenant Colonel George H. Mount and his Adjutant was Captain David Hilton.)

A large proportion of the 4th Bn was soon on detachment guarding vulnerable points in Kent, among them being all rail tunnels between Canterbury and Folkestone. Those between Dover and Folkestone could only be reached, in some cases, by rail, so a private train consisting of a shunting engine, one small passenger coach and a goods wagon was put at the disposal of the battalion. This was used to take reliefs, meals and visiting rounds from post to post.

Soon after we were concentrated in Canterbury an order came that all below the rank of full NCO in certain reserved occupations in civilian life should parade at the local Labour Exchange to be vetted to see whether they should be taken out of the army. We had about fifty of these so when they were paraded I spoke to them saying how sorry we were to think that they would leave their comrades, etc and sent them off under an acting corporal. A few hours later they were back again and the corporal said to me that when they were interviewed they all found that they were not as experienced in their trade as had been thought and in consequence they were all back with their comrades!

One thing we had to do was to get the whole battalion both vaccinated and inoculated in very quick time. Our MO, Dr Hammerton, dealt with this in a wholesale manner having an orderly with a swab dab the arm, he stuck the needle in, another orderly slapped on a pad and sticking plaster and it took a few seconds for each man to pass along. We nearly had the whole battalion done when some barrack room lawyer told the remainder that it was optional, so several of them said that they would not be done. We were prepared for this so we had the objectors in and the MO gave them a most lurid description of what might happen to them if they were *not* done and became infected with this or that in consequence. One man fainted with the horrible details but they all agreed to be done. Ours was the only battalion in the division to reach 100 per cent done.

After the War Office (WO) had moved all the troops from Dover and Shorncliffe, except National Servicemen, we found that our battalion was the sole unit for defence in case of any landing between Chatham and Hastings and we had at least one company on guard duty as previously explained. My defence scheme was to hold sufficient transport always available in Canterbury and to be ready to rush it to any threatened point! What a hope.

Among other duties I had to see that my company commanders were filing all their correspondence correctly and running their offices on business lines, so I made enquiries. One company commander said that filing gave him no trouble at all, he had just the one file marked miscellaneous in to which he put everything!

The spirit of the 4th Bn was one of the utmost keenness and crime just did not exist. The 4th Bn moved down to the Aldershot area and joined the rest of the brigade there.

A few days later I was invited to tea at his house by the Divisional Commander, Major General 'Snowey' Osborne and after tea he told me that he was recommending me for a job under AG14.[1] On my expressing my fervent wish to stay in command of the battalion, with which I had served for nineteen years and which I had largely recruited myself, he said, 'Well as a matter of fact I do not really want to have any Territorial COs in my division'. On my politely pointing out that the 44th Home Counties Division was composed entirely of Territorial Units he said that in his opinion no Territorial CO can possibly be as efficient as a regular officer of similar length of service, adding that he had picked out Major Adrian Marshall (a Buff) for the job.

My brigade commander, Brigadier Rupelle, who naturally knew me very well and who, I am glad to say, had a high regard for me, asked General Osborne to reconsider this but he refused to change his mind.[2]

This was undoubtedly the bitterest day of my life.

I consulted General Lyndon Bell, our Buffs' colonel of the regiment as to my best course and he strongly advised me to accept the position as any appeal by me would only put me in a most difficult position. Even if I were successful it might well recoil on the battalion.

As soon as Adrian Marshall came to us, I duly handed over to him. My last night in mess was spent showing my officers how to put together the webbing equipment issued to them in numerous pieces that day and in seeing that it was properly fitted and comfortable, as not a single one of them had ever worn webbing equipment or knew how to fit and adjust it.

I heard later that a number of our officers were unhappy with the new CO who did not understand that every officer and man was an enthusiastic volunteer, and got transfers elsewhere where, in many cases, they rose to the rank of lieutenant colonel before the war ended.

I did not see my 4th Bn again until it was reformed in 1946 and I was made Honorary Colonel of it.

CHAPTER 8

The Phoney War

In late October 1939 I was ordered to report to AG14 War Office for a new job. I found there my old friend Colonel J.V.R. Jackson who did so much unrecognized work, under very considerable difficulties for our very young and immature corps. He told me that I was appointed as a Group Commander in the AMPC. As I had never heard of such a post, I asked him first of all what 'AMPC' stood for, which shook him somewhat, and I also asked for a copy of the establishment and G1098 (list of stores and equipment) which shook him still more. [AMPC in fact stood for Auxiliary Military Pioneer Corps – Ed.] He had only his office copy of the Establishment and none of the G1098, so I hastily copied the former and was told to report to an AMPC Centre at Clacton. This I did, taking with me my batman from the 4th Bn The Buffs.

The Centre was very well housed in a Butlin's Holiday Camp there and I found large numbers of officers already on the spot. Practically all were middle aged or elderly, and all wore the uniform and badges of their former units. I found also a very mixed bag of other ranks, all except the staff being privates, mostly over military age, or of low medical category, but nearly all volunteers and therefore keen. One private, who was not picked by us but was a stout hearted volunteer, asked me in strict confidence whether he could continue to draw his old age pension as well as his army pay!

The Centre CO and the quartermaster were very co-operative and from the latter I received a typewritten copy of the much desired G1098, so with that and the Establishment I was able to start forming my Group HQ. I was given as an adjutant an ex-cavalry lieutenant, Leslie Ormerod, who had been on the reserve for many years, but had never been an adjutant, also a newly commissioned QM, Lieutenant Michael Browne, who had previously been a reservist company quartermaster sergeant.

My adjutant said that it would help him considerably in dealing with company commanders, who were all majors, if he could be promoted captain. There was then no regulation permitting this but few people at that stage knew their regulations, so I merely issued a Group Order promoting him to captain and adjutant and had this put in Centre Orders (we had no clerks or typewriters in the Group HQ at that time). It actually went through and he got his rank and pay without any later repercussions.

The first day there I found that the recruits were still being trained in obsolete drill and were still 'forming fours'. When I tactfully mentioned this to the Centre CO he told me that they had no training manuals and that he had spent the last twenty years in command of police in Burma so did not know anything about modern drill. The training officer eagerly borrowed my training manuals saying that he knew that the drill had been changed some time ago and that troops now 'formed threes' but he did not know quite how.

The Centre CO also asked me to help him to write a Defence Scheme. This we optimistically did although there were only a few rifles, no automatic weapons, no ammunition and, apparently, no information as to our role in case of hostile landings. My adjutant and I started choosing our Group HQ personnel as best we could knowing no man's capabilities; e.g. two privates were made Regimental Quartermaster Sergeant and Orderly Room Sergeant respectively.

A few days later I was ordered to France to report to the Director of Labour who was at, or near, GHQ. I was to be followed a few weeks later by my Group HQ, when it was fully formed. As a very friendly gesture by Colonel Jackson I was given a ticket to Calais on the civilian cross-channel boat instead of having to go a very long way round via Cherbourg, and, as I protested that I did not know where GHQ was, I was told, in strictest confidence, to go to Arras and then enquire.

I accordingly crossed to Calais with my batman and found Lieutenant Colonel Hicks, who was also a new Pioneer Group CO, travelling out. As there was no British Rail Transport Officer (RTO) or other representative in Calais we requested, and got, a travel warrant from the French Army authorities. Arriving in Arras we phoned from the RTO's office and were collected by the Director of Labour's car.

At that time the Director of Labour was a Brigadier Cox-Field with his HQ in Avesnes-le-Compte, a small village a few miles from Arras. He appointed me OC 5 Group and Colonel Hicks OC 6 Group. No. 5 Group was to comprise all AMPC personnel in GHQ Area. When I asked what AMPC companies there were in GHQ Area and their locations, he told me that as far as he knew there were three or four companies and he gave me their last known locations but said that my first job was to find them and let *him* know where they were.

Only one company, No. 47, which was stationed in Doullens, was available for general duties as the others were permanently attached to various 'Employing Services', either as a company or in sections. *Our* General A.L.I. Friend, then Brigadier, was at that time in command of GHQ Troops and he advised me to make my Group HQ in Doullens and he appointed me OC Troops in that town.

On searching round I found that No. 47 Coy had lost one section, dropped off under orders received en route from the Base Port, but no one knew where they had gone from there. We subsequently traced that they had finally got to Marseilles and returned to England. Six sections drawn from three different companies were working in or near Poix. Four of these sections had not seen anyone from their company HQ since they started work there. A number of Pioneers, all privates, were attached to a Royal Engineers Unit which administered them and provided NCOs, while other sections were the 'poor relations' carried round by the employing service.

Those working directly under the REs for example were being paid the same pay as the REs who were entitled to Corps pay, while our men were not, so when we did get them under our direct control every man was most seriously overdrawn and had to be put under the hated 'stoppages'. The position was slowly but steadily improved as soon as all our AMPC came under the wing of a group.

No one seemed to know exactly what the position or responsibility of a Group Commander was (including the Group CO himself) or what his authority was, but in GHQ area this easily resolved itself as I gradually wrenched the companies and sections from the employing services with the help of the GOC, who was delighted to have a proper pool of labour for special as well as regular jobs, and I also made myself Labour Advisor to GHQ.

I never received any instructions at all about the employment of civilian labour out there, but when I found that various services started employing civilian labour and paid them whatever rate they thought suitable, they were soon competing against each other. This being a labour matter I assumed control of it as a right and quickly got it under control so that all indents for civilian labour were passed to Group HQ which provided it, and thereby saved the employing service the bother, but also said what the rate of payment should be, etc. This was a most complicated business as we had to make certain deductions for French taxation and social services and also pay out certain additions for family allowances according to the man's age and the number of children and whether the mother of such children stayed at home to look after them or went to work herself, etc.

Being in GHQ area we had to comply with the French mission's request that these special methods of payment should be made. In consequence we had to engage 'clerk-accountants' with every body of civilians to work out the pay sheets. Civil Labour Units of the Pioneer Corps, for the engagement of civilian labour, did not then exist and we had no directives at all on the subject, so all this work fell on the shoulders of the Group CO.

The method of obtaining such civilian labour was first of all to see whether there was a French Employment Bureau and if so whether they had anyone on their books. Needless to say this very rarely worked in wartime, but having gone through the correct procedure we then got the men by other methods. Sometimes the mayor would help but we often used the town (or village) drummer, who was the equivalent of our town crier. Most of the mayors of small districts were helpful if treated with exaggerated deference to their rank and a few British cigarettes.

At that time Group HQ did not have a second-in-command, only a CO, Adjutant and a QM; while the companies had a major in command, one captain and one subaltern, which made very heavy work for all. The average age of officers was high to start with and in fact I found myself younger as CO at the age of forty-two than any of my officers, including subalterns. While some of these were excellent, a certain amount of weeding out was necessary as the smart and energetic young officer of the 1914/1918 vintage had sometimes turned into a stout middle-aged man with little energy and a big thirst.

One company commander for example drew about £250 from the field paymaster when he came to France with his company, had all his sections paid by the employing services, never visited them once, bought a typewriter for the company office without authority, out of this money, as he had been sent abroad without one, lived in a hotel in a large town some miles away from his company HQ and never accounted for the balance of the money.

Another officer, a captain called up against his will from the Regular Army Reserve of Officers (RARO), politely but firmly stated that he was a Conchie [conscientious objector] and therefore refused to go on parade in order to be court-martialled and so get out of the army. He was a nice fellow and I quite liked him, but there is a limit to what one can or cannot do in the army and this came in the latter category. I, with equal politeness and firmness, put him under arrest. He proved rather a problem for GHQ who had never heard before of a Regular Army Officer who was a Conchie, especially on active service. We finally got him discharged on medical grounds, without scandal.

After the first month or so we got some very good subalterns sent out and were able to weed out the officers who were hopeless for one reason or another (often heavy drinking) and we also got some first class work from those left.

Early in 1940, the Director of Labour was reported by Brigadier Friend as being drunk in uniform in a theatre box in Arras in front of the troops in the audience. Cox-Field retired to the UK and returned to civil life and Brigadier Friend was appointed as Director of Labour in his place by the GOC in France. This incensed the Secretary of State for War, Hore Belisha, who had appointed Cox-Field. He promptly appointed Mr L.W. Amps (an able civil engineer) to 2nd Lieutenant, Acting Major General as Director of Labour at the War Office, thereby out-ranking Friend. Hore Belisha then sent a signal to the BEF to the effect that Major General Amps was being sent to France to inspect the Pioneer Corps. The Commander-in-Chief sent back a signal that he was quite ready for a War Office representative to *visit* troops in the BEF, but that no one would be allowed to *inspect* his troops without asking his consent. Amps did not come out.[1]

When Pioneer companies were directly under their employing service for all purposes the employing unit arranged for accommodation, rations and clothing, etc. Once they came directly under Group it was found advisable to administer some companies direct under the Group QM while distant ones might be better served by doing their own indenting, being visited by the QM at intervals to see that their store ledgers etc were in order. While some of the employing services had looked after our men very well, there were cases where they had been treated as very much the 'poor relations' and had what billets were left after the employing unit had been settled, and rations drawn for them after the employing unit had had theirs first.

Originally the only transport in the Group consisted of a small car for Group HQ and ditto for each company, all driven by attached Royal Army Service Corps (RASC) drivers. These had not only to be used for visits to detachments, conferences, etc but often for drawing rations, stores and mail. The lack of any kind of water cart often created considerable difficulties for those in isolated billets, tents or huts and even when wells were available the water was open to grave suspicion when untreated.

No. 5 Group arranged for the attachment to itself of one lorry, supplied daily, which greatly helped the 'Q' side generally. At that time each man had only one pair of boots and we had no boot repairers or repair kits on our establishment. We managed, however, to get boot repair outfits in due course and could then keep more men properly shod, and at work, but this was only done with the active help of Brigadier Friend, who on one occasion even took a demonstration pair of boots, badly needing repairs, to a conference attended by DOS.

A trivial item that annoyed our men was that the pair of laces issued with each pair of boots was expected to last the life of the boots however many times they were repaired, or alternatively they had to buy their own replacements. I fought an unsuccessful battle over this first with DADOS then with ADOS at GHQ so then I put up a request through GHQ Troops for a ruling on 'What is the life of an army bootlace?' I never knew how far this enquiry got but we got replacement of bootlaces sanctioned.

We tried unsuccessfully for some months to get a suit of denims or a second battle dress per man until one day the Commander-in-Chief, 'Tiger' Gort VC, was being driven through Arras when he espied two disreputable looking objects walking along in old British uniforms smothered in chalk. They were in fact two of a working party from my group who had for some time been enlarging the tunnels and caves in the chalk under part of Arras which were to be used by GHQ, who had been constantly rubbing up against the wet chalk walls. The Commander-in-Chief stopped his car, sent an ADC to enquire who and what these men were and in due course I received, through the usual channels, a peremptory demand for an explanation as to why I, as CO, allowed these men to be seen walking in public; then followed some pithy remarks about 'disgrace to the British Army', etc.

I replied, through the usual channels that I entirely agreed that it was a disgrace that British soldiers should be seen in public in such a condition, but to rectify it I was faced with three alternatives:

1) To keep a proportion of my men off duty and in bed while their uniforms were washed;
2) To confine such men to barracks until their present uniforms were worn out and new ones issued; or
3) To issue all Pioneers with a suit of denims or a second uniform. That I had been pressing for weeks, quite unsuccessfully, for the third alternative but as the Commander-in-Chief was himself taking an interest in the matter perhaps this request could now be granted.

Brigadier Reford, Commanding GHQ Troops, sent for me on receipt of this letter and asked if I really wanted it to be sent forward as written, and, on being assured that I did, he gave me a friendly warning of possible unpleasant consequences. However, I was not court-martialled and we very quickly got authority from the QM General's office for an issue of denims per man. Upon our indenting for some 2,000 odd suits of denims I was informed that there were none available in France. My next action was to request authority for a second uniform in lieu of denims and this was granted both for my group and the whole of the AMPC in the BEF.

Some of our companies came out from England wearing RE badges, some with no badges at all and some with that of their original regiment or corps. Very few had the correct corps badge though later companies started coming out with this as they became available. For several months the officers continued to wear their original unit badges and referred to themselves as the 'Blank' Regiment *attached* AMPC, not as being AMPC, a practice that Brigadier Friend rightly and strongly frowned upon. Many of those men wearing RE badges felt a grievance because they did not get RE's pay.

After the original companies came out which were composed of reservists, the new companies consisted of men often with very little training indeed. Some counted it in days only and the discipline suffered accordingly. They were being worked seven days a week and got stale and browned off after a while and had no time at all for any training or rest or time for 'make and mend'. When I asked GHQ for a six-day working week I was told: 'The war goes on seven days a week so your men must work seven days a week'. Seeing how the wind blew I did not ask again, but gave every man a day a week off, staggering them so that the work was not interrupted. In fact considerably more work was done than before.

One company which was composed of Glasgow Irish (No. 47) gave much initial trouble. Nearly every man had a safety razor blade sewn in the peak of his fore and aft cap, which proved a ready weapon for slashing faces. They also had an undesirable habit of breaking the end off a bottle on the edge of a table and using the jagged remains for stabbing. (It is only fair to say that later in the war this company was one of the finest in the whole corps.) One day, I remember, they stole rum but as it was insufficient to give them all a good drink they diluted it liberally with stolen petrol! No one died, though several nearly did.

Other companies were giving trouble with thieving, drunkenness, rape, selling kit, etc, so at the same time as improving their living conditions, food, clothing and working conditions, very firm action was taken with malefactors, but mainly within the unit. After a certain number had been awarded detention and we found that GHQ could only take few if any into their detention barracks and then only after long delay, I decided that we must run our own. I asked the French authorities if they could help with a suitable building and they said, 'Well we have got a disused civilian prison in Doullens of course', so we borrowed this, staffed and ran it without GHQ knowing much about our troubles; the natural wish being to settle any difficulties within the family circle. After a few months, conduct was so vastly improved that we closed it down and handed the building back.

EXCERPT FROM A LETTER: FRANCE, 2 NOVEMBER 1939

Dearest Marjorie,

... I am very glad that I am partly under [Brigadier Friend] as he is a man who gets on with the work and is ready to help those under him with the same idea. I have mixed here with a varied bag. Some are out to get their job done and some are obstructionists while some are just plain useless; in the course of time, however, kindred spirits find each other and I am making new friends now.

My work is interesting as there is so much for me to do and I do not find much spare time. I have an Irish-Scottish bunch of men from Glasgow in one of my companies who are always getting into trouble but I feel sure that I can make something of them yet – many of the men have been treated without proper consideration but I am gradually getting this altered and think that this combined with considerable firmness will have the desired effect. There is one bad hat that I have treated leniently as an experiment as I hope to get the best out of him like this, but my officers tell me that this will be hopeless, however time will tell...

Early in 1940 a French major (whom we will call 'X') who had been appointed by the French Mission as a liaison officer with the British in a town in the Arras area, warned the British colonel (whom we will call 'Y') who was OC British Troops in that area,1 that the French authorities had expelled a number of prostitutes suffering from VD and that a number of them had crossed the Somme into the British Army area. Major X strongly advised Colonel Y to open a brothel without delay to safeguard the health of his British troops.

Colonel Y approved the idea and asked Major X to whom he should apply for a licence. X said that no licences were being issued and that Y should provide an unofficial brothel. Y said that he had no experience of such an arrangement and asked X if he could advise. X said, 'It's quite simple, you just put an advertisement in the local paper', and offered to do this.

There were several replies and the woman chosen as 'madam' said 'I was in a brothel in the First World War and know all about the running of one and I can speak English. After the War I retired and as I had a good "dot" I made a happy marriage but my husband is now dead.' When asked about staff she said, 'I have a daughter of twenty and a young niece so that should prove sufficient for a start and if there is a rush of business I can always help out myself'.

Colonel Y arranged accordingly, fixed up a house and arranged with a local French doctor for a weekly medical inspection of the women. Y put the local Deputy Assistant Provost Marshal in charge and never actually met any of the women, but until the British evacuation there were no known cases of VD in his town. He heard after the war that the Germans kept the brothel going with the approval of the local mayor.

As other troops were stationed in and around Doullens and there was a constant stream of traffic through the town, it required constant traffic control. I asked for and got a dozen Welsh Guardsmen from the 1st Bn and these acted both in lieu of MPs until such time as they became available and also as traffic police which did not then appear to exist.

All our companies were in those days supposed to be sent overseas armed with 25 per cent of rifles only, but hardly anyone had any musketry practice or instruction. We used to spend voluntary hours of the short rest periods in teaching musketry until finally every man out of the 4,000 or so had fired. This proved very popular and made the men feel and act more like soldiers. Valuable help was given by some of the CSMs who were old reservists. We also started a school of instruction for prospective NCOs and refresher courses for existing NCOs, all of which greatly helped efficiency.

During this period we very successfully demonstrated that, given the tools, there was no job that we could not tackle and that we could also give valuable advice and help on all labour matters, also generally supervise jobs and thereby economise in labour. For example when ordered to send 100 men to work at a railhead we would not normally send 100 but find out first the tonnage and type of goods to be handled, then allocate what we estimated would be sufficient to do the job, possibly only twenty men or less, thereby leaving men available for other work. If we found any job requiring more than we had estimated, for whatever reason it might be, we liked to have a small reserve to call upon. All the services, RN, RAF as well as the Army, were apparently only trained to ask for 'numbers' not for sufficient to do specific jobs, and they all over-insured by asking for more than necessary; possibly this was because their own men did not work so well, as they looked upon such work as a 'fatigue' not as a 'job of work'.

GHQ Troops were quick to appreciate the wisdom of giving us the jobs and leaving to us how we did them. Some of my men worked on fatigues round some huge army bakeries unloading flour trains and handling flour, loading bread onto lorries and trains, coke for the ovens and many similar jobs. Other parties of men unloaded stores from trains at railheads. We helped to lay railway sidings, erect hutted camps, worked on dumps, helped in stationery and map departments, quarried and mined a safe battle HQ for GHQ, etc. Many worked on aerodrome sites, but little did we realize that we were making or improving some of the finest airfields in Europe for the later use of the German Air Force. One of our smaller but much appreciated efforts was to form and run a hostel for casuals passing through the town of Doullens or neighbourhood, such as convoy drivers, leave men, men from hospitals, etc.

Once, I went visiting some of my scattered detachments as usual and passed through some of the old battlefield area where I had fought in the last war. Although most of the traces had gone, to the experienced eye there were many indications still in the form of pockmarked banks that were not worth the cost levelling to fill in the shell holes, cuts in the sides of sunk roads that used to be gun pits etc.

I had an amusing experience one afternoon when the representatives of the BBC called to make a recording from my men for a short broadcast the following Saturday night to encourage recruiting for the AMPC. The recording was done in a railway van in the station yard here and after the speeches the men actually did their job of loading a bread truck as recorded. We had the engine shunting round for sound effects and blowing of horns etc, but as the Frenchmen got so warmed up and excited it was a job to get them to stop.

EXCERPT FROM A LETTER: FRANCE, 2 NOVEMBER 1939

Dearest Marjorie,

I am just dashing off a note in haste before the post goes. This morning

I shook hands with the King who very nicely chatted with me and I was in fact the only one out of a line of colonels with whom he did chat in his hurried tour of GHQ as the generals quite properly were well to the fore.

I am very busy and have already over 1,600 men to look after, scattered over huge areas so my first job is to see them all or at least where they are and their officers, arrangements, jobs etc. The more I see of my job the more I think that it was highly desirable that someone took the job with energy, experience and push, in fact a good officer like myself (Loud Cheers).

I will write as soon as possible.

We thought that it would be a good idea to have a small pig to fatten on our swill for the men's Christmas dinner, so we detailed a Captain Verity to buy one in the next local market. He offered 200 francs, which was refused. While the haggling was going on the Frenchman lifted up the pig and extolled its fine points. Just at that moment the first air raid warning was given and everyone ran for cover. Finally, the only ones left were Verity and the Frenchman. The latter could not stand it any longer so he grabbed the 200 francs, thrust the piglet into Verity's arms and bolted, leaving Verity to walk home with a squealing piglet struggling in his arms.

We put this pig in the charge of the officers' mess cook, an Irishman, and all went well for a while. Unfortunately, the mess cook took such a fancy to the growing pig and made such a pet of it that when Xmas came no one had the heart to kill the pig. We finally solved the problem by sending the cook home on leave and dealing with the pig then. As Xmas had passed we sold it for 2,000 francs and bought two more pigs with part of the proceeds. These were kept until the Germans drove us out, but even then they travelled in sacks on our food lorry and were finally released in the streets of Boulogne when we embarked the remnants of the group under heavy fire.

One evening I was lucky enough to get a ticket for a concert given by Jack Payne and his Orchestra and Gracie Fields. This was the first time I had seen Gracie and she was certainly a very clever artiste as she could hold her audience wonderfully. When one or two fellows shouted loudly for special items she told them off in good Lancastrian and made them and the house roar with laughter, but they shut up alright. I thoroughly enjoyed the show and did not mind the drive back through a snow storm – I drove myself as I did not have a ticket for my driver.

For communication we had to depend very largely on civilian telephones, which meant that there was no secrecy and that we had to ask for our numbers in French. In Doullens we had much lack of co-operation from the local telephone girls who gave preference to French subscribers and would not understand our pronunciation. I finally instructed our interpreter, on his next visit to Paris, to get a really good fancy box of chocolates, not obtainable locally at that time, which I sent to the telephone exchange addressed to 'the charming young lady operator with the golden voice, and her colleagues'. It worked marvels. We later received a motor cycle at Group HQ and one for each company, which made it much easier to get orders out and supervise working parties etc as well as for collecting post, etc when necessary.

To start with we had no French interpreter, to which we were entitled. An ex-Australian soldier arrived in our town to report for duty to the town major who had not yet arrived. The man was enlisted in Paris owing to his fluent knowledge of French as he had been out there ever since the last war. He reported to me as OC Troops and I used him as my interpreter. This ex-Australian proved such a well disciplined man that I could not credit that he was Australian but this was explained by the fact he went from New Zealand to Australia to enlist!

When the official French interpreter turned up at long last, instead of being an officer, he was a lower rank who ranked as a corporal. Instead of having him in the officers' mess as we expected, I had to put him in the sergeants' mess. When working for me the interpreter felt very important and when I wished to speak to someone, whether it was the farmer, lord of the chateau, mayor or anyone else, he just banged on the door and if there was no immediate response, he would stamp inside shouting loudly, '*Personne?*' [A rather brusque way of asking 'is anyone here?' – Ed.] We had to restrain him several times from searching the bedrooms for someone to give information. After a fortnight we returned him to the French Mission as we could not stand his habits or smell.

We then got one who was popular and a success, and being a businessman he was able to help us with the French law on wages, social insurance, etc. One day my driver, who had taken the interpreter into Amiens on business in my staff car, came to me and said that he was worried about the latter as he acted so strangely, he stopped the car several times and chased cows round fields! When I enquired into this peculiar conduct it transpired that in the mess the previous evening bets were made as to whether a cow's horns grew in front or behind its ears, and the interpreter was instructed to ascertain the answer.

We quickly established the most friendly relations with the local French Military authorities though, as far as possible, French troops were kept out of British GHQ area. We invited a party of French officers, who were on leave, several times to our mess and initiated them into the game of darts, which was unknown to them. They were so taken with it that they tried unsuccessfully to get a board in Paris; we therefore had one sent out from England to them straight up to the Maginot Line.

When a French airman crashed into our area it was a party of Pioneers who pulled him dead out of the blazing plane, and in consequence we were asked to assist at the funeral. This we did with a very well turned out, smart and well drilled party who earned enthusiastic praise from the French, especially when we fired a volley over the grave, which was apparently not a part of their burial service. A few weeks later one of our Pioneers was killed and the French requested the privilege of sending a party to reciprocate.

To anticipate somewhat, when we marched out in May 1940 from some of the French villages where our Pioneers had been stationed, only a jump ahead of the invading Germans, we did not record a single instance of abuse or reproach from the frightened civilians left behind, but went off with the expression of most friendly good wishes and the hope that we would return soon.

CHAPTER 9

The Boulogne Debacle

10 May 1940 was the day on which the Germans really started their strong offensive and I give the day to day effects on No. 5 Group AMPC:

10 MAY

Heavy bombs were dropped near our Group HQ in Doullens, seventeen huts were damaged and five of our men wounded. One bomb burst twelve hours after being dropped. One more was suspected as having been dropped without exploding so an officer of RAOC arrived in the evening and requested my help in looking for this. It was a rather nasty job searching, but the delayed action bomb could not be found. This was our first experience of such delayed action bombs which later became so familiar.

One of my Pioneer lorries was being driven along the road taking a party of Pioneers back to billets when they came up on a line of halted vehicles. The driver descended to find out the cause and found that a German bomb had been dropped actually in the roadway and as it had not exploded everyone concluded that it was one of the delayed action bombs then new to us. The driver and his mate decided that someone must do something about it so they tossed up as to which one would carry out this dangerous job. The man who *won* the toss then proceeded to carry the live bomb across the field to a safe distance![1]

I sent certain sections to Belgium and forward areas for railheads etc under previously arranged orders should plan 'D' (for River Dyle) be put into operation.[2] A Church Army civilian canteen manager came in to my office to complain that a German plane had chased him half the distance from Amiens to Doullens. I congratulated him on the speed of his car and asked him what he would like me to do about it anyway?

11 MAY

Again searched unsuccessfully for the bomb. We had thirteen air raid warnings in twenty-four hours and turned out for each of them as per orders (four being during night hours). There were more warnings during the day, but I gave orders that no one would take special action any more unless enemy planes were definitely located and recognized by sight, or by offensive action from them.

12 MAY

I received a report from the French Commandant d'Étapes of some kind of parachute bomb dropped on or near the railway line on the west side of Doullens. We all thought this might be one of the often-rumoured Hitler's Secret Weapons. I informed GHQ and on their orders we stopped all rail traffic on the west of Doullens Station while I led a patrol to search, but being unable to find it we returned and discovered that the French Commandant d'Étapes had misinformed my interpreter and the bomb had fallen on the east side of town where rail traffic was still proceeding. We finally located the spot and on approaching it were warned by a gendarme that the 'thing' was heard to be ticking. A second gendarme informed us that the ticking had become slower, while a third Frenchman stated that he had seen blue smoke issuing from it.

The object had fallen close against the low railway embankment, so we all crawled up on the opposite side and had a look at it from behind cover. After a short while both the French and the British looked at me as the senior officer for orders. With inward trepidation but, I hoped, outward nonchalance, I walked over for a closer examination and found it to be a metal container attached to a parachute and was apparently a French meteorological instrument that may have been elevated by a small balloon. Anyway I picked it up, wrapped parachute and wires about it and took it back in my car, while all the onlookers kept at a respectful distance in case my diagnosis was at fault. I carried it into the office of the Commandant d'Étapes and placed it on his desk informing him that here was 'Hitler's Secret Weapon'. I had hardly finished speaking when the Commandant d'Étapes left by the open window behind him! On that same day further sections were sent to forward area as per Plan 'D' for railheads etc.

13 MAY

Many air raid warnings and constant stream of hopeless French, Belgium and Dutch refugees. Those with cars mostly had mattresses several thick on the roof for protection. Many of the refugees pushed the pathetic cart or pram and one very old woman was trying to push her treasured sewing machine on tiny castors. Most of these had eaten any food they started with and were unable to buy any on the way unless they were exceptionally lucky. About that time it was quite usual to see bodies lying by the roadside of those who had become exhausted and just died.

14 MAY

News most disquieting. I was called up twice during the night on false reports of approaching enemy. No. 47 Coy captured some reputed parachutists which were passed to GHQ but we never heard whether they were enemy, fifth columnists or merely armed refugees seeking food by force. I had been up all the previous night looking for reputed parachutists. The drill was that we should locate and spy upon any such parties, report same to GHQ, while still keeping a watch, and that the GHQ reserve consisting of 1st Bn Welsh Guards and some armoured troops should mop up. When the actual time came of course there was no GHQ Reserve as it had been committed elsewhere.

15 MAY

Major Hill, an assistant at the HQ, called with a verbal message from Brigadier Reford, who was in command of GHQ Troops, to the effect that we might expect enemy armoured cars or light tanks in four hours as they were breaking through and were already in the Albert district. I could do whatever I thought best for my troops (I was then OC Troops Doullens as well as Pioneer Group Commander), and any strays in the area.

I decided as we were not mobile and were only 25 per cent armed, to prepare the old citadel at Doullens for defence, and therefore sent in rations and medical stores, etc for our own men and all odds and ends. I arranged road blocks on both the Albert and the Arras roads to Doullens and sent CMP motorcyclists well up both roads to give early news of enemy approach. Nothing happened.

16 MAY

We blocked all roads into Doullens, collected all available rifles and ammunition, managing to arm about half our men. We found two officers and fifty ORs for an improvised lorry driving unit to remove any vehicles without drivers in vehicle parks and workshops etc in GHQ Area. It was now clear that there were no British or French troops in the district who would be at all likely to relieve us if we did get besieged in the old and very strong citadel so I altered my plan. Our men were then billeted in six different camps or villages and were still, in some cases, helping with petrol dumps and loading ammunition, etc, so I did not want to move them all the time they were doing something useful, but I arranged that if all or any had to move in a hurry, without further orders, they should all try and move northwest into the forest known as Bois Auxi-le-Château, where we hoped to reform.

17 MAY

Brigadier Rupelle came into Doullens during the night bringing with him 5th Bn The Buffs and 5th Bn RW Kent Regiment and we found billets for them all somehow. They did not appear to have any maps of that area in the brigade so I gave them what few copies I could spare. We also found billets for one battery with 12-inch guns moving back and personnel of four batteries (without guns) moving up! Many parachutists rumoured.

18 MAY

On orders from GHQ Troops, I moved Group HQ and the remains of seven companies in the direction roughly northwest to sidestep the Germans thrusting through Albert in the direction of Amiens. No. 48 Coy (I think it was), which was working under the RASC on the petrol dump at Villers-Bocage, I left to continue their lorry loading of petrol as I was certain that they could get away on the petrol lorries at the end. Anyway the petrol was vital so labour must be available. I told the company commander of the situation, but later we heard that for some unknown reason he had not pulled out with the petrol convoys and the whole company was captured before they could get across the nearby River Somme. It must be remembered that the only official transport we had was one 8hp car and one motorcycle at Group HQ and ditto with each company.

Acting as OC Troops I took with us from Doullens one medical officer complete with ambulance (which we stuffed with blankets and food), also such details of men as NAAFI staff, Army Printing Unit, CMPs, Bath Unit etc who had no orders to do anything or go anywhere. Two sections of our 121 Coy returned to us from Belgium having had some casualties. They came in two lorries which were joyfully received. The lorry that had been on daily attachment to us I also kept. I put a guard on it the night before and phoned the RASC company commander telling him that I was taking it away with me. He expostulated and ordered it back at once. I said to him, 'We need this for transport of our food and blankets as we have no transport of our own. What would you do in our case?' He replied, 'The same as you are going to do, damn you', and hung up.

Our mixed force numbered about 1,100 with no water carts, no cookers, no signallers and only half of us armed, but being Pioneers we could look after ourselves better than most troops. On reporting my positions that night to GHQ Troops, that I had men in six different villages widely spread apart, I had to use my DR as the civilian phones had gone out of use. I received orders to continue moving next day and to concentrate my force at Bruay. As our motorcycle broke down on the way back I received the orders late at night. We had of course no 2i/C, our adjutant was sick and the QM could not drive and my driver had to work on the motorcycle so it left me to take the orders round to all the companies myself. Although I knew of course to which villages I had ordered my companies, I had the utmost difficulty in locating them during the hours of darkness as some of them were in farm buildings outside the village proper and off the main roads, and there were no parked vehicles to indicate where. Also all civilians, without exception, refused to answer any knock on their doors when the area was swarming with refugees and possibly Germans. I finally located the last company well after dawn and got them all on the move once more.

Just outside Arras one of the British Military Police was on point duty when he saw a tank approaching down the road so he stopped the civilian traffic to allow the tank to proceed. As it passed him he saw to his horror that it was a German!

One of my Pioneer sections, unarmed except for picks and shovels, was returning along the Arras-Doullens road when they saw a German light tank following them so they quickly hid behind a wall and noted that the tank pulled up at a petrol filling station a short way beyond them. The crew went into the office to get the civilian to come out and unlock his pump and fill their tank. My men promptly hurried forward and whilst some stationed themselves outside the doorway other set about removing a tank track. As soon as the noise started the Germans rushed out and were promptly knocked on the head by picks while the others completed the job of putting the tank out of action.

19 MAY

On my return to my Group HQ I found that GHQ had just cancelled the move to Bruay and that we were to concentrate at three points on the La Bassée canal to help cover the flank of the BEF. Once again orders were sent out to all marching companies giving them a new rendezvous. Having got everyone on the move I had my own HQ start off also. We had spent the night in a chateau at Sains, looked after by a housekeeper who had a daughter with her. The housekeeper was very anxious to get said daughter away before the Germans arrived as she said that she knew what German soldiers were like. The daughter said that she thought she had better stay saying, 'After all war is war', with a not displeased expression!

Having got everyone moving I went to Avesne myself where GHQ and the Director of Labour had had offices as I thought I might perhaps find out where the Germans actually were. In any case there had been a NAAFI there and my troops' chief want at the moment was for cigarettes. In Avesne I found all the British had gone and that only a provost officer and two MPs were looking round all offices to make sure that all documents had been removed or burnt. They knew nothing except that the Germans might arrive at any moment.

I went to where the NAAFI had been and found the premises shuttered and padlocked and the door screwed shut. There appeared to be no back entry – the building was one of a continuous row with no side alleys. I enquired from the occupant of the adjoining house if there was a back door and he took me through his house and put a step ladder against the garden party wall. I climbed over and quickly forced the NAAFI's back door. Inside I found a quantity of goods, including several large crates of cigarettes. With the utmost difficulty I hoisted several crates over the wall and with the help of the Frenchman carried them out into the road.

The crates were much too big to be stowed in the car, so I broke them open and filled the whole of the back seats and floor with tens of thousands. When I had just about finished and was surrounded with smashed crates and debris, up came the provost officer and his two MPs. They stopped their motorcycles and the former said, 'Where did you get those cigarettes from?'

I replied, 'The canteen of course.'

He said, 'But it was closely fastened up and left.'

I said, 'Certainly.'

He said, 'Do you mean to tell me that you forced an entry and stole them?'

I said, 'Naturally as I am not leaving everything for the Germans.'

He said, 'Are there any left?'

Rations were my next problem but remembering that in the retreat in March 1918 the ASC (as they then were) had piled rations at or near strategic cross roads where retreating troops might find them, I reasoned that this might well be remembered by others and repeated. I did indeed finally find ration and petrol dumps at Brias and Ostreville and we were able to restock that night. Meanwhile I went ahead to Bruay to try and find where OC GHQ Troops was and I finally found him (Brigadier Reford) at Béthune. I received verbal orders from him to get my force to Boulogne so yet again altered the line of march of my six columns to Saint-Pol. All arrived safely, but some were so footsore that another march the following day was impossible. The staff work of Major Peter de Havilland (on the staff of GHQ Troops) was excellent right through. He had even arranged for a train to be available at Saint-Pol, also some bread. The bread was there, but by that time all trains had stopped running on that line. I was up almost all night conducting our three lorries and the ambulance to the food and petrol dumps. I found that the NCO in charge had orders to burn the remainder of the food dump with the surplus petrol to stop both falling into the hands of the Germans. I took it upon myself to countermand this, gave the petrol to the French Army Units that I found stranded for lack of petrol and dealt with the food by turning the stream of refugees onto it, when it quickly melted away. The only thing I destroyed was the rum as we could not risk this falling into the hands of British troops not under supervision.

20 MAY

Again, I went to petrol and food dumps, supplied the French army and fed refugees. I sent the road party to Boulogne. In early evening we found a train in a siding at Saint-Pol, consisting of the usual trucks labelled in French '40 men or 8 horses', which was quite possibly the one originally intended for us, and by heavily bribing both the engine driver and the stationmaster with imprest money, and thousands of cigarettes, got them to promise to try and get the train through to Boulogne. The stationmaster said that the railway telephone was working and that in all probability the railway points were set to give a through way on the main line even if the signal boxes were not manned still, but he knew nothing about the level crossings so great care must be exercised and we did it at our own risk, etc. All this took hours and it was late afternoon before we got the force entrained in the cattle trucks (more than forty *hommes* in each truck) but before we could move a messenger came running from the stationmaster saying that he had just had a message from down the line, at Petit Houvin, that a party of German Army fighting vehicles were on their way from Doullens to Saint-Pol and could we do anything about it. Being Pioneers we could and we did.

As I was organising my defence I found several lorries belonging to 'C' Coy 5th Bn The Buffs (a battalion that I had myself formed the previous year) with nineteen ORs under one of my old subalterns, Captain Smithers. He thought that his party was all that was left of the battalion which had been overrun that day trying to hold an impossible position in front of Doullens. After wandering over strange country, with no map, and no information, Smithers was as pleased to see his old CO as I was to have him and his party. The Buff lorries were quickly put across the road to block it while his men, with two 'Boys' anti-tank rifles joined the defence. We shot up the enemy motorcycles and scout cars which beat a hasty retreat then entrained once more. Putting some of our overflow of men into The Buff lorries I sent off the combined road party under my QM, Lieutenant M. Browne, to join us at Boulogne if we all ever got there. I went with the train party on its very slow journey to Boulogne which had to be done under cover of darkness but even then we were heavily bombed.

21 MAY

The train was diverted to Wimereux – the station beyond Boulogne – where we arrived in the early morning and in the train I managed to get nearly two hours sleep en route, thank God.

With the detachment of the 5th Buffs we prepared the defences of Wimereux and I reported to Brigadier Griffin, who commanded the Boulogne Sub Area. He said that he wanted 400 of our men to discharge an ammunition ship in the harbour which civilian dockers would not touch owing to the frequent dive-bombing by German planes. I supplied these men and even found some to man the electric cranes which had been abandoned by the French civilians.

I suggested that those Pioneers who were still unarmed might be sent back to the UK with the heavy stream of other British troops who were being evacuated and that I could stay with my armed party and see things through. Brigadier Griffin told me to keep all mine together. A few hours later, Brigadier Griffin himself left for the UK.

To remedy the arms shortage I boarded a transport and as the officers and men came up the gang plank I gave the order that those returning to the UK must leave their arms for the use of those staying behind to fight. By these means I gained sufficient revolvers, rifles and a few LMGs, also ammunition to arm the rest of my Pioneers.

That night I was again called out because of rumoured parachutists and fifth columnists. On this day all the many captive balloons flying over Boulogne, to prevent low flying attacks, were released and floated away out of sight, this giving a still further indication that the British Army was preparing to get out.

22 MAY

Who was in command after Brigadier Griffin had gone I neither knew nor cared. I received verbal orders from the Boulogne Sub Area that I was to send 100 men to hold the crossings of the River Canche from Étaples to Montreuil, inclusive. As this was such an impossibly small number of badly armed men for such a task, especially untrained men, I detailed 250 which I took myself and handed over command of the Group to my senior company commander, Major Gaden, an experienced infantryman. We collected lorries from the vast number left on or near the quay by troops leaving the country and proceeded towards the River Canche, in suitable formation.

Later we learned that the main road bridge at Montreuil had never been blown after all and found that the Germans were already over in full force. We met a reconnaissance party of Germans part way down. It was a bloody business.

After adequately dealing with this German party we returned with our casualties but without leaving any prisoners (or taking any) to Boulogne. There we found that a British Force had arrived from the UK consisting of 2nd Bn Irish Guards, 2nd Bn Welsh Guards and a few (possibly two) sections of anti-tank guns, all under the command of a Brigadier Fox Pitt. These proceeded to take up position on the outskirts of the town facing south.

I reported to Fox Pitt and was asked to send 150 of my Pioneers to the Welsh Guards to help reinforce them as they were weak in numbers. When I enquired whether the Guards would feed them he said 'no', so I took the men up myself and arranged for 600 rations to follow. No lorry could get through the several road blocks that scattered French parties had put up, but QM Browne finally managed to get through by off loading the lorry onto my baby Morris 8hp car which got through the road blocks.

Sending up *four* days' rations for my men shows my gross overestimation of the fighting abilities of this Guards Brigade; as was later proved. We learned later that the Welsh Guards ate all these rations in the next twenty-four hours as they had none. Had they mentioned this shortage we could easily have found them food. All supply services in Boulogne had by now faded away so we took the job unasked as we knew where the food depots were; and we fed various British stray parties, Royal Engineers, French Army Units and even, quite illegally, a few starving refugees.

23 MAY

At 01.50 hours I had a verbal message from Major Penlington of 5th Bn The Buffs who had arrived with thirteen more survivors of his battalion and who was in charge of Wimereux's defences that night. He had orders to evacuate Wimereux and retire into Boulogne as it had been decided not to try and hold Wimereux. The Germans were reported as coming in by the Calais road. I got the last of my men out of Wimereux about half an hour before the Germans entered. We evacuated Wimereux in a great hurry and went down into Boulogne town.

Major Verity found that he had left the tin box of his 47 Coy in the billet there with his documents and imprest money in it. His ASC driver, one Driver R.D. Beck, volunteered to go back for it on the company motorcycle. He did so and got the box safely fastened on the bike when he spotted the Germans up the street. He hastily mounted the motorcycle and started off but a burst of rifle fire followed him and put his engine out of action. Fortunately for him he was going fast and was near the top of the very steep hill down into Boulogne so he coasted down in safety. Verity recommended him for the Military Medal, which he never got.

The plan of battle given to me verbally by Brigadier Fox Pitt was that 2nd Bn Irish Guards were to hold that portion of the town of Boulogne right of the river; 2nd Bn Welsh Guards next on the left of the river; my Pioneers on the left of the Guards Brigade; while Major Penlington held a single post astride the Wimereux Road where it bordered the sea near the casino. I had to lend Penlington fifty men as it was more than he could manage. Actually he was never attacked.

This meant that 5 Group had to form and man eight road blocks, which we proceeded to do mainly with lorries abandoned by the quayside. As I had no signallers I arranged my Group HQ as near as possible to the Welsh Guards Bn HQ and left runners there to bring any messages. Shortly afterwards one of my posts was attacked by a German tank. Several rounds were fired at it from a Boys anti-tank rifle but the bullets just bounced off. It did, however, withdraw round the corner. Shortly afterwards either this or another similar tank tried another of our road blocks where lorries were merely placed across the road, these it just pushed out of the way and lumbered on towards the larger block we had been making slightly further back, again basically of lorries and cars reinforced with furniture and materials from bombed houses.

We fired at the tank with rifles, as we had nothing else, but naturally did not stop it. It shelled us with a light gun and caused us several casualties and then, after a pause for consideration, finding that we only had rifles, it proceeded to climb very slowly over our block. We were prepared for this and, the firing having brought me early to the spot, I had some lorry petrol tanks punctured with a rifle and my revolver, the tank being unable to shell us during its crushing climb, and we set fire to the lot. A sheet of flame went up and the tank backed hastily off and halted once more almost round the last bend.

Our road block burned for quite a while and allowed for a further block to be made under cover of smoke, which we kept going. Meantime we were being dive-bombed and shelled, mostly by mortars I think, and bullets were flying in all directions. We found that many of the latter were coming from over the river from the direction of the harbour where Brigade HQ was established with some odds and ends of troops. It was apparent that some inexperienced troops were firing wildly at anyone who moved on our side of the river so I got into my little 8hp car and dashed across the main road bridge to visit Brigade HQ and ask if this firing could be checked. While crossing the bridge my car was riddled by a burst of machine-gun fire (whether enemy or ours I never knew) and the engine put out of action; I was going so fast that I put the car out of gear and coasted the rest of the way across and under cover. Brigadier Fox Pitt promised to try and stop this promiscuous shooting but was uncertain whether his odds and sods could be restrained by the few Guardsmen he had with him.

Shortly afterwards Lieutenant Colonel Stanier, CO 2nd Welsh Guards, sent a similar request over for the shooting to be stopped. I walked back across the bridge, having now no car (this was the second put out of action while I was driving in twenty-four hours, the first was by bomb splinters) and rejoined my Group, where things had quietened down a bit.

All civilians, except a few dead lying about the streets, were well hidden. Some gendarmes came and told us that there was firing from a corner house *inside* our defences. I informed Lieutenant Colonel Stanier, but he said that he had no one left to deal with this. I therefore took a small party, posted some to fire at anyone showing themselves and to attract attention while the rest of us worked round back yards and got into the house. We found several men in civilian clothes firing at our men, but no one had the time or opportunity to question them. We assumed they were 5th Columnists and acted accordingly.

Some of my men shot a man dressed as a priest using a sub machine gun, thought to be of German make. Shortly afterwards the gendarmes brought three men to me dressed as civilians and asked me to shoot them as they were 5th Columnists and spies. I said, 'In that case why not shoot them yourselves?'

'Ah,' they said. 'If we do and the Germans get here tomorrow, we shall be shot ourselves but if the British Army does it, all is well'.

I saw their point of view and told my French interpreter to question them. He said that he could not say that they were Germans, though he thought so, but they were certainly not French![3]

We learned that the Irish and Welsh Guards were being forced back. There was much 'wind up' generally. Lieutenant Colonel Stanier and his senior officers were perfectly cool and collected, but I was very disgusted at the lack of control of some Welsh Guards junior officers. I had to stop two patrols of Welsh Guards, one under a CSM and the other under a very young officer, from shooting up the town as they fired bursts at every open window and while admittedly ricochets were flying around, I could not see any further signs of actual firing at us. Lieutenant Colonel Stanier spoke very highly of my 150 Pioneers attached to his battalion and told me that he had lost about 100 men so far and the Irish Guards about twice that number.

During the afternoon I got a message, by one of my runners, that the Guards were all withdrawing to the harbour, that the Welsh Guards were already crossing the river to get there and that the bridge would be blown up soon. I was surprised as I thought we had matters under control on our side but I had no option but to conform. Unfortunately the Welsh Guards had moved back before I had time to start withdrawing my roadblock parties and although I used my reserve (which being infantry trained I had naturally arranged to have), to cover my exposed right flank, the Germans already had parties behind my forward posts.

I took some of my scallywags of Glasgow Irish, No. 47 Coy, and we fought our way up and relieved two of them but two were overrun while the other four posts were able to retire without trouble. This street fighting with untrained and badly equipped men was a bloody affair and we had a number of casualties before all 5 Group still standing were across the river, where I followed them with the rearguard.[4] It was not a CO's job really but one could not expect our untrained men to do it on their own and they backed me up very well. I was very fortunate with most of my officers though the proportion of officers to other ranks in the AMPC as compared with the infantry is laughable when it comes to fighting.

After the Guards had left we followed them across a bridge and everyone concentrated in fish market sheds and docks and Gare Maritime. All our wounded were collected and looked after by our MO Lieutenant Mellow (stout fellow). Our unarmed men were still with us but further rifles were collected from the quayside. I collected all I could muster and manned the barricades. We were told by a Welsh Guards officer (name unknown) that they were all embarking on destroyers with the Irish Guards and it was up to us to look after ourselves. I tried unsuccessfully for an hour or more to find Brigadier Fox Pitt or Colonel Stanier for information, but by the time I got there he and the majority of the brigade had already embarked in some naval craft.[5]

I found some of my 150 men who had been attached to the Welsh Guards and they said that although they had fought with them and the Guards had eaten their rations, they had been told to stand back and let the Guards embark in the vessels, which were for the Guards! When some of these Pioneers tried to embark with them in spite of this strange order, they were accused of impeding the withdrawal of the Guards!

Meantime, of course, I and the bulk of my Pioneers were fighting a rear guard action and covering the Guards' embarkation. Having arranged my defence at the barricades I tried to find someone in any kind of command on the harbour station, but finally concluded that there was no one senior to myself left in Boulogne. The railway station there was crammed with empty trains, some of which had been smashed by bombing and by this time we were again being heavily mortared, also a German tank opened fire from the fish market across the river.

At one time we were very heavily attacked by three tanks from across the river firing with machine guns and pom-poms, also infantry from our side of the river. Just as we thought the end was near some shells from a warship out of sight landed unexpectedly and knocked out one of the tanks at least, silenced a second and the third ran away.

The dive-bombing was constant and frightening but not many casualties were caused by them considering everything. I was still going around trying to get my companies sorted out under their own officers again when a near miss knocked me unconscious and wounded Major Verity who was with me. I was left there for dead but recovered some time later, after dark, to find the station burning fiercely near me and the heat had even singed my overcoat. We were later told that this fire was very clearly seen from England.

On recovering I made enquiries as to what the situation then was and was told that during my blank period another destroyer had crept in and taken off some of our men, including my adjutant and QM. There were various weapons left on the quay belonging to the Welsh Guards and I was told that they had been ordered to leave them as 'nothing was to be taken on board owing to the terrible congestion'. This order could not have been given by any Guards officer but probably the RN, however I was glad of some of these weapons to arm a few of my men who had lost or damaged theirs.

I was also told on my recovery that a Guards officer, thought to be a Major Berry, had collected a few Guardsmen stragglers and had advised one of my majors to come with his Pioneers and try and sneak through the enemy to Étaples. Major Gaden, who had taken command of 5 Group automatically when I was reported killed, refused to do this, well knowing it to be hopeless, but apparently a part of AMPC believed to be under Lieutenant Timperley of 59 Coy AMPC had gone off with his men with Major Berry.

The fighting had quietened down after dark, though the station continued to burn and the German tanks from across the harbour had ceased firing at us. We had on the quayside with us a number of civilian refugees, including quite a percentage of Jews, also some stray Belgian and French soldiers, all hoping to get to England somehow. With the aid of my officers I continued to try and sort the men out but numbers of them had taken refuge under the many trains and no doubt some were asleep and it was most difficult to find them anyway. I decided that if no further destroyers came we would try and slip through to Calais in small parties.

24 MAY

At about 02.30 hours it was reported to me that a dark shadow was to be seen out to sea so I signalled SOS with my torch in case it was a British warship. Sure enough, it was the destroyer *Vimiera*, which was waiting off shore to try and see if there were any more British left or whether the enemy had overrun us. The *Vimiera* backed carefully in to the end of the mole. We started embarking across planks being much impeded by civilians, Belgian and French army men, Guards and AMPC, etc trying to rush it. Some fell off the planks and were swept away by the swift current.

We got our walking wounded on board but I realized that hundreds of my men were absent so arranged with the ship commander to hold up his boat for twenty minutes while I hurried back in search.

I ran off and withdrew the defenders of the barricades as the Germans were not then still attacking. I could not find any body of men left, but many were asleep under trains, in cars or under lorries etc, and although I woke a few, some were either too thoroughly fagged out or drunk to respond to my kicks. A certain number of Guards were among those lying about drunk or exhausted when I tried unsuccessfully to wake them. I warned all others in sight to make for the end of the mole. Major Verity superintended some of 47 Coy into the boat while his CSM tried to bring up the rear party. Major Parr also looked for his missing men but they had apparently been in the party that followed the Welsh Guards.

I arrived back at the *Vimiera* breathless and sweating and asked for longer time. The naval officer said that he was already most dangerously overloaded and top heavy, that dawn would break shortly, that he would not wait a moment longer and if I did not get on board he would leave without me. Feeling that we had done all we could and not wishing to be taken prisoner I walked aboard, the ropes were axed and we left; being shot at by badly aimed small arms fire and shelled unsuccessfully. I believe therefore that I was the last to get away from Boulogne.[6]

My *Agent de Liaison*, Marc Flury, stayed with me and acted bravely throughout, coming to England with us. Our casualties in two days were between four and five hundred killed, wounded or missing. The company commanders who crossed with me were Majors Verity of 47 Company (wounded but walking case), Gaden of 102 Company, Collier of 121 Company, Carlton of 122 Company and Garrard of 123 Company. Major Parr of 59 Company who was wounded beside me crossed on an earlier boat. We had collected our wounded in the customs shed but both our medical officer and the padre chose to stay with the wounded and were of course taken prisoner. They, like my Pioneers, were not regular army, but like my Pioneers they were British and acted accordingly.

After getting back to England, having been through some of the bloodiest fighting, including hand-to-hand street fighting in Boulogne, I phoned up my dear wife and said, 'I'm back in England alive and unwounded.' She replied, 'Well, why shouldn't you be?'![7]

After landing at Dover we went to a camp near Aldershot where I saw my old brigade commander Brigadier [...] and told him that I could not understand why we had left Boulogne at all, leaving the French on their own, that the AMPC had only left their barricades when deserted by the Guards and that I was very disgusted with the fact that certain British Army units would not stay and fight. He warned me not to repeat such a thing anywhere.

At this camp many thousands of mixed troops were being sorted out and catalogued. When I found out what was happening I reported that 5 Group AMPC, while being a shattered unit of approximately 600, was still a unit under its own officers, such as were left, and that we were ready to move as a unit and would not be treated as individuals in a rabble. The answer was, 'Thank God for that. What do you want to do now? Have you got a Depot to go to?' I said that any Pioneer Centre that could take us would suit us so they said, 'A special train will be ready for you within a couple of hours'.

A train was in fact provided for us but Brigadier Fox Pitt turned up and demanded and received priority for his Guards, so we were left on the station to wait for another train. Even before we got to the station we had a spot of bother as a line of buses were waiting to take 5 Group off when a 2nd Lieutenant of the Welsh Guards ordered them to move off to where the Guards were camped. When the leading driver said that he had orders to pick up the AMPC at that spot and that he would not move without orders from his own boss the 2nd Lieutenant pulled out his loaded revolver, pointed it at the driver and threatened to shoot him if he did not do as ordered. The driver shouted and

I came up, found what was happening and tried to make the 2nd Lieutenant put his revolver away. As he would not obey my order I called over two Guards captains, as I did not want to have further trouble with the Guards if it could be avoided, and left them to deal with their excited subaltern. We finally got a train to our AMPC Depot where we reformed.

After we got to the centre at Clacton, I sent a note to the CO 2nd Bn Welsh Guards, who were then at Colchester, saying that if they liked to send over I would let them have back the weapons they left on Boulogne Harbour and which our Pioneers had found so useful in continuing the fighting after the Guards had left – I was never thanked for this!

So ended a phase during which we had welded small units into a group as part of a corps in which we took great pride and we justly claim that we helped to build up tradition. The national press rightly called us 'The Fighting AMPs'. We were used for a short time in the defence of the east coast as we were formed and armed units and most of the infantry units were neither when they came back from France.

The commanding officers of 2nd Bn Irish Guards and 2nd Bn Welsh Guards each received the DSO for the Boulogne affair and later their brigadier also received the same. The Pioneers who fought before they arrived, fought alongside them and then covered their withdrawal and embarkation were not recognized, but we added an early chapter to our corps history of which no member of the AMPC need be ashamed.

Family press cutting from the London *Evening Standard*: Thursday, 6 June 1940

Last War Veterans Held on to Boulogne
TACKLED PARACHUTISTS

I learned today that the last men to leave Boulogne comprised a unit of the Pioneers – mainly men who served in the last war. After hand-to-hand fighting in which they suffered heavy casualties they boarded a British destroyer, still as a unit. In France, in addition to acting as a labour unit to the BEF, they have been active in rounding up parachutists, Fifth Columnists and snipers. This is the story from Boulogne. The Pioneers were sent out in support of infantry companies who were fighting a rearguard action. Armed detachments of Pioneers constructed and held a road block at the entrance to the town. To make this block they commandeered lorries, debris and furniture from the bombed houses. They held the mechanized columns of Germans by rifles until relieved by infantry units. They fought back step by step during the evacuation of the town until at last they were holding the entrance to the harbour. **Without this action, the remainder of the BEF would have been unable to embark.**

The Pioneers took over electric [cranes] in the harbour whose civilian workmen had either been killed or wounded. At a time when all the supply system had broken down, they not only fed themselves, but also a large number of detachments of other units. Under heavy firing and bombing, they did valuable work in unloading food and ammunition from boats in the harbour.

Family press cutting from the *Daily Mail*: circa July 1940

AMPs Now 'Fighting Pioneers'

So high is the reputation of the Auxiliary Military Pioneer Corps that the name they originally had when they went to France – 'the Pick and Shovel Brigade' – has been changed to the 'Fighting Pioneers.' Field Marshal Lord Milne learned this yesterday when he visited the Amps in his new capacity and Colonel-Commandant of the corps. ... Lord Milne was conducted on part of his tour by a VC colonel of the last war. The colonel told Lord Milne of the heroism of the AMPs in the recent fighting in Boulogne.

The AMPs came off in the last naval boat to leave Boulogne. Some of them had fought their way to the landing stage after being cut off by vastly superior German forces.

They suffered heavily, but their resolution was too much for the enemy. Many of them in the early stages were not armed, and the colonel sent men to the nearest casualty clearing station to collect arms from the wounded men as they came in. Only a few hours later these old soldiers and untrained troops were fighting their way back through the streets of Boulogne at the point of the bayonet. 'We would all have got out if we had not had to fight tanks and overcome machine-gun posts,' one of the older AMPs said yesterday.

The colonel himself was almost burned to death in Boulogne when he was knocked out by a shell. He found his clothes smouldering and fire all round him, when revived.

CHAPTER 10

Madagascar

My No. 5 Group AMPC reformed at Clacton after a brief stay at the Pioneer Centre at Caister, where we were assigned to coastal defence. We were one of the very few units of the British Army that was formed, disciplined and armed back from France during a period when there was near chaos in the army. Although armed we were only armed in a very modest way, as we only had what we collected and came back with from France.

As we were getting nowhere at Caister, we asked for and received permission to go to Clacton Centre where we originally formed our Group HQ. There we received several additional companies and then were attached to 11 Corps, which had its HQ first of all at Bishop's Stortford and later near Newmarket.

I set up my Group HQ at Buntingford as a convenient centre on 4 June 1940 and had companies spread over Essex, Hertfordshire, Bedfordshire, Cambridgeshire and parts of Huntingdonshire and Suffolk. At times my command exceeded in numbers an infantry brigade.

We were largely engaged in airfield construction, maintenance after bombing, camp construction, etc as well as RE and stores depot work. I had sent to me the first company of conscientious objectors wished on to me by the Director of Labour, now Major General Friend. They were called a 'Non Combatant Corps' and all officers and NCOs were provided by the Pioneer Corps. When they first came to me they seemed disappointed that they were not being treated any differently from my other companies, with the exception that they were not allowed to handle 'offensive material', but as no one gave me a definition of this I took it to be weapons and ammunition only.

They had apparently been fully expecting to be martyrs for the sake of their principles. As far as I knew they were all genuine and were mostly well educated. A very big proportion of them later transferred, at their own request, to other branches of the army, some even to combatant units.

Being for the moment at any rate on home service, and Sittingbourne being in a most doubtful area, I got Marjorie and the two children up into a furnished house, 'Rest Harrow', at Westmill on 16 July. One evening while we were there an enemy plane flew overhead and I heard the whine of falling bombs, a sound with which we were all too familiar. Marjorie was for the moment indignant with me as I pushed her down on the kitchen floor quickly and lay down with her. Several bombs fell with thuds, two of them within a few yards of the house, but they were delayed action. I went outside to see just where they were and found them far too close for safety although they had buried themselves out of sight. We quickly picked up young Susan who was in bed and by this time neighbours and Home Guard had arrived and they invited us to spend the night at their houses.[1] I with a Colonel Greg and Marjorie and Susan with Guy and Lorraine Morris. The bombs went up presently and made huge craters and much of the garden was sprinkled with clods but the house was not damaged so we returned there next morning. The ground being soft and the penetration being so great we were lucky.

One night while still at Rest Harrow we had a girl friend, Peggy Priestley, staying with us, when about 1 am, the phone rang. I dashed to it as at that time we were expecting an invasion at any moment, but the call was from one of Peggy's Air Force admirers in Scotland who had booked a call hours before and had not cancelled it. I hastily pushed the phone into Peggy's room on its long wandering lead and shut the door as far as possible but we could not help overhearing her refusing a proposal of marriage. The young officer flew down a few hours later and repeated the proposal but was still refused.

Not so long after this the phone rang one night: 'Duty Officer at Corps speaking, *Cromwell*'. I told him that I did not know what this code word meant so he must be more explicit if it required action on my part. He assured me it required urgent action, but said that he could not possibly say over the phone. I accordingly phoned up the CO of a nearby RASC unit, but he had no secret code book either. I then phoned up the CO of an artillery unit but he was on leave and although they had a secret code book, the CO had gone off with the key to the safe in his pocket. I phoned back to Corps HQ and told the duty officer that I was unable to find out what *Cromwell* meant and unless Corps sent me instructions I could do nothing and that I was going back to bed. It was of course a premature warning of imminent invasion which never materialized.[2]

Work continued as usual in a Pioneer Group for by this time we had settled into a routine. One of my scattered detachments showed an unduly high proportion of 'sick' so I went up there to investigate. I found that there was no Army MO near so the detachment had been put under the local medical practitioner who was a woman. I told her that in my opinion she was being far too kind hearted whenever any man reported a minor ailment, and I gave her a few details of 'sick' men who had gone off for the day enjoying themselves. After this a man almost had to have a broken leg before he got excused duty.

Being between London and so many airfields, enemy planes were constantly passing overhead and during the Battle of Britain in September 1940 particularly, they were a bit careless in their bomb dropping when they wanted to unload in a hurry.

We did everything we could to assist the local Home Guard in their training. The local platoon was administered by Colonel Greg who was a sergeant in the Home Guard but always wore his Sam Browne as well as his sergeant's stripes. One day a plane made a forced landing near us so I hurried over to help if necessary. I was told that it was piloted by either a foreign spy or that the crash had made him deaf and dumb. As I saw the plane was one of our fighters I asked the pilot, in English, if he was hurt. He said 'I am a Pole in the RAF and my English is so bad still that I was afraid that the Home Guard would shoot me as a spy if I opened my mouth'!

While we were stationed here, all Pioneer Groups were given a second-in-command which was very desirable as I had in my group over 3,000 men scattered round six counties. My second in charge was a Major Cannon, late of The Queens, a first class soldier and a very nice man.

A very big exercise was held in southeast England called *Bumper*, which was the usual type with Red Force invading and Blue Force defending, or the other way round. The defending force anyway was under Corps Commander 'Snowy' Osborne and because of secrecy, his HQ did not issue the addresses and phone numbers of his various units' battle HQs until the last moment, but they included in the distribution several of the 'enemy' formations thus informing the enemy of where to seek them. A mobile force of the attackers did a swift right flank swing and arrived unexpectedly at Osborne's HQ, but a staff officer just had time to rush down to the gate and stick up an 'Out of Bounds' notice. 'Snowy' Osborne was retired after this exercise, to my personal pleasure.

Finally in March 1942 the time came for me to go abroad again. The War Office ordered No. 5 Group HQ to embark once more for active service, on very short notice, for an unknown destination. A slight indication was given by ordering that tropical kit should be drawn. This was quickly followed by the order that we should move in two parts, the first consisted of myself as Commanding Officer; Captain J.G. Morley (Adjutant); Lieutenant M.F. Browne (QM) and ten other ranks. Major H.C. Cannon, the second in charge, was to follow with the remaining eight ORs including the RQMS and bring the group transport, which then consisted of one staff car and one motorcycle. In actual fact it was months before the two parties were reunited.

The reduced Group HQ left Stansted, Essex, for the port of embarkation on 20 March. We embarked on M/S *Sobieski*, a Polish merchantman, on 21 March

1942 at Glasgow and found ourselves to be part of 121 Force trained in assault landings. The *Sobieski* carried a number of landing craft in addition to usual ship's boats. Much speculation naturally followed as none of the other units had been issued with KD [Khaki drill, light uniform often issued for tropical service – Ed.].

On 23 March we sailed at 15.00 hrs and joined a large convoy off Greenock. Most of the army personnel fully expected a landing to be made by 'force' and most of them had much practice of this in mutual cooperation.[3] It appeared that there were no Pioneer companies included in the force so we could not understand why a Pioneer Group HQ was required.

First we sailed well west round north of Ireland, well into the Atlantic and then turned south. Our boat was No. 2 in 6th line. I counted twenty-six vessels in convoy in sight plus the escort. Circling the convoy there were a number of destroyers (I saw six at once), a cruiser and aircraft carrier, also with escort.

We went round with OC Troops and the ship's captain on Ship's Inspection and saw more corners and dark holes than one normally believes existed. I was invited to take meals in future with the ship's officers and OC Troops. Incidentally the food on board was excellent in quality, change of menu and cooking. I was asked to take charge of all 'Details' on board of both officers and ORs of army and Royal Marines. I had some difficulty in finding all my 'Details', which consisted of some 460 of all ranks from seventeen different units, but as I went round with OC Troops on his daily 'procession' of inspection I found them all in time.

For the first four nights we had to sleep in our clothes, for security reasons.

The washing water was only put on for one hour in mornings and one and a half hours in the evening. Although I wished Major Bellis (my cabin mate) would have gone to bed a trifle earlier, as he also slept late I got clear of the bedroom and lavatory before he rose.

One set of KD and topees were issued to all troops when at sea and they were told that a change would be issued on arrival.

We arrived off Freetown on 6 April and left on 9 April without being able to land. As we entered the harbour we saw our first view of Africa and I noted white bungalows on hillsides, many palm trees, native bum boats, and clouds low on hills. The town itself was at the foot of some hills and straggled up the hillsides with more hills and a range of mountains in distance said to be where river Niger rises. At one spot near the entrance to the harbour is a tropical island close inshore, with one spot, a sandy beach running up to palm and banyan trees exactly like coloured cinema pictures. There was much fun caused by the bum boats with green bananas being elicited away from ships by hose pipes.

We were warned to wear clothing over our arms and knees towards sundown because of mosquitoes. The weather was very close and sultry. The stifling heat on board a stationary ship, so near the Equator, after blackout, must be experienced to be believed. It was so great that as we sat playing cards in shirtsleeves and shorts (or trousers) perspiration poured off us, but during the day it was not so bad because of the breeze.

We crossed the equator on 11 April at 10.12 hours but owing to tropical rain the usual ceremonies did not take place. We reached Durban on 22 April 1942. The buildings made it look like a miniature New York as some of the skyscrapers went up to about sixteen or twenty storeys. There was a brilliant green on bluff sheltering harbour, a brilliant blue sky and sea, white or cream buildings and yellow sands. The men were given shore leave until midnight. Every opportunity was taken to do route marching and toughening up after a month at sea.

In the afternoon on leave I went shopping using rickshaws and taxis. The town was not blacked out and after dusk, which falls early, there was the constant undertone of crickets over the docks and the whole town – a sound not noticeable during daylight where it is perhaps drowned out by other noises.

On 24 April we made a route march in the morning to North Beach. We allowed the men to buy fruit for lunch: grapes at 6d per bunch, pears, apples, bananas, pineapples, avocado pears etc (oranges 1 or 2 pence each as the crop was short). In the evening I met Dr and Mrs Eddington, friends of the padre, and had dinner at their house at 7 o'clock. I tried the local drinks, i.e. brandy and ginger ale, pale sherry (very sweet) and Van Der Hum (a liqueur similar to Cointreau). On the afternoon of 25 April, the padre and I were driven by Dr (Miss) Eddington to the Valley of a Thousand Hills, which is part of a native reserve. En route I saw cane, mealies, palms, bananas, pineapples, orange and lemon trees, blue gums, mimosas, etc.

On 27 April I had dinner at a club, and went to the cinema in the evening at the Playhouse. Four thousand Australians came into port so all bars closed at 6 pm and hotels at 10 pm as the town had previously had a convoy of Aussies through and knew what to expect. I tried a pawpaw at dinner time at the club, also avocado pears and a bottle of Witzenberg white wine.

Much discussion was rife as to the final destination but no general disclosure of plans was made; however I was told by an Australian officer, met by chance in the club, that the objective was Madagascar [then under Vichy-French government] and he was laughed to scorn when I professed ignorance. So much for our careful security measures!

The Force left Durban on 28 April so suddenly that three orderlies who were emptying rubbish ashore were left on the quay but were put on board when the ship stopped to pick up some 'R' boats.

After putting to sea, a conference was held when all senior officers were told the destination and plans but were not allowed to inform the ORs until 2 May by which time they knew already, of course.

Madagascar is the fourth largest island in the world being over 1,000 miles long and 350 miles across at its widest point. It possesses only three good harbours, namely Diego Suarez in the north, which is unconnected by either rail or road with the capital Tananarive, Majunga in the west, which is connected by unmetalled trunk road only with the capital, and Tamatave, which is on the east and is connected to Tananarive by both an unmetalled trunk road and by a single-track railway.

The natives, who are called Malgache, are extremely mixed in type and vary from the chief tribe, the Hovas, who probably originated in Asia and are a superior and gentle type who would prefer to poison an enemy rather than stab him and who mostly become minor civil servants, down to rough and woolly types in the south who are not averse to cannibalism.

The plan in brief was to land at Courier Bay on the west side of the northerly tip of the Island and march east to take the large town and harbour of Diego Suarez from the land side. We subsequently found out that the French were expecting this but owing to the numerous reefs, small islands and submerged rocks, they did not think it feasible for large ships to get close inshore at night. By the help of two very stout-hearted Britons, who had worked for years in Madagascar and had reconnoitred this approach in a small yacht, and first class seamanship by the Royal Navy who laid a trail of marking buoys, the convoy crept in on the night of 4/5 May.[4]

On 5 May reveille came at 02.00 hours followed by breakfast an hour later. As daylight dawned we found ourselves among islands on the west coast of Madagascar. Leaflets calling for the surrender of the French were dropped on the local French Army airfield, shortly followed by bombs which destroyed most of their aircraft. Landings were made on three beaches as dawn broke and resistance was offered by the French Senegalese Regiment and a battery perched on top of a pinnacle of rock, nicknamed Windsor Castle, which was apparently a most difficult target for our naval gunners. Twice a white flag was flown from it and twice our troops were fired on when they went to occupy it.

The Pioneer Group HQ occupied itself in the usual way on assault landings, but instead of having any Pioneer companies who knew this work, it had to supervise the work of a mixed bag of spare drivers, gunners and details from about twelve units, men who had never landed stores, vehicles, ammunition, petrol, food, water, etc, on a beach from a landing craft before.

After the first few hours there was no more fighting near the beaches and the chief difficulty was to find strangers who did not relish the hard work which was new to them, and in that temperature, and work that they reckoned was not their job. Meanwhile, the attack moved forward and after a fierce struggle, in which the British had over 500 casualties, the airfield and whole town, docks and harbour at Diego Suarez were captured.

On 6 May at 04.30 hours I was told to get onto the main (Blue) beach at once to take charge of all working parties unloading and despatching ammo, food, water, vehicles, RE materials etc, which proved most necessary. There was some sniping and machine-gunning from air. It was a tropical beach of yellow, fringed with scrub and trees. We quickly formed our camp under a tree and bushes and everyone was soon caked with sweat and red dust. I went to sleep at 11.45 pm under a wonderful tropic sky.

This wonderful landlocked harbour, with a narrow easily defended entrance, was stated to be large enough to hold the whole Allied navies, while there was a dry dock which could take a cruiser. The French had not particularly wished to fight the British, nor they them, but while hostilities were in actual progress private sentiments went for nothing. However, after the surrender there was a philosophical acceptance of hard facts by both sides and even a small measure of cooperation for the mutual good.

It was found that the Allied blockade of several years had produced acute shortages of all articles not produced on the island. No clothes, nor materials of any description were on sale in any shop and one chemist even had a notice in his window which stated (in French) 'Repairs to toothbrushes from 5 francs'!

British supply ships came alongside the quay in the harbour for unloading and dumps were formed for the Force. When we unloaded the bales of clothing to issue the second set of KD, which by this time was most urgently needed, the bales were found to contain not tropical kit as expected but greatcoats, woollen underclothing and blankets; none of which we needed as the former were not worn in such a hot climate and we had all brought our own blankets. We hoped that Iceland or Murmansk enjoyed our KD![5]

In consequence most men were supplied with articles of captured French tropical kit in lieu, which created still further variations in the British uniforms. The order then in force, and strictly enforced, was that all ranks must wear topees because of the dangerous sun so near the equator and this was only disregarded by the senior officers entitled to wear red bands round their caps, thereby proving presumably that even nature has respect for army rank.

No. 5 Group HQ set up a civilian labour office and supervised the work of native PoWs (Malgache only, as the Senegalese were fighting men who could not be trusted to work for the British). The work at the harbour was supervised initially by personnel of a docks-operating company, but they were insufficient in number to do the actual work so 5 Group arranged with the *Monsieur* Jacques, the local manager of the Compagnie Maritime de l'Afrique Orientale, the company who owned the docks, for him to supply 100 of his Arab dock labourers daily to assist. This arrangement worked for exactly one week when the Arabs all went on strike and refused to work any longer for their French employers.

It was found that these Arabs were from Yemen, on a two-year contract which had expired some time before, but they could not be repatriated owing to war conditions. 5 Group HQ then took over all these Arab dockers and requisitioned their barracks and compound with everything in it which was found to contain certain families and even a mosque. Fortunately the Arabs did not know that army regulations strictly forbade the requisitioning of any religious buildings, so all was well.

The Group QM rose to the occasion and a ration scale was made up for these Arabs and then drawn from the RASC. They were rather doubtful about the correctness of it, but had to pass it as they could not prove it to be wrong. There was some difficulty in getting all the Arabs to work when required, but Group finally worked out that rations were issued only for the numbers at work, plus an allowance for families, so 'no work no rations' kept them up to scratch.

No one at Group HQ could speak Arabic and none of the Arabs could speak French, but one Arab spoke a little English so we made do in the usual Pioneer manner. This worked for a few days until a Sea Transport Officer [STO], Commander Griffiths, stated that he was responsible for unloading and loading all ships and that he had made a contract with the Compagnie Maritime de l'Afrique Orientale for this work. Force told Group to hand over the Arabs once more and the STO to carry on.

The result was that the Arabs went on strike again and work at the port was at a standstill. I was ordered by Brigadier Lush (who had no executive powers at all) to reengage the Arabs and work them as the French company had failed to carry out the contract for clearing the ships as made with Commander Griffiths. With the aid of my stalwarts at Group HQ, I did as asked and from then onwards the Arabs worked with little fuss under direct command of the Pioneer Group.

Each Arab was issued by Group with a homemade identity card, on which his thumb mark was placed; this was stamped daily as he entered the dock enclosure and on these numbers food was issued and later each man was paid on his number of days worked as shown on his card. I fixed the rates of pay for the Arabs, taking into consideration the housing and feeding provided, after consulting local employers who were not very cooperative, and these rates were paid by Group weekly with money obtained through their imprest account from the Force paymaster who paid over Madagascar francs taken from the local banks, rather than use prepared occupational currency.

The paymaster objected to this on the grounds that there was no authority so I asked the Force Commander, General Sturges of the Royal Marines, to put me in Force Orders as Acting Assistant Director of Labour. This the General did promptly. As A/ADL I then authorized certain rates of pay for Arabs and civilian Malgache labour and sent a copy to the paymaster. After this Group drew any money needed, quoting the authority of the A/ADL and everyone was satisfied.

When the first payment was made, each Arab had to receipt with his thumb mark after receiving his money. A number of them continued to hold out their hands after the paying officer had placed the money in them and it was some time before one gathered that they were waiting for the officer's private rake-off to be taken back as they had actually received in full the money promised. They then offered it to the Pioneer who was taking thumbprints as it was evident that the officer did not do this personally. They finally went off amazed when no one deducted anything.

Meantime, labour demands from all services were on a very large scale and as civilian labour was difficult to obtain, and very unreliable anyway, Group collected daily up to 2,000 PoWs from the neighbouring camp, split them up into suitable parties and saw that at least one could speak French before handing them over to the employing services who had to provide escort, which was rarely needed in actual fact. This arrangement worked only as long as the working sites were within reasonable marching distance, but many were not, so something further was needed and naturally the Force commander expected Group to find the answer.

About this time also, trouble was raised by a Frenchman who said that he was the local representative of the Red Cross and that Force was breaking the Geneva Convention by making PoWs handle offensive materials. This was quite correct of course, so again the Force commander asked me to find the remedy.

The answer to the difficulties was obviously to form labour companies of some description, and I had several times requested permission either for the importation of same, or for permission to recruit locally. I was told that the matter had been referred to the War Office, but had been turned down.

I then suggested to Force that Malgache PoWs might be released from their French Army engagements and formed into labour companies under Group HQ. As the matter was urgent General Sturges finally agreed to this as long as they were *civilian* labour companies only and a start was to be made with 500.

Accordingly I chose a camp site on a state farm where the only buildings were some good piggeries. Permission to use this was then sought but although on active service, believe it or not, Group had to get consents from, or to notify the following:

1) Force AA & QMG,
2) Town Major,
3) REs for water,

104

Donald John Dean [centre, standing] aged 2 years in June 1899, flanked by sister Elsie [left] and brother Graham Donald in June 1899.

Mother Grace Dean (née Walduck)

Father John Dean pictured in 1933.

Dean in June 1914, aged 17.

Private Dean 3692, 28th County of London Battalion (Artists Rifles).

Brother Graham Dean cheated the eye test to serve with The Buffs. He saw service in the Gallipoli campaign and was wounded in Mesopotamia.

Uncle Harold Walduck was instrumental in securing Dean a post with one of the 'fashionable' London Territorial battalions.

Brother Harold V Dean pictured here at 18 years old in 1918 in the uniform of a Merchant Navy Wireless Officer.

Dean in July 1915, one month before travelling to France. He had just completed his 14 weeks basic training, mostly using Boer War vintage equipment.

Dean was sent to a training camp at Richmond Park in May 1915. Heavy rain flooded the bell tents, giving a taste of the conditions to come overseas.

Dean's Artists Rifles pay book showing he lied about his age. It shows he enlisted on 19 April 1915, (his 18th birthday) but gives his age as 19.

Portrait taken in 1917 while on leave. Dean was posted as a 2nd Lieutenant to the 11th Battalion, Queen's Own Royal West Kent Regiment on 3 October 1916.

Lieutenant Dean in 1917 following his wounding in the Tower Hamlets attack. Dean went into the attack fully expecting a captaincy if he survived. Instead he was lucky to escape with his life.

This purse was in Dean's breeches pocket during the Tower Hamlets attack on 20 September 1917 when he was hit by 3 machine gun bullets. One passed through his left arm, one through his left thigh and the third through the purse, finally stopping against a flask in the same pocket.

A view of Lens taken by Dean's commander, Lt Col Wenyon shortly after the end of hostilities in 1918. This view shows the devastated town, looking northwards.

A view of Lens looking west. After fighting through the town sewers, a war weary Dean put in a transfer request to join the Machine Gun Corps.

Dean withdrew his transfer request after his VC action and was badly wounded on 10 October 1918. Sent to England for a third time, this photograph was taken in 1919 and shows his three wound stripes on his right forearm.

Lt Colonel Wenyon, Dean's commander in the 8th Bn RWK Regt. He described Dean's defence as 'magnificent' and recommended him for a Victoria Cross.

Dean's post. This exposed, shallow trench in the outskirts north of Lens was the scene of Dean's VC action from 24 to 26 September 1918. This photograph was taken by Wenyon at the end of the war, from Claude Trench, looking west.

Dean at Buckingham Palace after collecting his VC from King George V on 15 February 1919. He is accompanied by his parents and Aunt Jessie Walduck [right].

Dean's civic reception in Sittingbourne after returning by train from the palace. He had to be encouraged to open his overcoat and reveal the Victoria Cross to the massed audience.

Commemorating the fallen of the Great War became a constant in Dean's life. Here he is pictured visiting Flanders in the 1920s. This ruined chateau near Ypres was once in the German support line opposite Dean's position on the right of the Ypres/Commines Canal. The Royal West Kent veterans are the RSM, D.J. Dean, Lt Col Corfe, and R.O. Russell.

After threatening to work in the colonies unless he received a pay rise, Dean joined the family brick making business after the First World War.

Dean's future wife, Marjorie Wood.

Dean's Wedding in June 1923 at St Michael's church, Sittingbourne. His brother Harold [on Dean's right in bowler hat] was best man.

Dean [standing third left] pictured with the B company football team at Falmer Camp.

In July 1921 Dean was promoted to captain in the 4th Bn (East Kent Regiment). At the formation of this Territorial battalion it consisted of only one man: Dean.

4th Bn The Buffs at Falmer Territorial camp near Brighton in 1930.

Dean [centre with hand in pocket] pictured with his brother officers in jovial mood.

Caricature of Dean by R.J. Ballard [c.1930]

1930 portrait at the age of 33. Dean was promoted Major of the 4th Bn The Buffs in April 1930.

Dean [left] was made Lieutenant Colonel in 1936. As war approached he fully expected to lead his 4th Bn in action. When told he would not be accompanying his battalion to France he described it as the bitterest day of his life.

Landing party going ashore at Madagascar in 1942. Operation IRONCLAD was vital to prevent Japanese submarines using the Vichy-controlled island as a base.

Troops under fire from Vichy French positions.

Keeping the army on the move. Pioneers restore a mined road on Madagascar.

British Empire Pioneers clearing a roadblock in Madagscar. Dean's command was mostly composed of a wide variety of African and Indian troops.

French prisoners of War in Madagascar, October 1942. Although Dean allowed them to raise a Tricolor on parades, he did not allow their 'unofficial wives' to visit the camp.

Malgache workers in Madagascar. Ever the pragmatist, Dean released the Malgache from the French army and employed them as civilians in order to get round the restrictions on using PoWs for labour.

In August 1942 Dean was an umpire on Exercise TOUCHSTONE in Mombasa, Kenya, in preparation for second landing in Madagascar.

Dean as an Honorary Colonel of The Buffs in the 1960s. Among his many decorations he is wearing the insignia of the Commander of the Order of the Dannebrog.

Leading a Remembrance Day parade in Sittingbourne, 1970.

Remembrance of the fallen was seen as a sacred duty by Dean for the rest of his life.

The late colonel's resting place at the Church of St. John the Baptist, Tunstall, near Sittingbourne in Kent.

4) The Anti-Malarial Officer,

5) The Political Officer,

6) Hygiene Officer,

7) ADMS,

8) RASC for rations,

9) Force Transport Officer,

10) RAOC for tentage,

11) RE Dump for tools,

12) The ADL so that I could be quoted as being in favour.

I also had to get out and duly authorize rates of pay for various ranks.

These matters all being complied with, the following day myself and my adjutant visited the PoWs camp where 500 Malgache from various units, under native NCOs and one native *sergent chef* (chief sergeant), were drawn up. The French officer who had agreed to cooperate read out to them that they were temporarily released from the French Army. I then shouted out in my best French, 'You are no longer PoWs but are free men and will work for the British Army for pay; by the right quick march.'

The column then moved off to its new camp site and as it passed along the way a number of wives, official or otherwise, who had apparently been lurking in the undergrowth, fell in behind with their worldly goods upon their heads and straggled after their men folk, which rather spoiled the martial appearance of the parade. When they arrived at the camp I decided to put the single men into tents and that the men with expectant wives and/or children must build huts in the adjoining field. This was done but, as was found later, an initial mistake was made in not having town planning from the start.

The 500 were split into sections of 100 each as an easy unit for work and were placed under five Pioneer privates from Group HQ, clerks, store man, batman, etc. This arrangement proved so satisfactory that the process was repeated, and size of sections increased, until there were 2,000 natives in camp, plus hundreds of women, some children, goats, chickens, etc.

The authorities said, 'Why keep a PoW camp for a few natives when they appear to stay unguarded in a Pioneer Camp?' The balance of approximately 1,000 PoWs were therefore handed over to Group who now proudly had 3,000 men in their mobile labour companies, some 500 wives etc and soon easily the largest native village in that part of Madagascar. The whole became known soon as 'Dean Force'.

Sanitation among the men was adequately dealt with, but was a problem with the families until I picked out the wife of the *sergent chef*, pinned onto her the same badge of rank as her husband's and appointed her in charge of all women and children. At the same time she was put on the pay roll, but as nothing was said about this, and the paymaster did not know the difference between male and female Malgache names, all was well.

Rice and meat were drawn, but the camp had to grow its own vegetables to feed the hungry mob. It was found that the last contingent of ex-PoWs included nearly 300 Comorians, men from the French Comoro Islands in the Indian Ocean between Madagascar and Mozambique, fierce fellows who were all Moslems and therefore required separate rations, cookhouses, etc. They were all old soldiers and did not get on well with the Malgache, so it was decided to work them in the dock area alongside the Arabs of the same faith.

The actual work of making out payrolls and paying as well as rationing and administering 3,000 men without their own officers, plus dealing with families and doing the same for the Arab dockers and odd civilians working for various services, HQ and messes, proved too much for only three Pioneer officers and the devoted and overworked ten Pioneer ORs, so Force was asked to attach various officers and ORs from Details.

Force did this, but the personnel were constantly changing and at one time included several South Africans who spoke very little English. Force decided to form a battery of French 75 guns, but several of the breech blocks were missing, believed buried by the French on the arrival of the British. For several weeks an abortive search had been made for them, but the French officers would not tell where they were. Hearing about this I told the *sergent chef* to parade any natives from the battery in question. I then said to them, 'Do you remember where you hid the breech blocks'? They said, 'Yes', so I said, 'Jump into this lorry and one of you show the driver where to go and then bring the breech blocks back here'. This was done and the guns put into order.

The next demand from Force was for native drivers for this battery. Luck again favoured Group as some of their native Pioneers were the former drivers, who were even able to round up some of their battery mules. So together with certain gun numbers, all fitted out with the new French uniforms, Group helped substantially to assist in reforming the battery.

One Malgache Pioneer had stolen from him, while sick in camp, a sum of 845 francs, which was his life savings. An enquiry revealed little except that I was convinced that the Malgache all knew the thief, but would not tell a white man. The judgement was that all the eighty-odd suspects should have 10 francs each deducted from their pay, which was then due, and this was done next pay day. Two days later it was learned that the mulcted men had all forcibly collected their 10 francs from the thief!

Among the numerous jobs done by the native Pioneers was making an airfield. At least that was the order, but it was found that an airstrip was all that was required and this was done in record time because the wind obligingly blew in one fixed direction for six months and then still more obligingly blew from the exactly opposite quarter for the next half year. Work was done for the Royal Navy at times, as well as for the Army and RAF. One of the least pleasant jobs for the Pioneers was grave digging because after the fighting ceased in that area malaria claimed many victims.

Considerable excitement was caused on the night of 30 May when a tanker was torpedoed and sunk in the harbour and the *Ramillies* was also hit by two torpedoes; this battleship also being in the harbour at the moment, but though considerably damaged was not sunk. It was then thought that it was done by a French submarine. Guns were fired at imaginary targets and for a few minutes alarm reigned. One ship fired her 6-inch gun at a whaler picking up swimmers and it was also fired at by a pom-pom on the battleship but fortunately there were no casualties from this. Troops 'stood to' and the Force commander signalled to the *Ramillies* asking if any help was needed. The admiral on board signalled back in a typical naval manner, declining help with thanks and inviting the general to breakfast that morning.

It was feared that this presaged a general rising by the local French, and I was asked what troops I needed to deal with possible trouble among my ex-PoW Pioneers. On doing the rounds of the camp I found everyone apparently asleep. It subsequently proved to be a Japanese submarine that had done the dirty work.

Later some East African transport arrived on the island and I was loaned a van driven by an Askari so had to learn some Swahili. Private Guinness was a Group clerk who could speak French and did particularly good work during this period. Although a British private, he was known by the natives of various nationalities as the 'Sergeant Major'. One day after he had dealt in quick succession with Arabs, Malgache, Lascars from the sunken tanker, Afrikaans-speaking South Africans and French in the normal course of his duties, he threw up his hands exclaiming 'Oh for a second Day of Pentecost'.

Another job for a party of native Pioneers was cutting poles in the forest at Joffreville. This lush section was a great change from the arid dust-swept area round Diego Suarez as it was on hills which caught considerable rain. There was much competition between the members of Group HQ to visit this pole-cutting job. The lemurs occasionally seen in these forests, together with the crocodiles in the lakes and rivers, were the only wild animals ever seen in Madagascar, though some of the reputed 10,000,000 cattle were wild enough in practice.

On 6 June the christening of the baby son of my French foreman, Stannier, took place. As he was Roman Catholic and I Protestant I did not act as godfather as originally arranged, but gave presents and took an aperitif there. That same day I went to Orangea to the site of a new landing ground with 2nd Lieutenant Thomas.

Later that month a Lieutenant Colonel West commanding 2 Bn South Lancs Regiment went to my Labour Camp and, without reference to me, cancelled my orders (given after consultation with Force HQ) to certain NCOs put up to

'Acting Unpaid Local rank'. These NCOs were from his battalion, but had been attached to me 'for all purposes'. Not content with this he complained to Brigadier Festing who sent for me, although he had no authority to do so and viciously attacked me for giving such Acting Unpaid Local ranks. He was so obviously in the wrong that I stood up to him and finally got a half apology. Later Lieutenant Colonels West and Thatcher visited me in the mess when we tried to settle the matter. Lieutenant Colonel Elmslie (AA & QMG) told me quite unsolicited, that any army support I might desire from Force HQ would be freely given to me. I showed Elmslie the letter signed for by himself instructing that Acting Unpaid Local rank would be given to *all* attached NCOs.

At the end of July an East African Military Labour Group HQ, together with the HQ of three of their companies, arrived and relieved 5 Group of much of its worries, so Dean Force was handed over to them. On 8 August, Major Cannon and the eight ORs, who had formed the rear party when Group left England, arrived at last. They had left England on 24 May and had spent four weeks in Durban as the ship they left there after two weeks developed engine trouble and had to put back again.

Before we left Diego Suarez a newly formed battalion of King's African Rifles was brought in as a garrison to relieve the British troops due to go on to Ceylon or India and for the Askaris to continue with their training at the same time. It was rumoured that only a few weeks prior to their arrival they had been in their primeval forests in East Africa, but be that as it may, they had certainly had little training and had seen few white men before joining up.

A battalion of a certain famous Scottish regiment was detailed to meet this KAR battalion at the docks and to see them fed and happily bedded down for the night, in a way quite normal in the British Army with new arrivals. To the astonishment of most of these black Askaris they found white private soldiers for the first time. Up to then they had believed that white men could only be officers or WOs. By the next morning, however, they had worked it out logically in their own minds that there were different tribes of white men. The chief one called English found all the officers and sergeant majors, while an inferior tribe called Scottish produced only private soldiers.

When we first landed in Madagascar we came prepared with military occupation currency to be used if necessary, but right from the start we found sufficient local paper money in the banks in Diego Suarez for current use and as most of this kept circulating and coming back into the banks, it was re-used time after time. However, we finally began to run short of small paper currency though we still had a few notes of one million francs each, which were no earthly use to us, so on the wireless we contacted the Bank of Madagascar Head Office in the island capital of Tananarive (this used to be called Antananarivo in my school days), which was some hundreds of miles away and still in French occupation of course, asking them whether they would give us change in small notes for five notes we held of 1,000,000 francs each.

The governor of the island refused our request indignantly, but evidently the bank pointed out that if we were forced to put our occupation currency into circulation in the island it might well upset the currency for years, so, whether or not the governor gave permission the bank agreed to cooperate. Accordingly the bank officials set forth and travelled along hundreds of miles of dirt roads and crossed numerous rivers and finally arrived at our outpost line. The British Army blew the 'ceasefire'. The paymaster went out in his jeep into no-man's land and met the bank official, handed over five notes and received in exchange five large sacks of small denomination notes. Both cars turned about and hostilities nominally restarted.

While still in Diego Suarez we had a certain number of nursing sisters in a British hospital and they soon demanded starch for their uniforms, head coverings, cuffs, etc. Now this was one thing that no one had thought of providing and none was on sale in local shops and it would have taken weeks to get out from South Africa even. General Sturges asked 'Dogsbody Dean' to do something about it. I thought hard and finally went to some French Roman Catholic sisters and asked what they did for starch. They laughed and explained that they made their own out of rice so I got the recipe and all was well once more.

The original hard core of regular French Army officers who positively refused to cooperate when we first arrived and had taken the town and area of Diego Suarez were a bit of a problem, so it was decided to send them to England, but we never knew whether they were PoWs or were to be sent into France. However, they and their wives and children were put on board a ship bound for England. Their women wore all their jewellery when going on board. What we did not know, but someone told us, was they did not have to pay duty on what they were actually wearing; possibly they thought it safer on the person. A fair number of unofficial wives tried to go on the ship with their 'protectors' and there were some tearful scenes when we stopped them. However, when the ship cast off and was still in sight they dried their eyes and made a rush to my labour recruiting office on the quayside, and demanded that I find them similar positions with British officers and were quite indignant when I told them nothing doing. Many of the Creoles were extremely good looking too. Some of the French wives stayed behind as they had apparently changed partners without the formality of a divorce, but that was not our worry.

The British Navy brought into harbour an Italian merchantman and included in the crew were four natives from Eritrea. These were locked up separately from the Italians and no one seemed to know what to do with them. I asked for permission to give them jobs if I found them suitable and this was thankfully given to me. I found that they had been stewards and decided that they could well be used in officers' messes if they wished. They were only too happy about this and told me that as the British had conquered their country they considered that they were British subjects and should be treated as such. This seemed fair enough, if that is what they really thought, so I had them released without delay and used them as mess staff.

The Political Officer who arrived with Force HQ was a Brigadier Lush, accompanied by several British Army officers, also from Egypt, whose job appeared to be 'Civil Affairs' or in other words to look after the interests of the civilians *against* the army. A few weeks later a civilian, Mr Grafty-Smith arrived, appointed apparently by the Foreign Office, to do exactly the same job. Grafty-Smith thereupon ousted Lush from his office and took Lush's staff car. After a while, Lush flew to East Africa and returned with greater powers and reversed the situation, taking car and front office once more. This dual appointment continued, under strain, until we had gained control of most of the island when Lord Reading appeared on the scene as a third and overriding Civil Affairs officer to sort out the impasse. As I left the island at that time I never did hear who finally came out on top.

We had a number of South African Army and Air Force come out to us and apparently there was a strong move on the part of South Africa to take over control of the whole of the operations in Madagascar with, in the private view of many of us, the idea that after the war they would continue to exercise control or even ownership there. This appeared to be countered by the appointment of General Willy Platt, commander-in-chief in East Africa, who tried to boss everybody and everything even after South Africa sent an infantry brigade and a section of their air force to replace units of the British Army sent to India.

On 2 August, I had occasion to go to the sacred lake at Anivarano. The story that I was told was that many years ago the village of Anivarano contained a number of wicked people. The crisis came one day when a witch called at the village and asked for food and water, which was refused to her by nearly all the village. The refusal of water was too dreadful to think about. Finally a family on the other side of the village took her in and ministered her wants. The witch warned this family to go to the hill and stay there for the night. She then cursed the village and that night the curse operated and the whole of the village sank into the ground and became the present lake while the inhabitants, instead of being drowned, were all turned in to crocodiles with immortal life. The good family, with a few friends they took with them, were all saved.

Every year since, on the anniversary of the destruction, the good family, and then their descendants, arrive at the same spot by the lake where there is a grassy low bank. How long this took place I could not find out but it was 'a long, long time ago'. Arriving at the special spot on the given day they kill, cook and eat half of a bull. They then clap hands in unison and chant until some of the crocodiles come up out of the lake and eat their share of the bull. The largest crocodile, said to be more than 7 metres long (say about 23 feet), is the headman of old. None of the relations are killed by the crocodiles, but any stranger is most likely to be killed and eaten. The skulls of the bulls are then stuck on a pole and left to rot away. I saw a number of these skulls, but not the ceremony. It all sounds rather like a version of 'The Flood' story.

I also saw a tree with many hundreds of flying foxes hanging on it, which when disturbed flew round quite close, the largest having bodies about 15 ft long, with a wing span of about 36 ft. They can fly half a mile with apparent ease as they did not hesitate to fly across part of the lake.

On 23 August, the whole Group HQ sailed from Diego Suarez with 121 Force, who had handed over to East African Units and proceeded to Mombasa, Kenya.

Our Force arrived there on 26 August 1942. Actually, we docked at the port which is Kilindini. This was so that we could prepare for the next phase in occupying further ports in Madagascar, which might cause us serious trouble if they were occupied by Japanese and so cut our vital life line round Africa through the Mozambique Straits.

I was on the trooper *Dilwara*. In the afternoon I went ashore to stretch my legs, do some shopping and look around. It was very hot indeed. I found prices very high and many articles quite unobtainable. Next day I walked to Fort Jesus, which was on an island, now joined to the mainland by a causeway. This and a coastal strip were leased to Great Britain by the Sultan of Zanzibar for £12,000 per annum.

Fort Jesus was believed to have been built by Portuguese in the fourteenth century after a previous expedition had been massacred by the Arabs. The fort changed hands several times over the years with slaughter of the garrison each time. The Sultan's pink coloured flag was flying, though the fort was then being used as HM Prison we were told.

At the end of August we took part in Exercise *Touchstone*, which was a practice assault to test the defences of Mombasa and as a rehearsal for a landing at the Madagascan port of Majunga. I was an umpire in the exercise. It was hot but bearable.

While in Mombasa a local paper printed the news that all mail for the Middle East, which then included us, posted in London and Home Counties during 18/30 June was lost by enemy action. That accounted for some of our missing letters from home. We also heard that the 13th Infantry Brigade en route from Madagascar to India developed 800 cases of malaria, of which fifty-four proved fatal.

On 5 September, our Force sailed from Kilindini to make a forced landing at Majunga on the West Coast. No. 5 Group HQ Pioneer Corps left Major

Cannon (my second in charge) and a small detachment to do ditto at Tamatave on the East Coast. My party arrived off Majunga on 10 September.

There was not much resistance at Majunga when we attacked, but much confusion. The French officer in command there, together with the mayor, would not capitulate until we had made a considerable show of force and landed an assault party and fired a few rounds of naval gunfire over the town into the bush behind. French honour being thus satisfied they capitulated, but this did not get through immediately to all their troops who were the usual mixed lot of Malgache who did not want to fight anyway, Senegalese who fought well and a few French who formed a kind of defence force but were really armed civilians.

My orders were to get ashore immediately fighting permitted and help get guns and vehicles ashore at 'Green Beach'. Once more no labour was allotted to me for this purpose and no boat to take me ashore. I was supposed to be able to work ruddy miracles and being a Pioneer often did. I managed to get ashore when Brigadier Festing's 'R' boat came back for medical supplies, as I slipped on board with my batman, one Private O'Connor, who was a first-class soldier in times of danger or difficulty as long as he did not come over all Irish with the sorrows of a nation on him, which could only be drowned in whatever liquor was available at that moment.

When O'Connor and I landed, chaos prevailed as usual but fighting had stopped at that particular point, although there was still a bit of shooting going on further along in the town. I got hold of a party of Malgache soldiers who were still armed but who did not seem to worry, as they presumably reckoned that they need not fight without their officers directly ordering them to do so and they had none with them. So I led them down to 'Green Beach' with O'Connor bringing up the rear as 'whipper in' if needed and to see fair play for me. We stacked their rifles and O'Connor stood guard over them. Within a few minutes the landing craft with guns, etc started touching down and we got them, also ammunition, petrol, etc, ashore. It was a very near thing but we made it in time.

I was later joined by my adjutant, Captain Morley, my QM, Lieutenant Browne, and the rest of my Group HQ party so we found an improvised PoW compound and put our native soldier workers in. After that more trouble started, as follows: as the shore was soft sand it had been arranged that rolls of wire mesh track would be needed and as these were so important they were stowed first of all in the bottom of the ships and everything else on top at Mombasa, so naturally they were last off. To save the situation I had about 200 yards of reinforced concrete ornamental fencing hacked down and laid on the sand to get the wheeled traffic up the shore. The RA drivers were available to drive their vehicles ashore, but when it came to cars and lorries we found the drivers were being landed separately and had not arrived. So Morley, one man of mine who could drive, and I had a most hectic time climbing aboard the LCMs (Landing Craft Motor) as soon as their flaps were down and driving the vehicles madly up the improvised hard strip, which was now showing signs of wear, on to a hard road where we left them, doubling back for more. Although it was now evening it was still unpleasantly hot. We got ashore all that was due that day and then sank down exhausted to sleep where we were in the open.

Next morning, work unloading was resumed at dawn, but even now the drivers did not turn up so we continued as before. An hour or two later, General Sturges strolled along and said 'Have you seen General Platt this morning?' When I said 'No', he said 'Then you are the only senior officer in the force that has not been told off by him this morning'.

Later that day I was informed that Brigadier Lush had laid a complaint that I had 'wilfully damaged civilian property in tearing down the concrete fencing round the playing field'!

That day and onwards I collected labour gangs formed from PoWs, civil prisoners (natives of course), Arab dockers whom we paid, and also other paid civilians. Meantime, Major Cannon with the other assault party had reached Tamatave on the East Coast, which was taken after only a few token rounds had been fired by our Royal Naval guns but sufficient for French honour to be satisfied that they had resisted until overcome by overwhelming forces. Major Cannon organized very large numbers of civilians there for general work and repairing roads and railway.

We stayed in Majunga for a week or so while Brigadier Dimoline and a brigade force, which included some King's African Rifles, were pushing their way up, opposed mainly by the Senegalese, the biggest battle being by the Betsiboka River Bridge where no quarter was asked for, or given by either of the opposed fighting Africans.

Force HQ stayed in Majunga also and when they suggested sending more vehicles and supplies up to Brigadier Dimoline he sent back a signal that he wanted 'bodies, not stores'. A short time afterwards he sent an SOS for petrol so several lorries were loaded up and sent off. I was moving up that day myself, with my adjutant, leaving the QM behind in charge of our labour at Majunga, and came across a river in front of which the petrol lorries had all stopped as the river bed was very soft and muddy, although the water was only about eighteen inches deep at the ford.

Being the senior officer on the spot, and a Pioneer Corps officer to boot, I naturally took charge and prompt action. We cut down some lovely eucalyptus trees with straight stems and laced them with fencing wire into a mattress which we had floating on the water. As soon as a vehicle ran slowly onto it the mattress sank to the bottom and all the vehicles, including my own car passed safely over. Believe it or not, a few days later Brigadier Lush again complained bitterly about this and again reported me for 'wanton destruction of valuable trees and fencing'. This again illustrated why we fighting soldiers looked upon Civil Administration officers with grave mistrust.

On 26 September I left Majunga with other heads of services en route for the capital Tananarive, taking with me only Private O'Connor. The road was very rough in places, unmetalled and crossed mountains where the track had been blasted into the valleys and the river bridges blown. The River Betsiboka Bridge, a long suspension bridge, had been broken by cutting the cables but we managed to use it still as it had merely collapsed with most of it about three feet under water, with a 30ft ramp at each end of about 45 degrees.

I had sent up a labour party of 100 natives who had to unload most of the lorries and carry the contents across, tow the vehicles along the submerged bridge and reload them on the further bank. The car I was in had its petrol tank holed on a rock over 100 miles from the nearest repair shop. We enquired round but nobody had any chewing gum so we tried bunging up the hole with soap. This only worked for a short time but some bright lad got hold of some beeswax from a native and this did the trick until we got through a few days later.[6]

Arriving at the capital we found that the British Force had captured and then released on parole a number of French officers who in many cases were reserve officers with either civilian or purely administrative jobs, though there were exceptions. They were all in or near the capital. General Platt ordered that they should be put into a non-existent PoW camp immediately.

As usual General Sturges passed this job on to 'Dogsbody Dean'. I requisitioned a large empty seminary and ordered all French officers to report there within twenty-four hours; at the same time informing them that they should bring their own furniture, bedding, mess gear, etc, as there was none in the prison camp, but that we would provide transport. We had all their addresses of course. They all came along at the appointed time, some of them complaining bitterly that it was quite unnecessary and that we were only making the administration more difficult for ourselves by locking them up.

One of them told me that when they were released on parole he had collected his wife and family from the hotel where he had parked them but which had now been taken over by the British, and had returned home out in the country a few miles away, but he could not possibly leave them there in such an isolated spot without a white man to look to their safety. This struck me as quite reasonable so I gave him twenty-four hours' leave to move them to friends and a lorry to do it with, with a British driver of course who was nominally guarding him. He came back without any trouble.

The CO of the French Air Force found that things were rather primitive in the PoW camp and that I was running it on the 'Old Boy basis', so he himself suggested that he might return to the airfield and load up his mess gear, which he did, and he even brought back into camp a vehicle of his own.

The trouble was of course what to do about guards but this was soon solved as we did without any for the officers as I put them on a semi-parole. The next day, however, we had a number of both Senegalese and Malgache other ranks. As a temporary measure, with the cooperation of the French officers, we put the Senegalese acting as guards to the Malgache, which they did very happily, until we got a platoon of KARs for the job; then the French officers complained that they should not be guarded by native troops but I had a quick answer to that as one or two of our British officers, when wounded and taken prisoner had been guarded by French natives, so what the hell!

I was of course Officer Commanding the PoW camp with Captain Morley, my adjutant, to help and I requested the quick arrival of Lieutenant and QM Browne. They flew him up from Majunga promptly. We got on very well on the whole as the French got their own cooks and servants, etc from the PoWs and I merely drew the rations for them all. Fortunately the Senegalese could eat the same rations as the KARs and the Malgache could eat anything, though it was mainly rice.

Naturally I had to order the French officers to hand over their revolvers or pistols, which they did under protest as they said they were their own property and would be essential for their own protection when we left. Accordingly, I got the owners to label their own weapons and I took a French officer with me and we deposited the pistols at the local Gendarmerie which was also under the British Military Police. I refused permission for a flagstaff to be erected outside the PoWs' building for them to fly their Tricolor from as I thought that was a bit too much, but as they explained that for the sake of discipline they wanted a parade ceremony every day on raising or lowering the flag. I gave permission for this to take place in the inner courtyard and provided both flagstaff and flag. After about a week of this I even arranged for a visitors' day and allowed the French to have their wives or family or official fiancées in. We had a certain number of applications for unofficial wives to visit but I sternly refused. The KAR guards could not read English so I had some coloured cards provided by the local printing firm and put my censor stamp on each.

Naturally this was only one of the many jobs we had to do as the normal labour work had to go on. This was done partly with civil prisoners, partly with Malgache PoWs and partly with hired civilians, though as I had to keep either myself, adjutant, or QM at the PoW camp it meant increased work for all three of us.

One of the effects of the blockade by us of the island was an acute shortage of petrol so we found that all the cars were running on a special mixture called 'Carburol', which was one quarter petrol and three quarters a distillation from native sugar. If used on any vehicle not specially adapted for it, it just gummed everything up.

One day I needed a haircut so I went to a local civilian barber's shop. The barber was a native woman. When I sat down for my turn she carefully ran the metal comb through a spirit flame, which I thought most hygienic but I was not so pleased when she did the same thing after combing my hair, I also noticed that the same bristle hair brush was used, untreated, for each customer in turn!

I was billeted in one of the hotels in Tananarive which was staffed entirely by natives, some of whom had no room at all but just slept on the floor of the passages or landings at night. The first night the proprietor came to my room and asked if there was anything I wanted. When I said, 'No', he put it more plainly that if I wanted a sleeping partner I had only to mention it, 'Black, white or chocolate'!

One day I was taken violently ill there with a high temperature, sickness, etc, but the MO could not find out what was wrong. However, in a few days nature provided the cure that the army could not.

There was never any lavatory paper provided of course so I had my own closely guarded roll of Bronco. One day when I was in the loo, a lady rattled the door twice so I hurried up and left quickly and she popped in. It was only then that I remembered that I had not brought away my hoarded Bronco so I lurked just round the corner and as soon as she came out I popped in only to find that she had pinched my Bronco. What should a gentleman do in such a case? Should he go to the lady's bedroom and demand the return of his lost roll or ignore it? I must admit that I had not got the nerve to call her a thief so lost out.

It is worth recording that before we got to the capital there was a British resident who kept a transmitting set in his house there and sent out some most useful information to the British Army. When he was arrested by the French they were unable to find the set but they sentenced him to death. Undeterred, his wife kept transmitting and hid the set in her bathroom we were told. The British arrived just before this brave man was executed so all was well.

We met a British Bishop of Madagascar there. He told us that during the war he had been unable to visit Diego Suarez in the usual way by coaster and that the land journey was beyond his capability so some of the native priests up that way had finally elected their own bishop. I never heard how this matter was cleared up.

The French, of course, were most difficult over native marriages as they would not allow a marriage to be legal without the production of birth certificates by both parties. Very few indeed had such a thing and the only way to get one was for two people who had known the individuals from birth to come to one of the few centres and testify. This meant in actual fact that the two people, who were often elderly, had to walk anything up to 150 miles each way. Not unnaturally few would or could do this unless they lived really close to the centre.

116

Finally the day came when General Sturges was due to return to the UK so the night before his departure some of his staff gave him a farewell dinner. After dinner General Sturges came and sat by me and said, 'I do not know exactly what I am doing next, but I believe that I am going back for another combined operation landing, would you like to come with me?' I said, 'Yes, please.' So I hastily got on the phone to Major Cannon and told him to meet me next day at Tamatave as I was handing over to him and he was to take my place as Group Commander. I appointed Captain Morley my adjutant as second in charge and CO of the PoW camp, packed up and left early in the morning by the Michelin rail coach with the general and his staff.

So ended my interlude in Madagascar, which was full of incident and interest. A few days after I left a signal came for me offering me the job of OC Troops in Mauritius, but as I was no longer there this job naturally fell through. This would have meant the rank of full colonel for which I had to wait another two years, but I should have been in a backwater and away from the main action in Europe. I really do not know what I would have chosen had I had the choice, but the old army saying, 'never volunteer for anything or refuse anything', is a sound one, in theory.

Shortly before my leaving Tananarive I had to open a second PoW camp, mainly for natives, both Malgache and Senegalese, which I did at the barracks of the 'Direction Artillerie'. The HQ of two British Pioneer Corps companies arrived at long last from Majunga. I could not have found the officers to look after this extra commitment, so when I left on 17 October, there were sufficient to carry on all the jobs that my adjutant, QM and I had tackled alone.

Being now rated as on the Staff of 121 Force HQ as ADL (Assistant Director of Labour), we boarded the *Ocean Pride*, together with most of No. 5 Commandos who were also leaving, and sailed from Tamatave on the afternoon of 18 October 1942. During that morning I had further talks with Major Cannon and advised him to get to the capital with all speed and get his appointment confirmed otherwise they were sure to appoint someone else over his head from East Africa. There was always strong bias in favour of such people all the time General Willie Platt was GOC. Lieutenant QM Browne was then the only man left at Group HQ who had been with me since the formation of that HQ at Clacton in 1939.

On 24 October, we docked safely at Durban and got ashore. I dined that night at the club with Admiral Tennant, General Sturges, and Brigadier Festing, etc as a farewell between 121 Force HQ and 29th Infantry Brigade HQ. Next day we sailed again, the weather being so rough that even in our bunks we had to hang on tight to prevent damage to ourselves as we rolled and were thrown about so roughly. We were travelling very fast in spite of the weather as enemy submarines were reported. As our cabin was close to the engine room the noise was tremendous, so I spent nearly the entire night reading and slept from about

02.30 to 03.30 only. Next day one of our planes dropped a smoke flare by a ship's boat floating on the sea. A destroyer dashed past it at full speed but reported it empty.

On 27 October, we docked at Cape Town. Next morning I started shopping for food to take home. In the afternoon I was one of a party taken round the town by kind local inhabitants. We visited the zoo, Rhodes Memorial, etc. On the 29th I had lunch with General Sturges at the Civil Service Club and afterwards went with him by cable car up Table Mountain and after a short walk up on top, descended again by the same method. This cable is 4,000 feet long from the top of the mountain to a station part way up. The sensation of the down journey is somewhat like a parachute descent, I am told.

On 31 October, most of our party went to the races, but owing to shortage of cash I did not, but instead went with Lieutenant Colonel Moulton for a climb up Table Mountain. We went by the Blinkwater Ravine, which we were told was one of the easier routes, but as we had no guide we lost the track several times and got on to ledges that ended in nothing. However, we finally made it. The time taken in walking and climbing was about five hours.

During my spare time in Cape Town, I spent much of it buying food and transporting it back to the ship and getting it in cold store. We left Cape Town on 2 November without naval escort as we were not in convoy. Our maximum speed was stated to be eighteen knots so as we were under twenty knots, which was apparently the minimum which allowed us to take a full load of servicemen, some of the commandos were sent ashore to wait for a later ship and their places were taken by civilians, mainly women and children (so, what was unsafe for commandos was good enough for women and children). Amongst the former were a Mother Superior and several second class Sisters of Mercy. We insisted that even if they slept second class they should use the first class deck.

After circling round the harbour repeatedly testing out the new gear against magnetic mines, we finally cleared for the open sea going liked a scalded cat. Next day we should have had air escort, promised to us by Colonel Mostert of the South African Air Force, but this did not appear, probably because of torpedo attacks on our shipping off East London, which naturally had prior claim. We heard that one of the Empress ships had been torpedoed near us. An unidentified plane flew low over us that night so we promptly altered course as soon as it had passed.

Some 400 miles away from the nearest land we saw a lone swallow which stayed with us for several days; we did not see it perch but it may possibly have done so on the ship at night. We were not particularly cheered to hear of more ships being sunk when travelling not in convoy and, via Rugby Radio, rumours of seven German subs somewhere in our path, so we yet again altered course.

Talking of birds reminds me that we saw an albatross rising from the sea. Apparently it could not rise by just flapping its wings but had first of all to get up sea speed by furiously paddling. We later saw a parent albatross and a young one. The parent hardly moved its wings at all while in the air but the youngster while trying to glide also had to keep on flapping like hell to keep up.

After twenty-eight days at sea, going full blast all the time, we landed safely, and for my part, thankfully, at Liverpool, having been halfway to America I should think and coming of course round the north of Ireland. When I landed the customs officer asked me if I had anything to declare so I truthfully started telling him that I had half a hundredweight of sugar, a crate of oranges, 14lbs sultanas, 14lbs raisins, 14lbs currants, gin and tea. He stopped me saying, 'Ha! Ha! Very funny' and passed all my baggage through unexamined.

What we did not keep for ourselves, we gave as very welcome Xmas presents in a time of strict food rationing. Christmas was spent with Harold Walduck at his home in Elstree. The children's stockings that year contained native Malgache hats, jewellery and other native artefacts, which were much appreciated.

CHAPTER 11

The Invasion of Sicily

On 1 January 1943, I took command of No. 48 Group PC in the Chester area. The work was mostly the usual run but some of my men did work at an American Army depot on the Wirral. One day when I visited them there an American officer saluted me. I told him that he was the first of his nation that had done so and he drew himself up and said, 'I like the English, I admire the English, and those are my orders'.

Some of our men were employed in stowing various valuables down one of the salt mines. I noticed there, for instance, a huge pile of old records of The East India Company, crated works of art, a very large quantity of raw rubber, etc. All this was very safe there from any air raids with anything then being unloaded on us, and very dry.

When I took over No. 48 Group HQ I found that there had been quite a lot of trouble from the men overstaying their late passes, which were given to them up to midnight one day a week. I accordingly told them that in future they could stay out until midnight any day they liked, but that I expected them back then, although there would be no check on their return. I merely left it to them to comply. After that there was no trouble with any of them, probably because previously they had felt that they were not getting full value for their weekly pass unless they stayed out late whereas now they could do as they liked and felt was right.

Some of the billets up in that area had been most disgracefully treated by British troops. For instance, in one lovely old mansion an infantry battalion (not to be mentioned by name by me) had burnt its honoured regimental name with a red hot poker on an Adams fire surround! I accordingly gave a monthly prize to whichever company of mine had done most to *improve* its billets during the month.

While up in Cheshire, we did our best to help the local Home Guard with their weekend training. When I was out one Sunday with one of the Home Guard companies I said to their company commander, 'Sergeant *Blank* is doing it all wrong, would you like to tell him the correct way which is as follows?' The company commander told me that he knew his sergeant was wrong but that he did not like to say anything to him as that sergeant was the only blacksmith for miles around and might refuse to look after the shoeing of his horses! The following Sunday I was out with the Home Guard Battalion HQ and made a similar suggestion to the Home Guard CO who told me that he did not like to upset his company commander as he was the local butcher and rationing was so difficult!

One afternoon four of us went into Chester to see Noel Cowards film *In Which We Serve.* We had to wait in a long queue but eventually got in. The film was a masterpiece and many people shed a few tears of emotion at intervals. I was glad to have seen it, but it was not my ideal piece as it contained pictures of death and destruction during the war.

My dear wife came up to stay for a few days and the local vicar and his wife put her up. The vicar took her round in his car one day and said, 'Mrs so and so always does her cheese making on this day so we might visit her; and I hear that so and so has just killed a pig so we might well visit him.'

EXCERPT FROM A LETTER: BROXTON OLD HALL, BROXTON, CHESHIRE: 12 JANUARY 1943

Dearest Marjorie,

... On Sunday afternoon I went to tea with Mrs S-B ... She has a son of 39 and a younger one in the Welsh Guards. I saw the younger one's photo and thought that I recognized him, so on enquiry I found that he had been in Boulogne with me. His mother was most interested in this and suggested that when he came on leave that we should meet – I was secretly very tickled about this as, unless I am mistaken in the identity, I nearly put him under arrest – I can hardly imagine that he will be very keen on seeing me again to talk over old times! I told Mrs S-B quite a lot about her brother-in-law Gen. Willie Platt but I did not say what his officers really thought about him as I did not consider that this would be tactful; altogether the situation was ironical, not to say farcical.[1]

On 17 April 1943, I took command of No. 19 Group PC which was then being prepared for some overseas job. I exchanged Groups with Lieutenant Colonel Ballantyne who had been a subaltern of mine in France early in 1940. Group HQ went to a concentration area in Scotland for embarkation with X Force. We travelled up to Ayrshire in quite a good train and managed to sleep for a few hours on the way. Fortunately we had taken our thick overcoats, though one officer of another unit in our compartment had not done so and felt nearly frozen in the unheated train. Arriving in 'Bonnie Scotland', I began to understand why so many Scots leave home as it rained each day, was as cold as it had been in January and had a strong wind reaching gale force at times.

Four days later we were transferred to Y Force, so I reported to the War Office and found that we were destined for an assault landing in Sicily. I concentrated my Group HQ at Aldershot, meeting my new company commanders but not the companies themselves. We finally left Aldershot for Liverpool and embarked on the *Frankonia* at the end of June with four of my companies. The other four went in another transport. That was nearly 2,300 men in all, as well as numerous other troops. We tested new anti-submarine location devices and went up to the Clyde where we waited for the whole convoy to be collected.

It was an uneventful journey south, round Ireland of course, and a week later we entered the Mediterranean through the Straits of Gibraltar. When nearing Gibraltar we had our first air raid warning and, as subs were also reported, the escorting destroyers did their usual stuff in rushing about dropping depth charges.

We passed through the Straits at night so that enemy lookouts could not see who or what we were and anchored in Algiers harbour. We disembarked and the troops had one long route march though part of the town for the sake of exercise. While off Algiers it seemed very strange to us to see so many bright lights after black-out time. For some reason we put the clock forward one hour after having put it back one hour, so all was equal once more to England's double summer time. We next went to Malta but were not allowed to land. After lying there for a day or two we sailed for Sicily.

We started off in convoy but the *Frankonia* got a damaged propeller and dropped behind the rest of the convoy, which of course kept going. A bunch of German planes dive-bombed the convoy and seeing a lone bird a mile or so behind the rest, with no escort, made a run for us, hotly followed by one of the destroyer escorts. We naturally blazed away with everything we had, as did the destroyer. The orders were that all the men were to keep below on their decks unless or until ordered up and I was put in charge of boat deck port side.

I had been put in charge of a hundred or more odds and ends of men with no officers who were on a deck well below the waterline. My companies had their own officers to look after them of course, so knowing what those men down below must be feeling, I handed over my half of the boat deck to one of my officers and dived down to these odds and bobs and stayed with them. There was no panic amongst them once they saw me, but it was not at all comfortable for any of us.

I must admit that it was a bit trying being packed down in the bowels of a ship with bombs falling round making the hull shudder and the side plates buckle in on each near miss, wondering whether the sides would bulge in with a rush of water trapping us. With the bulkhead doors fastened it would have taken some ten minutes to move the men up the steep narrow iron stairs to the open decks some four decks up, but as is so often the case in war, nothing happened!

We landed in Augusta harbour on the east, or rather southeast, of Sicily in a great hurry as such a close packed convoy was very vulnerable. The orders were that on landing everyone was to have not only the 'unexpired portion of the day's ration' but also two days' compo rations on or with them. (These compo rations were excellent and contained not only food attractively packaged, but came with sweets and even toilet paper.) Unfortunately, the ships had no biscuits or dry rations on board and as the order came so late they could not make sufficient bread in time, so most of the troops landed without anything beyond that day's balance. I need hardly say that my Group HQ and the two companies of my men in the same ship had their rations all right as after all those years in the army I knew my way about in emergencies.

As the ships could not come alongside the quays everything had to be unloaded into lighters or small craft and this took so long that it was not finished before dark. At dusk the convoy mostly sailed away taking the balance of kits and essential stores with them and we never saw them again. The ship with most of our mechanical transport on board stayed in the harbour that night and was sunk in the usual nightly air raid, so most of the vehicles were lost.

There were about 40,000 men camped altogether under the olive trees near Augusta that night and I took charge of about 10,000 of them as I was the senior officer on the spot. Water was of course our chief trouble as we had no water carts and had to use the few, very inadequate wells from which the locals had of course removed the ropes and buckets. Signal wire and petrol cans or biscuit tins solved the problem of drawing water but did nothing to increase supplies for 100 times the usual number using the wells; we managed without more than discomfort but washing was sketchy. I shared out what food we had, rationed water, sorted out units, appointed camp commanders from my own majors and had a generally busy time. Hardly any officers or men had been abroad before and did not know the ropes but quickly learned.

My next job was to find out who was the nearest area commander and to notify him of the food position and to ask for orders. I had no transport and did not know the country, but I quickly found an AA site and borrowed a despatch rider from them to get a message through. We got some rations within twenty-four hours and kept everyone going.

My adjutant Captain Miles O'Reilley was taken ill shortly after we landed, with dysentery malaria and with later complications, so I finally managed to get a vehicle and sent him off to hospital. We never saw him again. I also arranged for an ambulance and first aid post, which were needed because of stray air raid casualties, from the odd booby trap, accidents, etc.

A day or so after landing my staff car was spotted on the road being driven by sailors from the RN who said that they were entitled to it as they had salvaged it. I had a party of my men waiting with orders from me to retake the car and turn out all naval personnel unless above the rank of commander (my own equivalent rank). If it was a captain or admiral, they were to hold the car and report to me. My car was duly recovered.

We were there about three weeks, but long before then we had our camps running on proper lines. Some Pioneer companies were out at work in various parts of the country and I had moved my Group HQ into a building which was cooler than being in the open under the broiling sun.

Malaria was particularly bad in Sicily and a large percentage of soldiers contracted this and it was often accompanied by jaundice. One of the difficulties was that on active operations men constantly had to sleep without a mosquito net in malarious areas. One thing which caused us considerable difficulty was that in 1943 we had men sleeping outdoors for months during the hot dry season and the mosquito nets as issued were all white so showed up most dangerously from the air. We did our best to darken them by steeping them in stewed up used tea leaves and, failing everything else, mud. Why could these not have been dyed khaki before issue?

Landmines were a source of inconvenience in Sicily as other spots, and in spite of all the precautions we had a few casualties from them and several lucky escapes. The seashore was a constant danger as men would slip down for a bath on unswept beaches. At the side of one path across a field in which one of our companies was camped for several days the local farmer was wounded and his son killed by a mine. One day I saw a donkey cart being driven across a field when there was an explosion and all that was to be seen was a donkey, less cart, at full gallop for home.

The Sicilians had an unpleasant habit of digging up our dead to remove the boots which were in great demand.

As soon as the important town and harbour Catania fell we moved up by sea with our companies to that locality. We took over Villa Ughetti, a large empty ducal house, as our Group HQ. There had obviously been some looting of said premises before we arrived, so being an old soldier, I had an immediate inventory made of the entire contents, noting any particular damage, had it signed by two officers and a copy deposited with the town mayor. It was just as well that I did as a few months after we left Sicily we received, through the British army, or rather from AMGOT (Allied Military Government of Occupied Territory), a claim from the house owner for over £600 for articles he claimed we had looted while in occupation. These included his wife's fur coat (what he thought we wanted with that in the height of summer, I cannot imagine) and 'six pictures by notorious authors'.

We had very heavily shelled or bombed the railway station at Catania, doing unfortunate damage to the nearby cemetery, and had of course put the electric power station out of action, so one of our first jobs was to clear out of the town refrigerator store about 100 tons of stinking putrid meat and then get rid of it, a problem in itself. We also had to clear the roads of debris to let the army vehicles through and get the port working. We found the labour for running the port and all the dumps of petrol, food, Royal Engineer stores, clothing and equipment generally for the Eighth Army.

When we first arrived in the Catania area we were permitted to work the Italian PoWs 'as long as they were guarded by the employing service'. After two days we had the whole thing sewn up quite happily, but our general said he was rather shocked after going round early one morning to the PoW camp and seeing my British Pioneers, mostly privates, of course, draw their squads and march them off 'under guard'. He found that in two days my men had got on friendly relations with the PoWs and they now just walked into camp where the Italians gathered together in a mob. My men called out in English, 'Fall in my squad', or words to that effect, whereupon his six prisoners came forward and he just said a cheery, 'Good morning, come on my lucky lads', turned his back on them and led the way off with the midday meal of biscuits or bully beef for them all in a sandbag slung over one shoulder, rifle slung over the other, and they just followed him like sheep. We never lost one working in these small squads with their own guard.

During this period we had our first Indian Pioneer companies, two Madrassi and one Punjabi. They were a mixed lot, either low caste or from areas not considered suitable to provide fighting troops, but we got really excellent results from them all and very little trouble, especially when one considers that they'd had very little military training of any kind.[2]

Similar remarks apply to Basuto and Bechuana Pioneer companies, which we had for the first time around about this period, though they all had British officers. The Indian companies were mostly commanded by a King's Commissioned Officer, though occasionally by a white officer with two Viceroy Commissioned Under Officers.[3]

One trouble of course was that of food. I found that my first Indian companies had had no meat for many weeks, they said several months, as Hindus would not touch the sacred cow in any form while Moslems would not eat beef unless it had been killed by one of their faith with proper rights. We acquired by one means and another certain unofficial small flocks of sheep and goats which followed us, as in Biblical times, the herders being our own men of course. 'Meat on the hoof' is a story in itself, but was most important in keeping our Indians happy. When the Indian Army divisions came over from North Africa 'meat on the hoof' became a normal, even if not regular, issue to them but not so normal to my scattered odd companies. Africans could eat anything but mostly had a special diet which included a liberal ration of maize flour. It is worthy to note that under army rations the majority of the Africans

125

improved in physique and stamina to a marked degree, which appeared to indicate that their standard of feeding at home was very poor.

We had frequent hospitality from our Indian officers, mostly Punjabis, with whom we got on best of all, and ate curry in all forms. Curried mutton, curried goat, curried livers, curried chicken, etc. The chicken was never on the ration but bought or traded for privately.

One of my companies commanded by a Punjabi Mussulman had been given several Moslem Indian prisoners to look after until they were given a court martial. We never knew nor enquired what their offences were but probably rape, I expect. The fast of Ramadan duly passed and the officers from Group HQ were invited to the feast immediately following it. That morning when I visited that particular company I noticed that there were no prisoners in the company lock-up, so I asked the company commander where they were. He told me that they were all in the cook house helping to prepare the feast for us and themselves. I did not say anything but the next day early I looked into the lock-up and saw that all the prisoners were safely under lock and key as if nothing had happened the night before.

One night there was a spot of bother with my No. 1239 (Madrassi) Coy under Captain Chengapa, when they all rioted over an identification parade arranged by their own company commander when two MPs escorted a Sicilian woman on to parade to identify some who were alleged to have been concerned the previous night in armed robbery. Apparently all went quietly when the woman picked out one man who happened to be unpopular with his mates but when she then picked out a popular man they all broke ranks shouting that they were not going to be insulted by parading for any woman, etc and then the fun began.

The first I knew of this was when their company babu (English-speaking clerk) came dashing up in their company truck with a message from the subahdar (platoon commander). 'Would the Colonel Sahib come at once with a number of armed British troops and stop a mutiny?' I said, 'Certainly not, we deal with our own discipline in the Pioneer Corps without outside help'. So I jumped into the truck and ordered the native driver to take me to the company billets. My adjutant, 'Charles' Chaplin said he would not allow me to go alone so I told him to leave his revolver behind and jump in.

We got to the company and found them trying to break into the armoury, into which the two MPs and the woman had taken refuge. Fortunately, all the company's rifles were in there or murder would undoubtedly have been done before we got there as they were out for blood. I enquired where the company commander was from the subahdar, who incidentally was still trying ineffectively to quieten his men down, and was told that Chengapa had retreated to his billet with a loyal guard. He refused point blank to come out when I ordered him to do so, but stood with revolver drawn at the top of his stairs. So my adjutant and I dealt with the 'mutiny'.

We extracted the MPs and woman from their refuge, which they were most reluctant to leave, and not without some bother got them into their jeep and sent them off with my adjutant. The jeep was stoned and damaged a bit before we got them off and I was hit by stones, quite unintentionally I am positive. Two NCOs under the orders of the subahdar tried to hustle me off for my own safety, but I just shook them off and with the help of the two Viceroy Commissioned Indian Officers got them back into their billets where they sobered down. Such was the prestige of an unarmed senior British officer in those days!

I got back to Group HQ and found instructions to telephone Area HQ instantly, failing which within a specific short time an armed party was being sent to find me. I phoned up and asked what they wanted and was asked, 'What British troops I needed to quell the serious mutiny?' I said, 'What mutiny?' and was told that a very serious and alarming report had come through from the Provost Marshal about attempted murder of some of his MPs and that troops were available. I replied that there certainly had been a small spot of bother, but that it was purely a matter for unit discipline and that we neither asked for nor wanted any outside help, thank you very much. Twice more they phoned me that evening to see if all was quiet and I told them under no circumstances did I want any MP or other patrol round my billets, that all my men had gone to sleep and would they please not phone me again as I was also going to bed. I don't mind admitting that twice during the night I went round to the company to make sure that they were in bed and asleep.

Next morning Area HQ did not know what action to take at all as these were Indian troops, but I told them that I had already suspended Captain Chengapa from all duty and that I merely wanted him sent away somewhere, I did not care where, and that I had already appointed one of my British captains to command the company. I was told (what I already knew) that only officers appointed by the Indian command could dispense any punishments, however minor, on Indian troops and that they really did not quite know what to do in the matter. I told them that I had solved the matter by appointing my captain as company commander for 'all purposes except discipline', but had attached the company to another Indian company for discipline, copy of such appointment enclosed for forward to India command.

My No. 1204 (Indian) Coy was used first of all to work on the railhead and then to march PoWs to and from their camp and to guard them en masse during that working time. One day the officer in charge of the camp complained that we had lost six PoWs and that he ought to report it. I told him not to worry and I told my Indian company commander that he would have to be more careful. A few days later the officer in charge of the PoW camp told me that we had already returned ten more than we took out and would we please stop it. On enquiry from my company commander he explained that there were many deserters from the Italian Army who had illegally discharged themselves and were roaming about, so if when marching PoWs to or from camp they saw a civilian wearing part of Italian Army clothing they just roped him in. Although they did not understand any Italian, if the man gesticulated wildly and jabbered hard enough they concluded that they had made a mistake and let him go; but if he came quietly they concluded that he was a deserter!

There was considerable looting from our army dumps by civilians at that time so I had to find guards. One night my 1236 (Madrassi) Coy was on guard at one of these dumps when a gang of civilians was discovered by the sentry. They promptly set about him but he just managed to fire his rifle as an alarm when the guard turned out and shot five of them; this effectively stopped looting for months. Not bad, I thought, of my men who were considered by the regular Indian army as good enough workers, but coming from a district without military tradition.

When my Basuto and Bechuana companies first appeared on the scene in Sicily, the locals were very scared, thinking that we had imported Abyssinians to use against them. (It must be remembered that old Mussolini had in recent years conquered Abyssinia and they had experienced some of the very unpleasant habits of the Abyssinians with helpless wounded or stragglers.) When they found that my Africans were normally quiet and well-behaved I had a packet of trouble from peddlers of cheap vino which they were not used to. I made one peddler drink a whole bottle of his wine in front of the company which made him very sick. Another lot we caught and smashed their bottles, but they still sold the stuff when we were not looking so the next couple we caught we poured all their vile vino over them and were they a sticky mess? This vastly amused the Africans and temporarily checked the trouble.

Before any of my African companies came to Catania the general told me at his conference one day that the Bishop of Bloemfontein (I think it was; anyway it was a bishop from South Africa) was coming especially to see his African converts and was arriving next day. What Africans were there in the area? I said that the only ones were a fire-fighting unit under a British warrant officer with no officer of their own, but as they were wearing Pioneer badges, I had arranged their pay. However, they were not under me and that in any case they had all been put into prison the day before for refusing to obey a lawful command by their warrant officer and were awaiting court martial. The general said that, 'From this moment they are under your command'. I went round to the prison and saw their white warrant officer. It appeared that they had all refused to clean up their billets as they said the WO had called them a lot of old women and that cleaning up the living quarters was women's work. I had the squad on parade in the prison and told them, through their corporal who could understand English, that I was now their commanding officer, that they were behaving not like women but like little children instead of like soldiers wearing a soldier's uniform, that they were to go straight back to their billets and clean them up for my inspection: 'March off!'

They all went like lambs and my only trouble was with the officer in charge of the military prison, who was horrified to hear me tell his warders to open the doors and let mutineers march off like that. The next day the bishop arrived and later told me how pleased he was to see his spiritual charges so happy – was there anything he could do to help them? I told him that what they needed above everything was a football. A few days later a football arrived by plane for them and they never gave me a moment's trouble all the time I was there.

During this time I had as my batman one Private O'Connor who had been with me all through my previous campaign in Madagascar. O'Connor was an extremely useful old soldier who on the outbreak of war had been on the reserve of the East Lancashire Regt while drawing a pension from the Irish Free State Army. The only real spot of bother I had with him was when he got drunk one night and decided that the rest of the headquarters staff were trying to 'get' him so he stalked them with a loaded rifle and nearly shot the RQMS before I got the rifle from him.

We tried to get up Mount Etna one day as it was close to the town and smoking a bit, but as the road had been blown part way up we did not feel like climbing the rest on foot. We saw many old streams of lava and were told that some of the best wine was made from grapes grown up its arid and inhospitable sides.

Some of my British Pioneers were also drinking too much poor quality vino so we showed them it being made in a country press by the locals. They were treading out the grapes as they had done since time immemorial and when they got tired and wanted a rest they just climbed out of the press, on to the dirt floor, after which they climbed in again muddy feet and all. Several of my men swore to sign the pledge!

One day a small party of Basutos (none of them from my companies) were being shipped back to Africa as they were real trouble makers, which was fortunately a rare thing with them. When their ship docked at Catania they broke loose and rushed into the town and drank, looted vino and became rather rough. I had early news of this so, although they were not under my command they were still Pioneers, I took immediate action without consultation and turned out one of my Basuto companies and returned the trouble makers to their ship. At the daily conference next morning at HQ General Clark said to me, 'I understand there was considerable trouble in the town last night with some of your Basutos'. I told him that there was no such thing but that there might have been a little trouble with some stranger Basutos that was dealt with and was not considered worthy of reporting. He looked hard at me and said,

'So that's the way you want to play it, all right, but for my private information come clean and tell me what actually happened'. So I told him that hearing of trouble I turned out Basutos to deal with Basutos, that they knocked out the rioters with their rifle butts, carried the bodies back to the ship and that was all. General Clark said, 'Dean that sort of thing won't do at all. If you go on like this before we know what is happening, your men may be damaging their rifle butts'.

I was gradually responsible for all labour, both military and civilian, from Augusta to the north of Sicily. Our most important job just then was the Port of Catania from whence we staged part of the assault on Italy with considerable follow-up of supplies. The ferry at Messina also became an important installation as soon as we had a footing on the Italian mainland. The area that my Group No. 19 had to cover towards the end of the Sicilian adventure was so large owing particularly to the difficulty of road and telephone communications, that before the end I had to send off my second-in-command, Major Keith Morgan, in charge of my northern section comprising roughly Messina and the northeastern corner of the island. This he did very well and I therefore recommended him as a Group commander, which job he got as soon as we left Sicily for the Italian mainland.

CHAPTER 12

The Italian Campaign

At the end of October 1943 my Group HQ and some companies embarked on the *Ville d'Oran* at Syracuse harbour bound for the Italian mainland. We were very crowded on board, so much so that men sat in passages all day and at midnight when the officers' lounge became empty, they came in and slept all over the floor. The harbour and surrounding rocks had a number of crashed gliders as they had been released too far out to sea during the initial landing and could not reach dry level ground. We all blamed the Americans which may or may not have been fair.[1]

We did not sail from Syracuse until 5 November, about a week after embarking. I was senior officer so was made OC troops. The ship was so top heavy with anti-aircraft guns, etc, that the men were not allowed on deck all at once and she rolled to an alarming degree at times. We landed at Taranto on 7 November and disembarked at once. Such was the hurry to clear the ship that she sailed the same day without some of the troops' kits and equipment being landed. These never reached the troops again. Of course *our* kits were all landed needless to say. Morgan left me to take command of 18 Group and the next day we left Taranto for Naples, travelling by the first train to do the journey since the Allies landed. This took us two days. At Naples we were joined by our road party under the QM which had crossed by the Messina-Reggio ferry and had since wandered about quite a distance.

In the country districts they bartered cigarettes for eggs on the basis of one-for-one. The exchange rate later rose to one egg for ten cigarettes, also a suckling pig for a pair of boots, part worn. By this time of course the Italians had stopped being our enemy and had become co-belligerents but no one seemed to know what that meant exactly. True, the Italians down in our part of Italy were not still fighting against us, though it was reported that some behind the German lines were still so engaged. All the Italian PoWs that we had taken up till then continued as PoWs but even in their prison camps they cheered every time they heard of a German set-back or defeat. They collaborated

131

whole-heartedly behind the German lines with the Germans and with us on our side of the line, but more anon about this.

I stayed one night in Naples as the guest of a local Pioneer Group HQ – this hospitality being normal among us Pioneers – and the following day (11 November 1943) went to Capua where I reported to the HQ of 10 Corps, which at that time formed part of the American Fifth Army on the Western side of Italy.

I was ordered to take command of some ten or a dozen Pioneer companies, including British, Indian and Basuto and was appointed Acting Assistant Director of Labour to 10 Corps where I quickly made friends.

I fixed up our Group HQ in Capua in a damaged barracks which we gradually roofed and made habitable. My quartermaster and adjutant, who had already become first class scroungers, found odd furniture and timber from bombed buildings while I concentrated on visiting my new companies. Naturally, when we arrived we had no tables or chairs for office or mess and no fireplaces or ovens, but these were soon made from local scrap such as bricks and oil drums. I had the one telephone instrument put on a very long wandering lead so that we could move it at nights from our offices to our upstairs mess and bedrooms by the simple expedient of lowering a bucket from an upstairs window, putting the phone into the bucket and pulling it up. It was pretty cold as it was November and with no doors or glass in the windows the wind rather whistled through, but we made ourselves as comfortable as possible.

On 12 November a signal came through that a certain Basuto company had mutinied and was refusing to do porterage up to the front line. I had no real trouble with the so-called mutiny as I listened to their complaints through their CSM, who was a minor tribal chief and spoke fluent English. They said that they had been on that unpleasant job far too long, had had a fair number of casualties and were fed up and it was the turn of someone else. I told them that I was their new CO, that I would look into their complaint as soon as possible, that I was going up with them myself that night, and that I did not know the way so one of those who did must come up to the front with me as a guide. They were to pick up their packs and follow me, which they did without delay.

Our companies at that time were doing real front-line work as much of the so-called front was up in the mountains. As we had no mules then, all food, water, greatcoats, blankets, ammunition, barbed wire, and RE stores had to be carried up on my men's backs right to the front posts at night. When we did later get mules we still had a final porterage as mules' iron-shod feet made so much noise that they always brought down fire and mules could not be trained to take cover behind rocks or in shallow depressions.

All our British wounded also had to be carried down by hand to the nearest safe road where ambulances could collect them. This type of work went on for some five months, during which we had a total of about 400 or 500 casualties ourselves, including killed, wounded and a few taken prisoner either by German patrols or by wandering into the German posts at night. One batch of Basutos, unarmed, were captured and released by the Germans who must have wondered what we were using in the way of manpower. At one time we had Italians, Basutos, Bechuanalanders, Mauritians, Seychellois and Swazis all on the job, as well as a diminishing number of British who were gradually taken away for the much talked about 'Second Front'.

In December 1943 they gave me 600 Italian soldiers for labour duties and I got very good work from them on the whole, even under fire. I put an English captain over this Italian lot as I was not sure how much trust to place in their own officers and everything worked well, though we had our moments of course.

At that time the British 10 Corps was running the theatre in Capua with ENSA artists or anything else available and the rule was that Americans and British entered freely as they arrived and if we got packed out the doors were shut. But when the Americans took charge they made the rule, 'Americans first, British stand aside', and then the British could fill in what seats were left, if any. This was *not* a popular action.

The Americans were always trigger-happy. In Naples one of their MPs thought that a staff car had too bright a dimmed headlight so he fired at it and wounded one of our staff officers. On New Year's Eve, I was woken up by an outburst of firing so I hastily turned out with a posse of my men to see what on earth had happened. It was only our gallant allies, the Americans, welcoming in the New Year by firing rifles and pistols into the air! I got something out of the Americans, however, as I voluntarily did some porterage for a newly arrived American infantry brigade and got one of their jeeps in exchange for a bottle of whisky!

While we were still in Capua, occupying some old barracks with most of the window glass gone, it was rather freezing as winter crept on. Snow in the mountains also made porterage even trickier at times. There was a skinny Italian lad, who might have been anything from fourteen to sixteen years old, who would keep creeping into our barracks however many times we pushed him out. I rather suspect some of our Group HQ men fed him on the quiet. Anyway, he was under our feet so much that I finally decided that we had better take him officially in hand as he either had no parents or did not know where they were. His name was Michaeli; we never knew his second name as far as I know. Anyway, I asked him, through my interpreter, whether he would like to work for and live with us and he jumped at the chance. I told him that the first thing he must do was have a bath. He rather funked this as he said he had never had one yet. My men prepared a tub full of warm water and made sure that Michaeli had his bath. Afterwards he said, 'I rather like that, I would like some more baths', so his education had started.

We rigged him out in some old clothes between us and made him clean and respectable and he loved it all and was probably happier than he had ever been before. No one bullied him, all had jokes with him, he was fed regularly and we even put him on the pay roll as an employed civilian for a trifling weekly amount. He moved when we moved but a month or so later, he slipped down a bank and broke a bone. We could not put him in a military hospital but managed to get him into an Italian civilian one. Some few weeks later, miles away, I saw Michaeli standing in the soaking rain just on the edge of our camp so I went over and spoke to him and he said very pathetically I thought, in broken English, 'Please may I come home?' I have no idea what happened to him after I left that Group but I have no doubt he finished the war as a happy camp follower, paid or unpaid.

At the end of 1943 we moved under canvas near Sessa. It was bitterly cold and very windy. Each night for about a fortnight we moved the snow off our tents before going to bed in case the weight of it increased too much during the night.

My Pioneers helped considerably in the battle in the crossing of the River Garigliano, which was for some time the dividing line between us and the Germans just then. Prior to this attack it had been arranged that a landing should be made during the night north of the Garigliano (the German side of course) and included in this landing party was half a company of my Indian Pioneers. On the night in question, the troops set off from Naples in American landing craft escorted by an American destroyer and approached the coast, but as shells were falling near the shore they backed out twice and finally ran into shore and hurried everyone off, unloaded part of the stores and then ran like hell. Our Indians looked about them for a while and the infantry also sent out patrols to locate the enemy posts but it was not until someone discovered a wide river mouth to the north instead of the south that they realized that the Americans had landed them behind their own lines. Our Indians first packed up and just walked back to their previous billets, less than a mile away and went to sleep!

During the assault I was up sheltering under the river bank when some of our infantry were trying to cross by folding boat, but the current was too swift. One of my Mauritian Pioneers thereupon volunteered to swim across, in icy water, and he took a signal wire with him and pulled a rope across to assist the boats. One of my Basuto companies put a Bailey Bridge across in a fully exposed position and to make this possible, another company of mine, a smoke-laying company, smoked a long stretch of the river so that the Germans would not see where the bridging party was working. We also ran a ferry service with folding boats across under frequent shelling.

Several times during the winter we had so-called mutinies of our African troops, which were merely sit down strikes when they thought they'd had too many casualties or required a rest. On each occasion I hurried up to the scene and talked to them as follows: 'If you don't carry these loads up to the men in the front line who are shooting at the Germans they won't have any ammunition to shoot, they won't have any food or any water even, so we must get busy.' I then gave the order to 'pick up loads and follow me' and without a murmur they did so. I also had to go up at intervals with all the non Europeans just to encourage them. Of course, I often went up alone by day as until one got within rifle range it was not considered worthwhile to waste shells on a single man, then also some of the posts were on the reverse slopes of the mountain and could be approached under cover, even by day.

Our Italian troops were mostly in rags when they arrived and took a very poor view of the fact that we did not immediately give them at least the scale of clothing and toilet items, food etc, that we gave the Italian PoWs. The real answer of course was that as PoWs we had to look after them according to the Geneva Convention but that the Italian nation should be responsible for its own troops in its own control. Three mornings in succession I was 'told off' by Brigadier L ... of 10 Corps for raising the question of Italian clothing and asking for 600 pairs of British Army boots for these men, as not a single pair of Italian ones was available. My request was refused and I was finally told 'not to mention the subject again'. I waited two days and then announced that morning that there were 150 fit Italians unable to go to work as the soles of their boots were worn completely through and I would not allow them to go out barefoot in the snow and mud. Brigadier L ... said 'Why was I not informed of this situation before?'

To get out of this I did something in which I take pride. I went to a friend I had made in the Polish Corps (which was equipped entirely from British Army sources of course), and asked him if he had any condemned boots on his salvage dump. He did not know but we went and looked and found about 250 pairs there. I asked if I could have them and he told me I could do what I liked with them as they had no further use for them anyway. I collected them and had them put through for exchange for new British boots, which was merely a routine matter. I then spoke to my RQMS and said that I believed he was friendly with the WO in charge of the salvage dump in our area. He said that he was, so I told him I had done all I could at officer level and he must try at WO level now. He therefore collected the same 250 pairs of condemned boots and we put them through for exchange a second time. Both parties were now satisfied and the Italian soldiers were more than willing to work.

The Director of Labour had agreed shortly before that a staff such as I had for an ADL was quite insufficient for the work I was supposed to do, so I got a Lieutenant QM and a RQMS and I made up the balance mainly from Italian army personnel. One of the Italian officers spoke good English so I used him as both liaison officer and interpreter. One day he told me that his family would so like to get a letter to his brother who was a prisoner of war of the British in North Africa but could not do so; could I help? I told him to write a letter in English to his brother which I then posted under a covering letter addressed to the officer in charge of the said PoW Camp asking him if he agreed to deliver this letter. This was duly done and a reply came back by the same route.

I repeatedly asked for mule companies to be sent to us from North Africa, where there was no longer any fighting, to help with this blasted porterage fatigue, but nothing happened for several months. I finally got permission to form two mule companies of my own. One party were Italian cavalrymen, without horses of course. So I made a pack mule company out of them and made another pack mule company from my Mahratta (Indian) company, which was largely composed of small farmers who were used to animals, though not mules perhaps.

We got our mules by local purchase. The mules to start with were a small Italian type. The British had great difficulty in getting animals in exchange for a requisition note as the Italians seemed to prefer to deal with the Americans who paid cash! Not unnaturally, the British could not buy a single mule so had to get them from the Americans, however, I got my mules for these two mule companies. Our pack saddlery was weird and wonderful but it worked. A few months later regular mule companies turned up from Africa and I thankfully made full use of them.

About this time I had Major Coventry as my second in command and I told him I would visit our series of relay stretcher posts and carrying parties up the mountains every second day and that he must do ditto on alternate days. I often used to ride a pack mule up the mountains, which would otherwise mean a two-hour climb each way. But Major Coventry was an ex-cavalry ranker who had risen to be RSM and considered it far beneath his dignity to ride a *mule*! So I jolly well made him walk.

During our operations in Italy, just as in Sicily, constant care had to be exercised against landmines of various types but in spite of all due care we had some dozens of men become casualties, mostly loss of a foot, through stepping on a mine, generally at night while on porterage in forward positions. The Germans displayed great ingenuity in placing mines round orange trees laden with fruit, up tracks, on bathing beaches, near wells, booby traps in houses (a favourite trick was to arrange one operated by the next person pulling the toilet chain), attached to or under dead bodies, etc. I was very lucky myself as well as being both knowledgeable and careful.

About Xmas 1943 Corps HQ was forced to go under canvas, but I quickly got two lorries temporarily fitted out as office caravans and had a cave dug into the soft stone bank to which we fitted a door and stove with chimney sticking out through about five feet of the roof as a mess. We then dug a shallower cave next to this with a communicating door and a timber lean-to as a kitchen, so did not fare too badly.

Most of our Pioneers were within artillery range and some within mortar range at this time, so we never knew quite what to expect. Two of my officers were wounded one day by a shell while talking to me, but I was lucky, though a bit shaken up.

I was interested to have under my command No. 47 British Coy, which was my Glasgow Irish company from France in 1940. While mainly made up of bad lads at that time, it had fought well at Boulogne and was now a very fine company trained in Bailey bridging and road-making (they went to France again in 1944). Knowing where they were working up a mountain track, I went up in my jeep and stopped near them. Some of them recognized me. Two of them came running over and said, 'I don't suppose you recognize me do you, sir?' I said, 'Yes, I do! I gave you twenty-eight days detention about Xmas 1939 didn't I?' 'That's right,' he said looking pleased. I looked hard at the other man and said, 'If I'm not mistaken, I gave you twenty-eight days twice in quick succession about the same time, didn't I?' 'That's right,' he said grinning broadly, both as pleased as punch at being recognized and remembered.

Bathing was a great problem in the forward areas, but I found a hot sulphur pool and spring and after getting a few mines cleared away and a tent erected, it made a most useful bath for those within walking distance and, being on a hill, was out of enemy sight.

Prior to the main battle for Cassino, fighting for which was spread over quite a long period, we Pioneers had a rather sticky job turning the unused railway line running into Cassino town into a track for jeeps and tanks, etc. Work went on day and night. During the day it was under full observation from the monastery hill, so if a working party was too large, or the enemy thought fit, down came their artillery fire. Monte Cassino was another very unpleasant spot. I had to take a turn going up with the nightly carrying parties myself naturally, but I never got hit, although we had casualties almost nightly. All took their share of work and casualties, including the attached Italian soldiers who worked as well as the others.

When the thaw came Corps HQ got well and truly bogged down. They had been using a number of caravan and lorry offices parked in a gully up in the mountains and it was frozen hard when they got there, but was over the axles in liquid mud when they had orders to move forward. It took them three days to get out and there was quite a lot of pithy comment from higher command.

One day I got a lorry load of twenty sheep and twenty goats up to Capua to go forward next morning. I told a Mauritian company to water and feed them and lock them up in a stable for the night, which they did. When reloading the lorry in the morning, they let the lot go and chased them round the town and neighbourhood before catching them and sending them safely off up the line to be delivered to four of our Indian companies up there. The Mauritian company commander told me, as a huge joke, that when they were all in the lorry he had counted twenty sheep and twenty-one goats. I said 'Good Heavens, you surely haven't sent up for slaughter the magnificent goat which is the prized mascot of my Madras Company have you? If you have and the lorry goes first to either of the other three companies they will probably pick out that mascot as their part of meat on the hoof and there may well be real bloodshed over it'. So I tore off in my jeep, as the mascot had disappeared, fearing the worst. When I finally got to my said Madrassi company, the company commander met me and said 'How kind of you to take the opportunity to send our mascot up to us, it was such a pleasant surprise to find it in the meat lorry'!

When we were out in Italy in 1944, one of my friends, who was then a lieutenant colonel, was commanding a Pioneer Group. He bought, or was given, a goat by an Italian farmer to supplement the rations. To the surprise of all the officers what was delivered was a live kid just old enough to leave its mother. This was such an engaging little fellow that no one had the heart to kill it and it was given the freedom of the mess and became a great pet. The colonel's batman was put in charge of it.

Time rolled on and the Headquarters were then billeted in a large old house; first one then another of the officers complained about the smell round the house. One suggested that it was the drains while another said that all Italian houses smelt during the warm weather anyway, while yet a third said that he thought that a dead German must be buried in the garden. Finally, however, there was no mistake and it was clearly traced to Wilfred (for that was the name of the pet goat).

The colonel said that in future Wilfred must be kept outside. This was easier said than done as Wilfred could not understand why, having had the run of the house for so long, he was suddenly debarred from entering. Every time the front or back door was opened Wilfred would streak through, and he even managed to jump through an open window of the office one day upsetting all the papers and overturning the military phone. This rang the military exchange automatically and when the signal orderly enquired what number was wanted all he got was a loud bleat.

The batman of course got all the blame for Wilfred so he tied him up after that, but each rope was soon eaten until a lorry driver missed his wire rope used for towing! Wilfred's temper underwent a change for the worse due either to his ageing or to his objection to being tied up, or both, but the sad fact remains that anyone who got within the circumference of the rope was lucky if he could jump for it before being torpedoed in the rear by Wilfred.

Things went on like this for a while and in spite of many threats not a soul did anything about Wilfred. The colonel because he was too soft hearted and the other officers because they did not dare to upset the CO. Then one day the brigadier said that he was coming to make an inspection. The CO gave strict orders that Wilfred was to be kept out of sight and smell all the time the brigadier was about. The batman had by this time managed to get hold of a chain so he took Wilfred out that morning and chained him up well away from the house.

Everybody cleaned up the place with the usual spit and polish finish and the brigadier arrived. The batman now had time to think of Wilfred and looked to see that all was well, but found that Wilfred had run round and round the post so much that he had nearly strangled himself with the chain. The batman therefore tried to loosen the chain but in so doing he untied it from the post. This was the moment for which Wilfred had been waiting, so off he galloped hotly pursued by the batman who caught hold of the end of the chain and was dragged along the ground vainly trying to stop the flight.

The brigadier was at this moment inspecting the guard of Basuto Pioneers drawn up in front of the building and such a tempting target was just too much for Wilfred; he made a rush for the brigadier's rear with the batman manfully hanging on. Complete disaster was just averted by the colonel who, realizing all too well that his military career was at stake, literarily stepped into the breach and received on his person the assault meant for the brigadier. The CO slipped up and the brigadier turned round to find the colonel on the ground, a savage goat trying to butt him and a dusty private soldier also on the ground but still holding tight to the chain. The sight was just too much for the Basuto guard who first tittered and then laughed aloud each time the goat made a charge or attempted charge. Needless to say the brigadier demanded to know what it was all about and if it was a mess pet why were regulations being so flagrantly disregarded, etc.

Before the CO could find a suitable reply the batman quickly said that it belonged to an Italian but that as it had got loose he had tried to keep it away from the parade. The brigadier by this time got to windward of Wilfred and immediately decided it was unreasonable to suggest that anyone would be such a bloody fool as to have a stinking so-and-so like this as a pet anyway. So Wilfred was led away and by this time the Basuto guard was standing strictly at attention. The brigadier was taken off for the day inspecting various Pioneer companies by the colonel who managed to give fierce and very terse orders that Wilfred was to be disposed of for good and all before they returned to dinner that night, otherwise ...

The brigadier and the colonel returned at the end of the day, had a drink and all was well. When they started dinner the brigadier said that this was a very tasty piece of meat and where had it come from. The mess president said it was rations but they had a cook who could disguise anything. The colonel had a mouthful, looked very thoughtful, turned a little green and said that he regretted that he was suffering from a slight touch of malaria and asked the brigadier to excuse him. He went out and found the batman and said, 'Is it?' The batman said, 'Yes sir!'

I was ordered to send up 100 men for work in Sessa which at that time was well within artillery range but was not being shelled just then. I sent up British troops for this job as I did not know what we could arrange for billets. Snow was on the ground and all habitable dwellings either still had civilians hanging on in them or British troops, or both, and it looked as if my men would have to go under bivouacs on the snowy ground. I went up on a reconnaissance and the only possible building was a small monastery. Now, the army was not allowed to requisition any church property, so I knew there would be no troops in it but hoped that the monks would voluntarily permit my men inside, if room permitted, for about a fortnight which was all I needed for them.

I took my interpreter and knocked on the door when a nun opened it. I apologized saying that I had expected monks in a monastery but she explained that the monks had been moved elsewhere and they had been put in as their nunnery had been badly damaged. I explained that under those circumstances, I could not ask for accommodation naturally. The nun said that the Mother Superior would be much annoyed with her if she (the nun) let us go without the Mother Superior seeing me. We went inside and I again apologetically explained to the Mother Superior my mistake. She told me that she had two unoccupied rooms to which we would be welcome, so I had a look and decided that with very close billeting in those two rooms and the corridor we could accommodate eighty men. The Mother Superior said that the only place left was the Chapel and I told her that we could not possibly use that as my men would be eating and smoking as well as sleeping there. The Mother Superior said 'I think it is much better for your men to use the Chapel for a fortnight than that they should be forced to sleep in the snow, bring them in and when they go we can re-consecrate the Chapel!' We of course put them in. I was most struck by this notable example of practical Christianity.

One day I got in touch with the Pioneer Group Commander operating next door to me on my eastern side and told him that I had heard that No. 1204 (Indian) Coy had arrived that day from Sicily to join his Group, but as I had known them well when they were in my Group, had he any objection to my making a friendly call on them? He said that he was thinking of visiting them himself and would be pleased for me to come with him there and then. Off we went and as soon as the Indian sentry saw me he recognized me, turned out the guard and presented arms. I quickly pushed forward my friend, their own Group CO, and hid round the back of the cook house while he inspected them. By this time, the Indian company commander had arrived and greeted us both. After a while their Group CO said he was off, but I asked if he had any objection to my staying and having a chat with the Indian company commander to which he readily agreed. We accordingly retired to his tent and after a while an orderly came to say something to his company commander, who then turned to me and told me that the company was now on parade for *my* inspection. I told him how irregular this was but I thought it best to do as asked, so I inspected them thoroughly after which the subahdar said to me, 'This company has a request to put to their Father (me)'. So I asked what it was. He replied, 'Well, we have had no meat to eat since you left us in Sicily so will you please do something about it?' Luck was on my side as I had some sheep coming up by lorry that day so I told them ten sheep would arrive for them that day and they had better get their butchers ready. Little things like that made a lot of difference when handling these non-European troops in a land strange to them.

About that time I had another stroke of luck as a Basuto company asked me whether I thought they did the same work as the Mauritians. The answer was, 'Yes'. Did I think that they worked as hard as the Mauritians? 'Yes,' again. 'Then why do we not get the same pay as the Mauritians?' All most logical but very difficult to explain that the cost of living was much higher in Mauritius than Africa. All I could say was that I would pass on their complaint to the general. About a week later it came through from High Command that the Army Pay and separation allowances had been raised for all our Africans. My Basutos and Bechuanalanders naturally gave me the full credit for this which, if correct, would have been a blinking miracle, however it did me no harm with my men.

After I left that Group it was taken over by another, much younger, officer with fewer medal ribbons. Africans respect their tribal elders of course and are very snobbish over their officers. They gave a spot of bother so their new group commander had them all on parade and through their English speaking CSM gave them a real pep talk which they received in silence. He then turned to go, feeling that he had settled the matter, when they started throwing stones at him!

One punishment I used to give to such men was a week without sugar in their tea. This may sound childish but meant that when the sweet tea was issued, the naughty one had a mug brewed and drawn which he had to drink while his mates roared with laughter at him. It had a most salutary effect even if not in King's Regulations as a punishment.

In March 1944 I was appointed Assistant Director of Labour to 5 Corps which was then fighting on the Adriatic coast, so I said a regretful farewell to 19 Group. I was mentioned in despatches a second time for work while with 10 Corps.[2]

On 7 March 1944 I travelled by jeep, with my batman, across Italy from one coast to the other via Naples, Vasto, etc, to Paglieta near the mouth of the River Sangro, which was another hotly contested river crossing. An Indian division in 5 Corps included a number of Hindus. When they had one or two killed, their brother Hindus clubbed together to send their ashes back to India to be thrown into the River Ganges. After Sangro there were far too many casualties for this to be possible, or their mates would never have had any money at all, so it was arranged that the senior Hindu priest, holy man or whatever he was called should publicly and solemnly declare that 'the mouth of the River Sangro was the River Ganges for the duration of the war'. After that the ashes were thrown off the railway bridge near the mouth to make sure that they got well into the main stream.

After the battle and both prior to and later, the British dead of all colours and creeds were buried close to where they fell as quickly as ever possible, as a temporary matter of course and the sites both marked and carefully noted. Later General Montgomery himself chose a wonderful site for a cemetery on the hill overlooking the Sangro and the Adriatic and ordered the concentration of all bodies there. I was ordered to get the bodies dug up and dealt with, but I had no Pioneers available for this job so was told to use civilians. I duly started with civilians whom I collected but they struck within half a day for very understandable reasons, which I need hardly go into, but a buried body, in a blanket, after a few weeks?

The extra pay I could settle myself of course, but they needed soap and cigarettes as a bonus. The latter I had no authority to issue so I asked the Brigadier A/Q for it. He apparently could not or did not like to have these issued from canteen stocks without any authority but as I was unable to comply with Montgomery's orders without such help I asked to see the corps commander. Apparently this was an unheard of thing and everyone was absolutely horrified at such an idea, but I finally won my point, after a warning that it might well mean an adverse confidential report or worse. The corps commander could not have been nicer, however, when I explained as a business proposition that I could only do as ordered with his help, which I promptly got and the work went on without further delay. That was one advantage of being a Territorial Army officer who did not know any better!

We buried everyone according to their religious beliefs as far as we knew, Moslems lying facing Mecca, Jews with a Rabbi saying whatever their burial ceremony is, etc. Then little school children gathered wild flowers and laid them on each grave which was such a charming action on the part of co-belligerents whose land was being devastated.

On the subject of General Montgomery, when commanding Eastern Command in England in 1940 he had his own peculiarities, of course. For instance, he would hold an officers' conference and say, 'As I will not tolerate any coughing while I am speaking I am giving you half a minute in which to cough'. He was so keen on officers being physically fit that he gave orders that all must do a five-mile run once a week, or resign. The commandant of the Women's Services told Monty, most indignantly that she would not allow *her* officers to do such runs!

I did not serve under Monty again until 1943 in Sicily and Italy but I never liked him as he was so greedy that any other unit or formation could go without if he wanted their stores or equipment, and he ruthlessly sacked any officer whose face did not fit. However, as I said at the time, and later: 'It is difficult to criticize a general who wins battles in wartime.'

Monty had a carefully calculated but successful method of inspiring confidence in his troops. He was a great showman. One of his habits was to address his men informally before a battle such as driving into a market square when his men were off duty, standing up in his jeep and calling them to gather round. He could then say to his aide-de-camp 'Have we any cigarettes'? (which of course had been specially brought as Monty never smoked himself) 'Pass them round'. Monty would then give a pep talk saying why he was certain that they would win and this was well received.

My greatest admiration was for General Alexander, but we had able corps commanders in Italy also. Monty, though junior to Alexander, was appointed a field marshal before Alexander. Many of us were very pleased when Alexander was also promoted as field marshal with seniority one day prior to Montgomery. Alexander was both a brilliant strategist and a gentleman; towards the end of the Italian campaign, when the troops there had been considerably thinned out for the coming invasion of France, he continued to defeat the Germans with fewer troops than they had, in repeated attacks against well prepared positions and, in my opinion, he was a better general than Monty but Monty appealed more to the rank and file as an inspired leader. We were most fortunate in having them both.

With the warmer weather came the mud. I should write MUD. The indifferent roads under the military traffic were indeed a problem, one which I had to deal with a lot, with Pioneer companies and civilians.

As ADL 5 Corps I was a staff officer and not a commanding officer, but I much preferred to deal with the Pioneers of different nationality myself rather than let them be dealt with by officers from Corps HQ who did not understand them, naturally. Corps did not want to be bothered with them in any case as they had more than enough on their plates while fighting, so they happily put me in orders as having powers of discipline as a CO.

When the Germans got pushed back they always blew up all bridges and culverts so we were always hard put to it repairing same. If it was a dry or nearly dry creek we used to start bulldozing a track down one side of the cutting and up the other and roughly surfacing it when it got too badly cut up for use. Later on we used to repair the original bridge when possible; to replace perhaps a Bailey Bridge we might have thrown over the ravine when there was too much water for a dry crossing on the bottom. On one such site I gave the Chief Engineer all the civilian male labour available, but when he demanded more I told him I would send him fifty women. He was quite rude in his refusal, but I told him it was women or nothing so he most reluctantly agreed to try them out.

This was one of the many jobs where we cut the stone from the hillside above the bridge, carried it down to the bridge and the masons laid it. After the first batch of women had done a day's work, however, the Chief Engineer asked for more of them as he found that, whereas it took two men to carry a stone block on a kind of stretcher down the hill side, many women carried everything possible on their heads instead of by hand. They just put a cloth as a pad on their heads and then a lump of stone up to half a hundredweight and strode down the hill with it balanced there.

Talking of civilians I recall that when I was with 10 Corps there was an outbreak of typhus among the civilians in Naples. We stopped this remarkably quickly by simply arranging for males to deal with men employees and females with the women; they just puffed DDT powder down their necks, back and front each morning when they reported for work and also did ditto for all civilian volunteers not employed by us.

When I started as ADL 5 Corps we had the usual difficulty in getting any staff for my job, but I finally got Basil Burton as my staff captain (he afterwards became a major), two clerks, one batman and one driver.

On 10 June 1944, we left Paglieta and Corps HQ moved under canvas in the San Vito area. There was much planning for a push up the Adriatic Coast, but this attack did not immediately develop as we were all the time losing troops who were sent back for the French front.

On 16 June, we moved to Campobasso training area and while 5 Corps was engaged in this I had the offer of a holiday in Egypt. What happened was that the army commander's plane was going to Egypt for stores and he decided that eight senior, war-worn officers might go on local leave in it. I was one who presumably filled the requirements, so off we flew on 2 July.

We landed in Alexandria where we stayed for the night. This was a Saturday, so there was no army paymaster open to change our Italian occupational money and the hotel would not accept it. As senior officer I had a chat with the hotel manager and explained our difficulty. He said that he could not change our money or accept our cheques, but that he was quite ready to lend us anything we wanted and that we could pay him back before we left Egypt. I told him that this might well be in a fortnight's time as we were off the next morning, Sunday. He said that he had no worry about lending us whatever we needed as we were British officers, but added 'I would not do this for the Americans'!

Next morning four of us decided that we would like to fly to Beirut and the pilot being quite happy about this, that is what we did, asking him to fly low over certain biblical towns such as Bethlehem. We stayed the night in Beirut, had a good look round and then flew straight to Cairo airport. One of the party and I put up at Shepherd's Hotel which was, at that time, the old hotel of course before it was burnt down. After a week in Cairo we flew to Alexandria for the second week. While in Cairo we went to the Pioneer Corps depot at a desolate spot in the desert not far from the canal. I cannot remember how it was spelt but it was pronounced 'Cas-a-sin' though the name started 'Qu....'. I also met Brigadier Prynn in Cairo; he had become Director of Labour Middle East. We stopped for a meal en route both ways at Benina Drome (Benghazi).

On 14 August 1944, my team and I left 5 Corps, who had just moved up to near Assisi, saying goodbye to my many friends there with some regret. Our first job was to form twelve companies of Italian Pioneers, get their clothing and equipment and to form a British cadre for each company. These cadres consisted of one captain, one CQMS and one corporal and it was largely due to their work that the Italian companies were normally a great success. The British captain did not command in theory, but in actual practice he had to do most of the work of supervision and acted always as liaison officer between the British authorities and his company. He with his two NCOs had to draw rations, see the clothing was obtained as far as possible, see that men turned out for work as and when required, that the sick received attention, billets were provided, bathing arrangements were improvised, etc. One of our senior Pioneer officers once remarked, 'Englishmen make good mothers' and this was indeed true in the case of our liaison officers as immediately they took on the job they ceased talking about the 'Ruddy I-ties' but instead talked about 'my men' and worked hard and frequently illegally, acquired clothing and blankets, soap, etc for them. These companies when formed were moved up to work for the British Eighth Army. I was also appointed Labour Adviser to 71 Sub Area (Colonel Woodhouse).

On 19 September 1944, we moved to near Arezzo and I took over a number of companies from Lieutenant Colonel Jack Whitfield, OC 39 Group.

When we had troops in or near Assisi, this railway station was used as a railhead for all purposes but when we opened up a railhead at Arezzo we still used Assisi as a railhead for the evacuation of our wounded. The ambulance train would come in perhaps once a week, or perhaps twice a week according to the number of wounded. My men moved the stretcher cases from ambulances to the trains, but when I had no troops of any kind in that area I was faced with a difficult problem. I could have got civilians to do the job no doubt but it was of such a casual nature that it would have meant taking men straight from dirty jobs to move our wounded and might have meant delays or unsuitable men trying to do the job. I thought hard about the problem and decided that as Assisi was the headquarters of the Franciscan Order and appeared to be thronged with monks, why could they not help?

Naturally nothing would be arranged except on a very strictly arranged, voluntary system as Religious Orders were entirely outside the scope of the army. I went with my interpreter to call on the head of the Seminary in Assisi to ask whether he could help. He said that he could not possibly do anything about it without orders from 'the general'. When I asked what general, he replied in a shocked way, 'Why the general of our Order of course'! I then asked where the general lived and was told Rome. I then enquired if he ever visited Assisi or district and was told that as it happened the general was due there the next day. I therefore asked for an appointment and the next day turned up with my interpreter and was graciously granted an audience.

When I started explaining what I wanted, the general replied in English and said 'That's all right old boy, you tell me direct what you want'. I did so and he said he would arrange it. He was as good as his word and for several months after that the drill was for the Railway Transport Officer to notify the town mayor of Assisi when a hospital train was due in. The town mayor arranged for a lorry to pick up monks and notified the head of the seminary who had them ready. It all worked perfectly. This was probably the only known squad of monks to ever work for the British army.

The town of Assisi was never bombed or fought over at all and I personally found it tranquil and soothing to the spirit to wander round its chapels and memorials, in peaceful setting, an oasis of quiet in a country at war in which I took my busy part.

In Assisi there lived an Englishman who was a well known art critic and expert. Before the war he wrote articles asserting that the murals in the Basilica were genuine works by the famous Giotto di Bondone. After war was declared by Italy this Englishman was interned for a long time but was, of course, released when Italy became our co-belligerent. He thereupon wrote a learned article proving conclusively, to his satisfaction at least, that these murals were only painted by a pupil of Giotto.

Having arrived in Arezzo in September, I had an extremely busy job running the equivalent to a Pioneer Group with the small staff of an ADL (Assistant Director of Labour), and was also Labour Adviser to 55 Area (Brigadier Moseley) and 71 Sub Area. The most important of our jobs was running Arezzo railhead, which supplied 13 Corps (British) and certain American divisions. The tonnage for the American divisions as compared with British divisions was five tons to three tons. The weather was very bad and the mud shocking. The railhead failed to deliver the supplies as quickly as required, so no less a person than Field Marshal Lord Alexander came along in person to enquire into the reason. I assured him that labour was not the reason as I could produce all that was required, but getting it working was a different thing. As a result Brigadier Moseley was sent home and another appointed in his place. Moseley was too much of a quiet gentleman for the difficult job; it needed a strong ruthless type for this particularly trying situation, with all the roads getting impassable.

I had by this time a very large number of Italians, including a complete battalion with officers, and all as part of my labour force. The first day I did what a British officer would normally do, namely inspected the Italian dinners. I knew exactly what the rations consisted of as my headquarters had drawn them and handed them over to the Italian QM the night before. The dinners were most inadequate and I found that when we delivered them in bulk the Italian officers' mess had first share, the Italian warrant officers and sergeants had next share and the bulk of the men had what was left. After that I had the food divided by my own staff, per capita, and to the amazement of the Italian other ranks, daily inspected their main meals myself or had one of my own officers do it. This appeared to be unheard of in the Italian army and while it upset the Italian officers, I could get any amount of cooperation from the men when extra effort was required.

In December, Colonel Blanchard, DDL 1 District, went to Burma and I was appointed in his place and at last got the rank of full colonel.

Our HQ was then at Foligno; Major General Hyderman was in command. While there, a complete Italian division was sent up to us to be trained by the general for the job of holding a quiet spot in the line. General Hyderman came back one day from inspecting this division and remarked that they would be, 'a good fighting division if only they had *white* officers'!

I took over a badly damaged lunatic asylum for my I-ties and got them to re-roof sufficient for their needs, but had no medical inspection room for them. So I went to see the Italian RC bishop and got from him the use of a disused chapel, most unofficially. He said that if that would not do I could have a room in his bishop's palace – another example of practical Christianity.

The mess to which I belonged was in a kind of manor house about 2 miles outside the town and was reasonably comfortable, while our offices were in a technical school building which was always inadequately heated. The weather was very cold at this time.

My area covered a very large chunk of Italy, but this grew larger and larger as the front line gradually moved north. Our chief port on the east coast was Ancona where I had a group of Swazi Pioneers and we handled about 4 to 5,000 tons net per day there, but much of it had to be handled several times: ship to lighter; lighter to dock; dock to rail or lorry; lorry to dump and then into lorry when it was collected from dump, so tonnage handled daily was 12,000 to 15,000 tons. I also had thousands of civilians working at the docks, dumps, petrol filling, roads, bridges, repairs of vehicles, etc. Much of the work was done by civilians during the day and by Pioneers at night.

On 1 January 1945, we moved to Perugia in a snow storm. The snow much delayed the move as vehicles could not move without chains on the wheels. The same storm blocked the passes over the Apennines so snow clearance was added to my other jobs.

Our mess was in part of the Brufani Palace hotel which was an officers' transit hotel, while we tried to get reasonably near to the offices. Perugia is a very ancient town with a university. It is the town from which the Fascist march on Rome started. The town itself is built on a hill and on spurs of the hill that radiate from it. It overlooks part of the upper valley of the Tiber and across the plain one can clearly see Assisi perched on its hill: for centuries the two towns were constantly in conflict.

Early in 1945 our mess moved into a ducal villa on the outskirts of Perugia, much against the wishes of the countess of somewhere or other, who had taken up residence there purely to hold it against requisition while her husband continued to reside at the main residence in the country somewhere near. When this lady was informed of our intention she was furious, so 'Dogsbody Dean' was detailed to make the final arrangements with her. I duly called on her, by appointment, and said how distressed we were that it had been found necessary to disturb a lady, particularly such a charming one, that I had noted how well the garden looked and that we hoped she would continue to have the gardener look after it and take the flowers or produce as she wished, etc. One could not apparently lay it on too thickly to please her. Anyway, after she had showed me round the house herself and I had picked out in my own mind which room I would allot to each officer, she asked me which room I had chosen as mine. Next morning when we moved in I found a bunch of flowers placed in my room, which I thought a very nice gesture under the circumstances.

As the British Army was fighting its way northwards, and it was clear that we should shortly reach Perugia, the *podesta* or mayor of that town, who had collaborated fully with the Germans, saw the red light so he had a number of glazed earthenware cigarette ash trays made at the local potteries, which were famous during peacetime but could now only make rough ware as we had cut off all power when we bombed the electricity station. These were inscribed 'Good Luck 8th Army, Perugia wishes you well'. On the arrival of the army he distributed them to senior officers and I received one which I brought home with me. We graciously accepted them and then put him straight away under arrest as a collaborator.

I had to cross the Apennines a number of times, both during the snowy period and later as I was supplying Italian army labour to keep the passes open and also had companies on the east side of the mountains. During March 1945 I saw a number of primroses in one area and also picked wild tulips near Macerata. I took these tulips back to Perugia and handed them round to the various HQ offices. One was occupied by the chief woman of the nursing staff, a full colonel as far as I can remember. Anyway, she was a real battle-axe of a woman, feared by most people, but when I carried in these tulips and asked if she would accept them for her office, she came over all girlish and apparently appreciated the gesture.

While in this area I had a brief glimpse of Rome where I attended Allied discussions on Labour problems. My hotel room was on the fourth floor and as there were no lifts working because of a shortage of electric power it meant a pretty stiff walk up 108 stairs every time I wished to visit my room. On 5

April I had the morning free so, with two others who were there for the same reason, I went to the Vatican City and had a long look round the museum and the Sistine Chapel. Of course, we could not begin to see it all but we had a very fair view and walked some miles. We saw sculpture, maps, pictures, ancient ornaments etc. Of course, it was not looking at its best after nearly five years of war as it was not so clean, prosperous or well dressed as formerly, but it was still worth a visit.

During my work in Italy I found the Roman Catholic religion much more colourful than anything I had experienced before, although it did not change my basic ideas. For instance, just outside Assisi was a bothy used by St Francis when he went into the woods to pray and commune with nature; it is now preserved by having a huge basilica built over it so that the hut or bothy comes just under the dome. In Perugia cathedral on very special occasions they produce a ring said to have been the signet ring of one of the Apostles (I have forgotten which one now). At Loreto there is a famous cathedral where they house, on the floor under the dome, the Virgin Mary's small house brought over from the Holy Land. At Assisi they dug under the altar and extracted the embalmed body of St Clare and now show it off in a glass-fronted coffin for anyone of the faithful to see. Many evidently find this of interest, but I thought it a bit hard after she had lain peacefully for 600 years under the altar. Several of the famous places of worship have a splinter of the True Cross or a thorn from the Crown or something for the public to venerate, and so on.

About this time we had some difficulty because civilian employers were finding it so difficult to get labour that they were in some cases paying more for it than either the Italian government or the Allied armies in our No. 1 District and this led to labour unrest. Some of the civilian firms were working for the Allied army on work of utmost priority, such as liquid fire for our flame throwers. They paid absurdly high wages in order to get men as they were reimbursed for all wages paid whatever they were. The Americans immediately followed suit but one better.

The position became very difficult, but by tact and firmness I settled each problem as it arose; I busted several strikes by drafting Pioneers in temporarily to do the work until the civilians saw reason. The attitude adopted unfortunately by a number of senior officers was, 'What does it matter what we pay as it is only in paper money which the I-ties will have to redeem after we have gone.' My general was always open to reason, however, and backed me up in all my efforts to stop inflation, but still to get the work done.

Incidentally, some idea of my job can be guessed as during March 1945 in No. 1 (my) District we averaged over 42,000 civilian employees. We had to increase the use of Italian army units to replace Indian Pioneer companies, which were sent back to India for use in Burma and their own country no doubt. Nearly all our British Pioneer companies had long since gone home for the Normandy invasion of course.

Our No. 1 District was just behind our 8th Army, backing them up in many ways and now and then we did not even know where the dividing line came.

One place where we were making a jeep track in the foothills as a supply line for the front, almost in no man's land, we came across a cave with a dead family lying in it – man, woman and two small children. We never knew whether they died of starvation, gas or disease so we just blocked up the mouth of the cave and left it to them. Close by were several caves which a detachment of mine used temporarily. The first night a small boy crept in and asked for food which he of course was given; he then went off and returned with several other children in a similar state, who all said that they had got lost from their parents, had been out in no man's land for days and that their families had been displaced when the fighting flowed past them and the children did not know whether their parents were alive or dead. Of course it was strictly against all regulations to use army rations for civilians but...

After a few days we were moving on so I took the children to the nearest town and asked the *podesta* to take them off my hands. He said that this was impossible as he had nowhere to put them, etc. I made an impassioned speech, standing up in my truck, speaking through an interpreter, in front of a gathering crowd, saying that we all knew how the Italians loved children and were very good to them, that we had done what we could, against all regulations, to save them, but that we could do no more and I knew that the warm-hearted Italians would not let little children be starving or homeless. I had hardly finished when the onlookers, men and women surged forward and took the children in their arms; I beat an immediate retreat.

At one town up in the hills, Isernia, there was a pile of rubble at one end of the square where buildings had once stood and the inhabitants told me that there were a large number of their dead buried in the debris. Their story was that when the armistice was signed in 1943 between Italy and the Allies, they thought that this meant the end of the war as far as they were concerned. The local people gathered together in the square rejoicing and when they saw Allied planes coming over they waved joyfully to them only to find a few seconds later that the planes bombed the entrance and exit of the town to block the only road through the mountains in that area to prevent the Germans either escaping or reinforcing. Some bombs fell on the edge of the square killing a number of the civilians (reputed to be 1,500). When they told their story to me they said that it was American planes and when they told it to the Americans, they said British planes; anyway one of the many tragic happenings during war. Large numbers of the Allies seemed surprised that they were not universally popular in Italy!

As we were at times fighting side by side with the Americans, we were constantly in touch; this happened when we took Bologna – British on the right

Americans on the left, each occupying part of this ancient town. That evening the price of drinks in the hotels and bars had a habit of rising steeply between rounds as there was a constant passing of messages between the I-ties from one zone to the other, saying for example: 'Americans now paying 10 lira more for a whisky or gin' or 'British now paying 50 lira more for a bottle of Chianti'.

When we took Florence we found all the bridges destroyed by the Germans except the historic Ponte Vecchio and in this case they were content with blowing up the buildings at either end so as to block the bridge. Our first job therefore was to build a Bailey Bridge across. The town itself was fortunately not too badly knocked about.

About this time also, part of the road making and repairing by civilian labour was taken over by the American civil affairs officers, although I was nominally responsible for civilian labour in my area. These same American civil affairs officers ran their own court for trying cases amongst employed civilians. On doing spot checks on the labour gangs I found that in those paid by the Americans the Italian foreman or ganger who kept the tally was recording as present and at work a large percentage of absent or non-existent men. The Americans paid out the money for each gang to the ganger who paid the individual on the daily attendance list. I arrested the first half dozen gangers thus falsifying their accounts and reported same to the Americans who promptly released them. I reported to my HQ that my estimate was that over £1,000 per week was being stolen in this way and was being shared between the gangers and the two American officers and that I had positive proof of this gross irregularity. I was told not to make any official report or take any action as the road work was being done and the British higher command could not care less as the swindle was an American one and the British had not the time to deal with it and would not be thanked by our gallant Allies for finding out a scandal.

Talking of the get-rich-quick methods of the Americans, there was of course an acute petrol shortage among civilians, but the Americans sold so much petrol (gasoline) to them on the quiet that at one time the black market price for gas dropped to the controlled ration price. American rackets grew to such a size that they even ran black market convoys by deserters in uniform in and out of the docks at Naples. We knew all about it of course and some of our Military Police were killed trying to stop these convoys when going through British areas, but again we had to stop taking any action as it would only have made friction with our gallant Allies. These were American stores and lorries and the Americans knew all about it anyway. It was no doubt difficult for them as quite a number of men in the US Army were of Italian origin and it was all too easy for them to dispose of anything through their own relations. Al Capone and many of the other greatest gangsters in America were of Italian origin of course.

One time I was talking to a British civil affairs officer and said that I could not get sufficient salt for my Italian army units. He said that he was desperate for salt for the civilians as they could not even cure a pig for want of it. He said that salt was available from civilian sources about sixty to seventy miles away but that transport was his difficulty. I arranged with him that if I supplied the transport I wanted 10 per cent of the salt for my army. We arranged this and got the salt but when the lorries came back with twenty tons of it he would not let me take my two tons. I said in that case we will not unload but I will just send it all back where it came from. We got our two tons! A few days later my Italian officers told me that they had done a barter and had got a pig for themselves and pork for their men out of it and plenty left.

One night I went to the local cinema where we had a talk on war news etc followed by the film *The San Demetrio*, which was about the oil tanker that was brought home by its crew after having been set on fire when the *Jervis Bay* was also sunk. It was an epic of British heroism by the Royal Navy and Merchant Service. The following evening I attended a 'do' at the Sergeants' Mess. It was supposed to be a musical evening but later developed into a dance as the sergeants had invited some ATS and some local 'floozies'. I faded out of the picture at what I considered to be the right moment, but one or two officers who stayed on regretted it as is always the case!

On 9 April I entertained His Honour the High Commissioner for Swaziland to dinner. The visit passed off all right and he was most surprised at the condition of our Swazi troops who were well, apparently happy and certainly doing good work. He said out in Swaziland the whites considered them dirty, lazy and generally poor workers, but then out there of course they were not under Pioneer officers, which makes considerable difference. We had our Swazi dancing team over to perform at the local ENSA theatre and their performance went off very well indeed. There was a back screen painted to represent an African kraal and a very well done camp fire on the stage with a flickering red light among the logs and they entered into the spirit of the thing very well. Instead of kilts of leopard or similar skins they wore kilts in red and green (our Pioneer colours), which looked very effective. I wondered if on their return home this would become a tribal custom among ex-servicemen.

Every Saturday evening there was an educational show put on in this theatre. We called it ABCA (Army Bureau of Current Affairs), which included such items as talks on war situation, food, hygiene etc and some entertainment to draw the audience, generally films. This time a short talk on Swaziland was given before our dancers did their stuff. This was only the second occasion upon which I had been there as it started at 7.30 pm and ended at or about 9.45 pm. It was rather difficult for officers to fit their evening meal in and this applied to all our evening shows, which were quite rightly timed to suit other ranks.

One night I won a prize of 40/- in our weekly football sweep, the tickets for which were 1/-. I also discovered that a Lieutenant Colonel Hargreaves, then a newcomer in our mess, was a keen crib player so I got out my board and much enjoyed some games with him. It had been many months since I had a game of cards with anyone as I didn't play bridge and few played anything else, except occasionally poker for high stakes which did not interest me.

I spent so much time with my comrades that to prevent myself going crackers I had to occasionally get right away from the lot of them and out into the country where I couldn't see anyone in khaki. Some officers get their relaxation with feminine society and this was quite an easy thing to do out there, but being married, when I took time off from work, I just walked. During wartime I could not use an army car or use up petrol and rubber for joy rides. If one suffered a little occasionally from years of war strain, to tire oneself out with physical exercise ensured sound sleep.

On 4 May 1945, our No. 1 District moved from Perugia. Before leaving several of us thought it was full time that we had a really good look round the town so we arranged for a guide and had a conducted tour. Perugia is one of the very old hill towns that have about 2,000 years of recorded history. One archway for instance is mainly Etruscan and is reputed to be 6 or 700 years BC. There are reputed to be 110 churches in the town, which may be correct but it is full up with chapels and churches. The guide was surprised when I asked whether one church had not been used by the lepers in times past, as it had, but he wondered how I knew? It was only guesswork on my part but the floor sloped as certain of them did to enable easy washing down of the place. I believe there is one near Canterbury that slopes in a similar way. I also learned why there were so many old doorways walled up. It is because the old houses owned by the nobility had a door which was only used for funerals and was walled up in between times. Some even had a door which was only used for a bride to enter by. Some of the churches out there had a door which was only used once every twenty-five years for their quarter century anniversaries and is fastened up and sometimes walled up in the intervals.

We moved 150 miles by road to Forli, wandering about rather a long way over repaired mountain roads. Forli is a town in the Po plain near to which Mussolini had been born. It had been very knocked about in the fighting. Our offices had no glass in the windows and no doors, so it was particularly draughty and cold, but we later moved on to Ferrara and the weather improved.

8 May 1945 was the day of the General Surrender of the German forces in Europe or in Italy anyway. The celebrations were very quiet with us. We had a wireless rigged up at several spots in the afternoon so that we could hear the Prime Minister's speech on that historic day.

Considering that in this area we had such a mixed party including British, a few Americans, Italian Army, Italian Patriots, Indians, Africans, Mauritians,

Poles, New Zealanders, South Africans and goodness only knows what else, such as Cypriots and Palestinians, there were potential elements of danger; but apart from a few accidents and a surprisingly few drunks there was little difficulty. That night a certain number of troops fired off Verey lights and homemade fireworks, liberally reinforced by anything that would make a noise, such as hand grenades, machine guns and other small arms (fired mostly into the air of course), so that it paid to keep away from windows or doorways but nothing really to worry about. The ATS girls were annoyed of course when a stray bullet came through their mess window, but no one was hurt.

EXCERPT FROM A LETTER HOME: 8 MAY 1945

At long last the great V Day has arrived, or should I say V1 Day as we still have Japan to settle of course? My thoughts turn instinctively to you my Dearest Wife who has so nobly born the heavier end of the load in looking after the children and home needs under shocking difficulties and dangers all these years. I have of course had my moments of danger and periods of bodily discomfort but have on the other hand had excitement, change and a more interesting job – the chief hardship of all has been the long periods of separation from you and the children. This period will no doubt end in a few months time when I shall be 'disembodied' or whatever the new correct term may be for an embodied Territorial being stood down.

We shall have many years of struggle and difficulty before us. I to keep the house and family going and pay our way and you to keep the house and family going with little domestic help but thank God we shall be doing it together once more so can face anything.

My job won't take me into Austria as far as I can see so I shall miss the army of occupation this time as I did in 1918 but not for wounds this time. It is over thirty years since I first joined the army now and I shall not really be sorry to get out as I have had enough and have done my share I think. After nearly six years in this war I feel without boasting that I have always given of my best, though like so many others without much reward, but then we did not volunteer with that in view.

Even though the actual fighting eased there were certain problems still facing us. We had to consider how best to deal with PoWs, surrendered German forces which were apparently subtly different, Italian Patriots who had to be disarmed as quickly as possible but were friendly, ditto who fought for the Germans and were *not* friends; displaced personnel of different nationalities and some who might have been anything from enemies to just plain refugees.

We suddenly heard that a few thousand Chetniks were being passed back to us. These birds were apparently formed of partisans fighting against Tito at one time and were unable to return home without being liquidated. No one seemed to know what they were and as a matter of fact we never did either get to know even how they spelt their names or whether they were allies, enemies or co-belligerents, or even refugees; but the fact remains that when they came back to us from the front somewhere they were armed to the teeth and included about 1,000-odd pregnant women also armed. The first thing seemed to be to disarm them, which they refused to permit, and we had not got any men on the spot to make them. We did, however, say 'no rations until you hand in weapons'. In the case of the women and children we put them in the sports arena and fed them and after a few days the men went through the motions of handing over their weapons though we knew full well that they were bristling with concealed daggers and pistols, but it was not policy to press the matter further. We never did hear what finally became of these unhappy people after they departed from our immediate area.

Naturally, we had vast numbers of German PoWs moving about, still rather dazed and wondering how it had all happened. After the surrender of the German Forces the 8th Army could not get rid of them quickly enough, so to start with some of their staff officers were given a map reference and told to motor down in their own vehicles. We were therefore faced, within a day of the fighting stopping, with a German staff car calling in at our petrol supply point and getting served, also the sight of a German lorry which had broken down and both the driver and a British Military Policeman had their heads together under the bonnet.

We were told to be ready to receive 2 or 3,000 Germans a day, coming by lorry from the front, to bed them down for one night and feed them and pass them on the next day; in other words to act as a staging camp for them. The first day a convoy of huge American 'trucks' (lorries) arrived, each with 120 German soldiers standing up packed like sardines. We learnt that coming round a mountain bend the sides of one of the lorries broke with the weight of so many bodies swung against it and about ten were killed. The next convoy had only 110 per truck but a similar accident happened so the Americans said that 100 was obviously the answer. Now the Americans are very good at lorry work and to give them a job of 'trucking' was right up their street. The first twenty-four hours we received 200 lorries or 20,000 bodies so we had to do some very quick re-arranging to bed down and feed such numbers.

Fortunately the Germans did not need any particular close guarding. As a matter of fact they well knew that if any ran away they would have been very quickly killed by the Italian partisans who sprang up all over the place and were not over particular whom they robbed or killed, but Germans for preference of course. One has only to remember how they killed Mussolini and his mistress and hanged their bodies upside down in the market place.

DONALD DEAN VC

The Communist element was very strong in parts of Italy as was the Fascist party still, so peace celebrations gave rise to a certain amount of strife, which was fortunately curbed by the presence of the Allied army. Many processions toured the towns carrying red flags with the hammer and sickle and large numbers of houses were decorated with flags of various types. Of course, the Italians did not have to worry about the Japanese problem so peace in Europe is all they really worried about, but it would take them many years to rebuild their rather badly shattered towns, remove mines from the fields, rebuild bridges and re-lay railways etc as so much damage had been done. It was not wise for a stranger to try cross-country walking owing to the uncleared minefields, which might have been known to the local inhabitants but they wouldn't tell anyone if they could help it as they didn't want troops camping on their land. In fact, I sometimes wondered if they didn't put up some of our warning signs deliberately and they certainly didn't remove them after mines had been lifted.

I went to Bologna where the Germans had for a long time stabled large numbers of their animal transport. This no doubt accounted for the plague of flies there. Bologna was badly knocked about round the station and some of the suburbs, but the centre of the town was untouched. It had some nice old buildings in it but I did not think much of the cathedral. The shops had plenty in them at a price. I was told that within twenty-four hours of the Allies entering the prices had doubled. A story is told that the first few days drinks at the hotels were raised between rounds as a man would slip out after serving drinks to find out whether any more was being obtained at the place next door and so if you ordered a second glass it was frequently more than the one just drunk.

I then went to Ancona for a couple of nights. It was a grand sight my officers told me seeing some of the German U-boats or E-boats coming in to give themselves up there. On the Sunday we had a special church service in the local stadium there followed by a march past of the services. As the civilians in the town were very bolshie it did not do them any harm to see strong contingents of the navy, army and air force still in their area.

Work for me and my troops did not ease up at all after the armistice. Our numerous Italians deserted in swarms and even I found it a little difficult to keep up the same enthusiasm now that war in Europe had been won. I stated quite firmly that I had no wish to stay on in the army after my age group were released and I did not anticipate there would be any need as several senior officers wished to stay on as they had no special job to hurry back to and some of the good junior men wanted to stay on if it meant promotion. I was not getting any younger and began to feel that I had done my share in two wars and wanted to get out as soon as the government felt it could release me. I felt deflated and very tired after six years of war, much of which was a trifle hectic,

156

and for a long time I had been dealing with non-European Pioneers and one never knew when one of them might run amok (for that reason I always kept a metal ruler on my desk, just in case). I knew that I should miss the army very much at times, but not nearly as much as I missed my wife and family.

Towards the end of May 1945 the first men in Age/Service Release Group No. 1 started going down to Naples for home. As we had a fairly large number of senior officers of fifty or over, our Corps perhaps lost a bigger percentage than some of the others. All those going meant that others were promoted to take their place, so quite a large number moved from one job to another.

No. 1 District HQ moved to Padua, an old university town only about twenty miles from Venice. Things were very quiet with us, though there was of course constant work of repairs to everything going on, roads, bridges, buildings, railways, docks, etc. Our offices were in a huge block which must have been flats as well as offices in peacetime. I was up on the sixth floor but fortunately the lifts worked. The lifts were self operated *if* you had a key, but to start with no one had any. I managed to get one myself and got some more cut for 35 Lire (or 1/9) each, or ten cigarettes. Needless to say, we were paying in cigarettes which we bought at special prices from the NAAFI. This was of course quite illegal but...

One Sunday afternoon I ran over to Venice with Major Tryon for a few hours. No bombs fell in the town as far as I could see, though very considerable damage was done to the approach on the mainland side. We were quite unable to book a gondola as the men were making so much money that they didn't work many hours a day. The water was covered with Americans who paid above the fixed tariff so got preference. Venice looked rather dirty and was in want of a good clean and paint up, but still retained much of its charm in spite of this and the swarms of Allied soldiers of different nationalities. Americans were in most evidence, and then came British, New Zealanders, Indians, a few Poles, ditto Brazilians and two Canadian nursing Sisters, though how they came to be there was a mystery as all Canadians were supposed to have left the country a long time before. A 'Duck' service was running to and from the lido (a 'Duck' is the dual purpose boat on wheels that runs on land or sea), and looked rather out of place in this old town.

On 12 June 1945, I had notice that if I did not wish to stay on I was due to go home, leaving Naples in exactly one week. I started clearing up but there was no one to hand over to. Accordingly, I phoned up the DDL 8th Army and arranged for him to send down a senior lieutenant colonel to take my place and I informed AFHQ (Allied Force Headquarters) that I was leaving and who was taking my place.

I handed over on 13th and on the morning of 14th June said goodbye to my staff and friends and set off in my staff car. I left Padua for Naples, sleeping the first night at Florence and the second night in Rome. I arrived at the Labour

Directorate HQ in Naples on 16 June and reported to Brigadier Carter and had a warm invitation to stay the night, which I did. I was informed that I just had to go to Caserta about twenty miles away for a medical inspection. I rather wondered why there was no senior medical officer in Naples of all places capable of giving me a medical inspection, but orders are orders so an appointment was made for me on 18 June. 17 June apparently did not give time for this.

Anyway on 18 June, I went for my medical but was not expected so was ordered to go again on the 19th. This meant that I did not manage to get my kit onto the boat in time but had to leave much of it behind. All I could take on board was what I could carry up the gangway myself but I was past caring much anyway. The ship was the *Carnarvon Castle*. It was dry, as were all transports, by arrangement with the USA. I found that six colonels were sharing a cabin that pre-war had been a single berth cabin so it was rather a tight fit with what little kit we each had, and only two could dress or undress at one time.

We arrived at Southampton on 25 June. A band was on the quay to welcome us. As I was a full colonel, I was entitled to 'direct release' instead of going to a depot first, but as no one knew what the correct arrangements were for 'direct release' it was 1 am the next morning before we finally got our papers signed. Reveille was 04.30 hours the same morning. I went to somewhere near Aldershot, got my civilian suit free issue and went home for my release leave to which was added an increase for length of foreign service.

So ended the Second World War for me.

Epilogue

After the Second World War Colonel Dean became Hon. Colonel Dean of the amalgamated battalion of The Buffs and The Royal West Kent Regiment, a position he held for eighteen years. Colonel Dean was appointed a JP in 1951, a Deputy Lieutenant for Kent in 1957 and received the Order of the British Empire (OBE) in 1961. Through The Buff's association with the Danish royal family, he was also made a commander of the Order of the Dannebrog by the Queen of Denmark.

As President of the Sittingbourne branch of the Royal British Legion he was responsible for twinning his home town of Sittingbourne with Ypres. In 1983 he was presented with the National Certificate of Appreciation, the highest award of the British Legion. He had been chairman of the Sittingbourne branch for fifty years and saw Remembrance Sunday parades as a sacred occasion to remember lost comrades.

Dean was of strong Church of England faith. He was church warden of his local village church at Tunstall for forty-six years, the last few years being emeritus as well as treasurer etc at different times. He died at his home in Sittingbourne on 9 December 1985, survived by his wife and daughter. He was the longest surviving VC winner from the Great War. He was buried at Tunstall Church, Sittingbourne, Kent. At the service the Reverend David Matthaie said of him, 'Donald Dean will always be remembered for his courage. The courage of overcoming one's own doubts, fear and feelings of hopelessness and inspiring others to resolute action.' By popular request, a memorial service was held at St. Michael's Church, Sittingbourne, in January 1986. It was attended by members of the British Legion, Masons and the public who came to remember him. The epitaph on his tombstone reads: 'I have fought a good fight, I have finished my course, I have kept the faith.'

In 1997 the Royal Pioneer Corps Association presented 168 Pioneer Regiment with a silver bowl commemorating the Pioneer's spirited defence of Boulogne in 1940.

APPENDIX A

Lieutenant Dean's VC Citation

The following citation appeared in the *London Gazette* on 14 December 1918.

Near Lens, France, 24–26 September 1918, Lieutenant Donald John Dean, 8th Bn, Queen's Own Royal West Kent Regiment

For most conspicuous bravery, skilful command and devotion to duty during the period 24th to 26th September 1918, when holding, with his platoon, an advance post established in a newly-captured enemy trench north-west of Lens.

The left flank of the position was insecure, and the post, when taken over on the night of the 24th September, was ill-prepared for defence.

Shortly after the post was occupied the enemy attempted, without success, to recapture it.

Under heavy machine-gun fire consolidation was continued, and after midnight another determined enemy attack was driven off.

Throughout the night Lieut. Dean worked unceasingly with his men and about 6 a.m. on the 25th September a resolute enemy attack, supported by heavy shell and trench-mortar fire, developed. Again, owing to the masterly handling of his command, Lieutenant Dean repulsed the attack, causing heavy enemy casualties.

Throughout the 25th and the night of the 25th/26th September consolidation was continued under heavy fire, which culminated in intense artillery fire on the morning of the 26th, when the enemy again attacked and was finally repulsed with loss.

Five times in all (thrice heavily) was this post attacked, and on each occasion the attack was driven back.

Throughout the period Lieut. Dean inspired his command with his own contempt of danger, and all fought with the greatest bravery.

He set an example of valorous leadership and devotion to duty of the very highest order.

APPENDIX B

Colonel Dean's Medal Entitlement

Victoria Cross

Officer, Order of the British Empire (OBE)

1914–15 Star

British War Medal (1914–20)

Victory Medal (1914–19) with 'Mention in Despatches' (MiD) Oakleaf

1939–45 Star

Italy Star

Defence Medal (1939–45)

War Medal (1939–45) with Mention in Despatches (M.D.) Oakleaf

King George VI Coronation Medal (1937)

Queen Elizabeth II Coronation Medal (1953)

Queen Elizabeth II Silver Jubilee Medal (1977)

Territorial Decoration (TD) + 4 Bars

Knight, Order of Dannebrog (Denmark)

APPENDIX C

An AMP Song
[circa summer 1940]

We are not as young as we might be,
Our figures are not what they were.
You'll find when we take our hats off,
That some of our hair is not there.
But what we may lack in precision,
It won't pay the Army to count us,
As simply a lot of 'has beens'

We'll never go short of our rations,
Our kits will be always complete.
We'll always look after the Rum Jar,
And get the best cuts of meat.
Old soldiers we are, don't forget it!
Or you may learn with regrets,
We know all the tricks and then some more,
We are not just 'dear little pets'.

Our faults may be many and varied,
With virtues we may not all shine;
But at least it can't be denied us,
We turn up just time after time.
We don't hold with new-fangled notions,
Like drilling in 'threes' and not 'fours'.
We don't do the 'Kick Step' in marching,
We walk and don't 'Bus' to the wars.

We've foot-slogged in many a climate,
Enlivened by songs and by cheer;
We've marched from Cape Town to Pretoria,
Lamenting the death of good beer.
And now that there is this big war on
We've turned up to serve once again.
Old soldiers we were once aforetime –
And soldiers we wish to remain.

And now that our worth is acknowledged,
For our chief they thought wise to elect,
A man with more service than we had,
One for whom we should all have respect.
But decided that none filled the bill,
Till they turned to the list of Field Marshals,
And gave us our old Chief, Lord Milne.

Glossary of Military Acronyms and Terms

2i/C
Second in command

AA&QMG
Assistant Adjutant and
Quartermaster General (Personnel
and Logistic Branch)

ADC
Aide de Camp

ADMS
Assistant Director Medical Services

ADOS
Assistant Director Ordnance Services

AMPC
Auxiliary Military Pioneer Corps

ADL
Assistant Director of Labour

AFHQ
Allied Force Headquarters

A/Q
Chief Administration Officer

ASC
Army Service Corps

ATS
Auxiliary Territorial Service (for
women)

BEF
British Expeditionary Force

Bn
Battalion – normally comprising of
three rifle companies; commanded
by a Lt Col (CO)

Brigade
Smallest tactical formation in British
Army, composed of two or more
battalions, commanded by a brigade
commander, or brigadier

C-in-C
Commander-in-Chief

CMP
Corps of Military Police

CO
Commanding Officer (usually Lt
Col)

Corps
 i) Generic term of a military
formation
ii) Military formation comprising
    two or more divisions

Coy
Company – normally composed of
three platoons and commanded by a
major (OC); deputized by a captain
or senior lieutenant

CQMS
Company Quarter Master Sergeant

CSM
Company Sergeant Major

D of L
Director of Labour

DADOS
Deputy Assistant Director of
Ordnance Services

Division
A division is composed of several
brigades or regiments commanded by
a major general

DOS
Director of Ordnance Services

DR
Despatch rider

ENSA
Entertainments National Service
Association

G1098
List of stores and equipment

GHQ
General Headquarters

GOC
General Officer Commanding

Group
An army group consists of several
field armies operating in a
geographic area, usually commanded
by a full general or field marshal

HQ
Headquarters

KD
Khaki Drill – a light cloth uniform
often worn in tropical service

LMG
Light machine gun

Lt Col
Lieutenant Colonel

MG
Machine gun

MO
Medical Officer

MP
Military Police

NAAFI
Navy Army Air Force Institute

NCO
Non-commissioned Officer

OC
Officer Commanding (typically a
major)

ORs
Other Ranks (those without a
commission)

QM
Quartermaster

Platoon
Smallest military unit commanded
by a platoon commander (normally a
lieutenant) and a sergeant; typically
thirty men in strength organized into
three sections

PoW
Prisoner of War

RAF
Royal Air Force

RAOC
Royal Army Ordnance Corps

RARO
Regular Army Reserve of Officers

RASC
Royal Army Service Corps

RE
Royal Engineer

RN
Royal Navy

RPC
Royal Pioneer Corps

RQMS
Regimental Quartermaster Sergeant

RSM
Regimental Sergeant Major

RTO
Rail Transport Officer

Section
Sub-division of a platoon comprising
of seven men commanded by a
corporal

STO
Sea Transport Officer

Notes

EDITOR'S INTRODUCTION:
1. One of these 50ft Thames barges (number 109961) was named *Donald* and was launched in 1898. It was renamed *VC* in the 1920s and ended her days as the housebarge *Annabelle* at Chelsea, until broken up in the mid-1970s. [Ed.]
2. *The regimental Roll of Honour and war record of the Artists' Rifles* (London, Howlett, 1922). [Ed.]
3. Major E H Rhodes-Wood, *A War History of the Royal Pioneer Corps , 1939-1945* (Gale & Polden, Aldershot, 1960). [Ed.]
4. H J Wenyon and H S Brown, *The History of the Eighth Battalion, The Queen's Own Royal West Kent Regiment, 1914-1919* (Hazell, Watson & Viney: London & Aylesbury, 1921); Christopher Thomas Atkinson, *The Queen's Own Royal West Kent Regiment*, 1914-1919 (Simpkin, Marshall, 1924). [Ed.]

CHAPTER 1: THE ARTISTS' RIFLES
1. Dean's mother, Grace, was a member of the Baptist Church and a strict teetotaller. [Ed.]
2. The Prince of Wales was the future Edward VIII, perhaps better known as the Duke of Windsor after his abdication in 1936. [Ed.]
3. Haig became commander-in-chief of British forces on the Western Front on 16 December 1915. GHQ moved from St Omer to Montreuil on 30 March 1916. [Ed.]
4. 'Plug Street' was the British nickname for Ploegsteert in Belgium. [Ed.]

CHAPTER 2: THE YPRES SALIENT
1. Lieutenant Colonel Arthur Cecil Corfe was an Australian who went to South Africa at the beginning of the war and fought there. He then came over to England and was straight away put in command of 11th Bn. He was awarded the DSO and two Bars before being given command of a brigade. [Ed.]

2. Kingsley Thompson-Smith was killed on 23 March 1918, aged twenty-seven, in the fields north of the farming village of Beugny (20 miles southeast of Arras). Transferred to 10th Bn Royal West Kent Regiment, K. T. had the misfortune of being present on one of the costliest days in the regiment's history. An order to withdraw did not arrive and 10th Bn was left in an exposed position during a German attack and subjected to heavy shelling and machine-gun fire. By the end of the day, only 120 out of 598 officers and men were still in a cohesive unit. K.T. was posted as missing during this action and his remains were never identified. His name is engraved on Bay 7 of the Arras memorial. [Ed.]

CHAPTER 3: PASSCHENDAELE

1. The Battle of Messines opened on 7 June 1917 with the detonation of nineteen mines under German lines. It was a prelude to the Third Battle of Ypres which opened on 11 July 1917. [Ed.]
2. According to the official history of the 11th Battalion, the casualties in this one action were 260 all ranks out of a total who went in of 388. Dean wrote: 'We were shockingly under strength before the action of course, but it was by no means unusual for us to lose, wounded or killed, two out of every three who went into action.' [Ed.]
3. The battalion lost forty men in this bombardment while moving up into position. [Ed.]
4. Second Lieutenant Harold Charles Came has no known resting place. His name is inscribed at Tyne Cott memorial. [Ed.]
5. This was Dean's youngest brother. [Ed.]
6. This is a reference to an infamous Gotha air raid on the night of 24/25 September 1917. A 50kg bomb landed outside Harold Walduck's Bedford Hotel in Southampton Row, killing thirteen people and injuring twenty-two on the hotel's steps. This raid is still marked by a plaque on the modern Bedford Hotel. [Ed.]

CHAPTER 4: REFLECTIONS ON TRENCH WARFARE

1. The 11th Bn was disbanded on 16 March 1918. [Ed.]
2. Australians, unlike the British, were not subject to the death penalty for desertion. [Ed.]
3. According to the battalion history, this race was won by Diana, the veteran 'C' Company charger. [Ed.]
4. The French franc was, during the war, pegged at about 25 to £1, or near enough; 1 franc equalled 10 pence. As some of the French towns in our area ran short of small change and we were always paid in 5 franc notes, a number of the towns printed their own local currency down to 25 centime notes. These we could only cash either in that particular town or at the Expeditionary Force canteen. [Dean]

5. In 1924 a party of Territorial Army officers went over on a battlefield exercise close to Noeux-les Mines so a friend and I went to call on my miner friends. The door was opened by a fat, cow-like blowsy woman looking about 30, with several brats around her. When I enquired whether Lorraine still lived there she simpered and said that she was Lorraine! [Dean]

6. The German Maschinengewehr 1908 (MG08) was an almost direct copy of the Maxim machine gun. The German manufacturers did indeed pay license royalty fees to Hiram S. Maxim, a British subject. [Ed.]

7. The Germans first used chlorine gas on the Western Front against Canadian troops on 22 April 1915 during Second Ypres at the Battle of Gravenstafel Ridge. [Ed.]

8. The PH (Phenate Hexamine) helmet was a chemically treated, gas-permeable hood introduced in October 1915. In January 1916 the PHG helmet was introduced, having rubber sponge goggles to give better protection against tear gas. [Ed.]

CHAPTER 5: THE LENS FRONT

1. News of this attack had come from a German POW. It was scheduled for 22.30hrs on the night of 9th May 1918, involving twenty-two divisions. [Ed.]

2. Elsewhere in his notes Dean recorded: '[The Germans] disliked the fighting in these underground places as much as I did, I think. Our policy was to block up all possible underground runways and fight above ground for preference.' [Ed.]

CHAPTER 6: DEAN'S POST

1. Wenyon and Brown, *History of the Eighth Battalion QORWK 1914-1919*, pp 217-24 [Ed.]

2. The course of Twisted Alley is now followed by the rue Jean Moulin in the suburbs of modern Lens at the point in question. Canary Trench is now covered by the private gardens of the houses on the southern side of the nearby rue Pierre Bérégovoy and then follows on the east side of the rue Jean Moulin. Claude Trench follows roughly the line through the gardens of the northwest side of the rue Lazare Hoche. [Ed.]

3. *East Kent Gazette*, Saturday, 21 December 1918. [Ed.]

4. The 8th Bn history gives the date of Dean's wounding as 11 October in a position south of Rieux. Commenting on Dean's wounding the history records (p.238): '[Dean] was loudly cheered by the Battalion, and particularly by No. 16 Platoon, as he was carried away on a stretcher. ... After the charmed existence he had had during past weeks, it was the irony of fate which decided that he should be the only casualty in the Battalion on the day when he was wounded.' [Ed.]

5. I recalled that when my Great Grandfather Smeed lay in bed dying his relations were called and gathered round him and just at that moment a dog howled round at the stables. They all took this as a certain omen of doom but it amused Great Grandfather so much that he laughed heartily and lived for years afterwards. [Dean]

6. The 8th Bn history records the news was announced to it earlier, on 12 December 1918 at Nomain in Belgium during a concert after the ballot for the General Election. It records (pp.224-25), 'The news was telephoned through to us when the whole Battalion was in the village school at a Battalion concert. Such a scene of tumult and enthusiasm as greeted the announcement is impossible to describe. The events of those September days were still fresh in our minds, and a few of Dean's platoon were still with us. Every man in the Battalion during those frenzied moments of cheering took Dean to his heart, and felt that he was the man who would stand at the head of the Battalion for all time.' [Ed.]

7. The investiture took place on 15 February 1919. [Ed.]

CHAPTER 7: DISAPPOINTMENT WITH THE BUFFS

1. AG14 is the acronym for Adjutant General Branch 14, the department responsible for Pioneer officers' careers. [Ed.]

2. In 1940 Osborne, who was then a Corps Commander, was retired from the Army for inefficiency after Exercise BUMPER in which he was in command of the defending force during a mock invasion. [Dean]

CHAPTER 8: THE PHONEY WAR

1. After the BEF returned to the UK on the fall of France this made two Directors of Labour at the War Office. Major General Amps became a Colonel in the Royal Engineers and took up a position in the Northern Command, which he filled adequately and Brig. Friend remained at the War Office as Director of Labour until the end of the War, subsequently being prompted to Major General. [Dean]

CHAPTER 9: THE BOULOGNE DEBACLE

1. Private F. Wilson was later awarded the Military Medal for this feat (*London Gazette*, 3 September 1940). [Ed.]

2. Plan D was the Anglo-French plan to move the BEF 60 miles into Belgium should the Germans advance into the Low Countries. The position would stretch along the River Dyle between Wavre and Louvain. [Ed.]

3. Dean's notebook and diary entry records three civilians were shot at request of French gendarmes, along with a man dressed as a French marine. [Ed.]

4. Dean's notes record that some men dropped their rifles and bayonets in the street fighting and fought how they knew best: hand-to-hand with their cut-throat razors. [Ed.]

5. The Guards had reported the defence of Boulogne as untenable. The decision to evacuate the two battalions went right up to Churchill for approval. Much to his regret he consented and eight destroyers were sent to collect the Guards. Churchill makes no mention of the Pioneers in his history of the Second World War. [Ed.]
6. The defence of Boulogne continued until 25 May when the last of the French garrison surrendered in the citadel. [Ed.]
7. According to his daughter Susan, when he called their Sittingbourne home, she answered the telephone while standing on a chair. The voice on the telephone said, 'It's Daddy,' so Susan ran outside to tell her mother, who was up a ladder mending the clothes line. She nearly fell off at the news as a telegram had earlier reported Dean missing presumed dead. They were reunited at the Imperial Hotel in London. [Ed.]

Chapter 10: Madagascar
1. Michael had returned to boarding school by the time of this incident. [Ed.]
2. With the Battle of Britain at its height, the moon and tide indicated there would be favourable tides and moon for a landing between 8 and 10 September 1940. In order to bring Home Forces to a state of readiness, the Chiefs of Staff issued the codeword 'Cromwell' just after 8pm on Saturday, 7 September. [Ed.]
3. Brigadier Festings' 29th Independent Brigade, which formed the nucleus of Force 121, had been training for a year in Scotland. [Ed.]
4. Percy and Berthe Mayer were employed by the Special Operations Executive (SOE). Their role is told in Colin Smith's excellent *England's Last War Against France: Fighting Vichy 1940-42* (London, 2009) [Ed.]
5. Dean may have been the unwitting victim of an operation initiated by the secret deception organisation, the London Controlling Section. Author Denis Wheatley describes in his memoir, *the Deception Planners*, how the Germans were led to believe the troops employed against Madagascar were in fact destined for an attack on Norway, an operation codenamed SOLO 1 – 'Solo' being an obvious anagram of Oslo. [Ed.]
6. There is another tale from the Betsiboka Bridge that Dean did not recall in his memoir. It comes from the book *Into Madagascar* (Pengiun Books, 1943) by K.C. Gandar Dower. He wrote of an incident involving Dean: 'A senior officer arrived at the crossing in a car that had no brakes, and he very sensibly produced a rope and a team of Malgache. But Equatorial labour is proverbially unreliable, and his team did not appreciate the fact that, if you intend to lower a car down a steep place, it is necessary to tie the rope on first. The car, therefore, shot down into the water as fast as it could fall and, according to reliable witnesses, vanished completely beneath a wave of water. To everyone's amazement, when the fountain subsided, the senior officer drove calmly across the bridge. A gas-cape over the radiator had

saved the engine, and as for the nerves of the senior officer – well, he already held the VC'. [Ed.]

CHAPTER 11: THE INVASION OF SICILY

1. The sequel to this story is Dean did indeed meet the Welsh Guards officer. They recognized each other, but as gentlemen did not acknowledge the fact. [Ed.]
2. Madrassi Pioneers were from the Madras Province in southern India. [Ed.]
3. Basuto Pioneers were from the Territory of Basutoland now known as Lesotho, a kingdom entirely landlocked by South Africa. Bechuanaland is now called Botswana. [Ed.]

CHAPTER 12: THE ITALIAN CAMPAIGN

1. On the landing further to our left, in which we were not implicated, the initial attack was accompanied by a number of our airborne troops in gliders being towed by American planes. The American pilots misjudged the wind presumably as they cast off too soon so most of our men were drowned a few hundred yards form the shore, being much too heavily loaded to be able to swim [Dean].
2. Dean was mentioned in despatches on 24 August 1944. He had previously been mentioned after Boulogne on 26 July 1940. [Ed.]

Index